Solanus Casey

For more information or materials
on Solanus Casey, contact:

The Father Solanus Guild
1780 Mt. Elliott Avenue
Detroit, MI 48207

Solanus Casey

The Official Account
of a Virtuous American Life

Edited by

Michael Crosby, OFMCap.

A Crossroad Book
The Crossroad Publishing Company
New York

The Crossroad Publishing Company
370 Lexington Avenue, New York, NY 10017

Printed in the United States of America

Library of Congress Cataloging-in-Publication Data

Crosby, Michael, 1940–
    Solanus Casey : the official account of a virtuous American life /
by Michael Crosby.
      p. cm.
    Includes bibliographical references.
    ISBN 0-8245-1835-7 (pbk.)
    1. Casey, Solanus, 1870–1957. 2. Capuchins – United States
Biography. 3. Christian saints – United States Biography.
I. Title.
BX4700.C2527C76 2000
271′.3602–dc21
    [B]   99-32998

3   4   5   6   7   8   9   10   05   04   03   02   01   00

Contents

Part Two
THE PRACTICE OF THE VIRTUES BY
SOLANUS CASEY

Foreword

I met Father Solanus Casey only once, when I was about twelve years old. It was a memorable visit! My cousin Virginia, wife of a well-known Detroit physician, had been diagnosed with a serious heart malady. A visit to Father Solanus was recommended. So my mother and an aunt joined Virginia in seeking the prayer of the kindly and prayerful assistant porter at St. Bonaventure Friary in Detroit.

To this day I remember Father Solanus's gentle manner. He greeted each of us and then drew Virginia aside so that he could speak with her personally. He prescribed certain daily prayers and also the reading of a spiritual book entitled *The Mystical City of God* by Mary of Agreda. Father Solanus promised his prayers for Virginia and for us all; we received his blessing.

Father Solanus returned my cousin to her family, full of confidence in God's love. She lived a long and full life. Two of her sons became Capuchin priests. Another son and a daughter established wonderful, loving marriages. Virginia and all her loved ones felt that Father Solanus had brought many divine blessings into their lives.

Little did I know then, as a boy, that someday I would serve as an archbishop, a cardinal, and, for a lengthy period, as a member of the Congregation for the Causes of Saints. In all those responsibilities, I have had wonderful opportunities to attest to Father Solanus's holiness. In so doing, I have reflected what thousands of Catholics in the United States have believed for many years: that Father Solanus was a man of great holiness and a most worthy candidate for sainthood.

Father Solanus is a model of evangelization. He never preached to enormous crowds nor did he travel from place to place giving parish missions. But from his humble station at the friary door, in Detroit and elsewhere, Father Solanus manifested the loving face of our heavenly Father. This good Capuchin priest was completely in love with God and at the same time very approachable. Thousands laid their burdens before him. He drew thousands close to the Lord and to the Church.

It is my hope that all who read this volume will allow the life and witness of Father Solanus to touch their lives with the truth and love of Jesus. I ask the readers of this volume to pray earnestly for the Cause of Father Solanus Casey, that he may some day be numbered among the saints whose holiness the Church recognizes and celebrates.

JAMES CARDINAL HICKEY
Archbishop of Washington

Editor's Note

This book contains virtually everything found in two of the three volumes of the official *Positio* (Official Record) needed by the Vatican's Congregation for the Causes of Saints for the Cause of the Canonization of Solanus Casey. The third volume submitted, the *Summary of Testimonies,* contains the official testimony of the fifty-three witnesses who testified before Detroit archdiocesan officials regarding Solanus Casey. This volume can be found in the Archives of the Vice-Postulator for the Cause at the Solanus Casey Center at St. Bonaventure's in Detroit or with me.

The remaining two volumes represent the core of this book: Solanus's biography of 327 pages, with pictures, and a presentation of Solanus's virtues in 145 pages, with appendix. The main sources for these come from the *Summary of Testimonies* as well as the *Collected Writings* of Solanus Casey. The only parts that have been deleted in this book are the historical overviews and documentation related to the various periods covering each chapter.

No citations will be noted in this book if they come from the *Summary of Testimonies* or the *Collected Writings.* The main reason for this decision rests in the fact that these generally are not accessible in libraries. Another reason is their sheer numbers. For the volume on Solanus Casey's "Virtues," there are 1,304 footnotes. Some of these 1,304, in turn, contain dozens of citations themselves. One footnote contains over sixty references to sources in the *Summary of Testimonies* and/or the *Collected Writings.* Full citations, overviews, and documentation can be found in these volumes and the official *Positio* in the Archives of the Vice-Postulator for the Cause at the Solanus Casey Center at St. Bonaventure's in Detroit or with me. Only sources not found in the *Summary of Testimonies* or the *Collected Writings,* therefore, will be cited as endnotes in this book.

MICHAEL H. CROSBY, OFMCAP.

Introduction

Hagiography and Heroicity

Hagiography: How the Study of a Holy Person's Life Offers Insight into the Moral Life[1]

*It seems to me that, were we only to correspond to God's graces, contin-
ually being showered down on every one of us, we would be able to pass
from being great sinners one day to be great saints the next.*

— Solanus Casey

This book, covering two of the three volumes in the trilogy of material
considered by the Congregation for the Causes of Saints for the Cause
for Canonization of Solanus Casey, OFMCap., focuses on his life and the
way the virtues were exemplified in it. Sources are his writings (*Collected
Writings*) and the testimonies of those who knew him (*Summary of Testimonies*), as well as other biographies and pieces written about him. Within
these pages will be found his biography and a discussion of his virtues,
especially details noting how he vigilantly practiced the theological and
cardinal virtues, the spiritual and corporal works of mercy, the evangelical
counsels, and humility. In this volume, it is hoped, there will be sculpted
an image of a person born in the United States of America whose life and
spirituality have a definite and hopeful message for our age, and all ages.

Traditionally, moral philosophy, or ethics, has considered the virtues
as necessary to and constitutive of ordered social interaction. Until very
recently, however, the virtues often have been relegated to a minor consid-
eration in reflections on the moral life. Indeed, in his influential book *After
Virtue*, philosopher Alasdair MacIntyre claims that we have abandoned altogether the essential language of virtue. The consequence has been the
lack of culturally accepted norms of life and behavior.[2] While courses in
moral philosophy linked to a "Catholic" approach never lost total sight of
the role of the virtues in determining rightly ordered human relations, only
recently has their value been discussed by secular philosophers or ethicists.

In her book on contemporary morality, *Saints and Postmodernism: Revisioning Moral Philosophy,* Edith Wyschogrod contends that in this "postmodern" era generally accepted norms as articulated in the virtues no longer have the strength to sustain community. Consequently, any moral system or ethical norms based on the virtues is debatable at best, or at least irrelevant. Contemporary ethics, the author insists, can no longer be limited to that level of abstraction found in a purely philosophical approach to the virtues. What society needs is a "new path in ethics." She contends that ethics can find more adherents if it stresses the role of "literary narrative," such as that contained in hagiographies, the stories of people considered "holy" (after the Greek word for holy: *hagios*).

According to Wyschogrod, a "stories of the saints" approach "exposes the presuppositions of the conventions of modernism as modernism encounters the actuality of our 'mascara and soap-opera age.' "[3] Rather than reverting to "an older hagiographic discourse," the highlighting of people considered by society as models and exemplars offers a "plea for boldness and risk, for an effort to develop a new altruism in an age grown cynical and hardened to catastrophe: war, genocide, the threat of worldwide ecological collapse, sporadic and unpredictable eruptions of urban violence, the use of torture, the emergence of new diseases."[4]

Solanus Casey himself stressed the value of hagiography as a model for the moral life. In 1915, having read the *Autobiography* of Sr. Therese Martin (just one of the many times he would do so), Solanus wrote a letter to his sister Margaret. He mentioned his admiration of the "Little Flower," not yet officially determined to be a saint, and suggested that Margaret's daughter, Therese, might benefit from emulating her life:

> Therese ought to imitate the little Servant of God, Therese of Lisieux, the "Little Flower of Jesus."
>
> Dear Margaret, if ever there was a good for a family like yours, her autobiography is one. She died only fifteen years ago. Her cause for beatification is now in Rome and I am asking her for entire reconciliation between J.T. and T.J., as well as other favors.... You ought not fail in procuring this book. She makes sanctity so really attractive and so beautifully simple. I think the book costs $2.00 at P. J. Kenedy and Son's, Barclay, N.Y. Do not fail to bless your family with its presence.

Many, including those in the Vatican who determine the necessary qualifications for sanctity, might have good reasons to consider an elaboration of the virtues to be necessary in determining whether someone like Solanus Casey lived the Christian life to a heroic degree. However, Solanus looked at the goal of sanctity from another perspective. In his mind there had "to be ways and means close at hand whereby, according to the lives of the saints, we may, if we try, ascend to great sanctity and to an astonishing familiarity with God even here as pilgrims to the Beatific Vision." Another letter, written around the same time, intimates that Solanus had found a possible way whereby one could "ascend to great sanctity." In his mind growth in holiness was synonymous with progress in knowledge of God and neighbor; this knowledge would lead naturally to increased appreciation of both: "To know and appreciate is to advance in the one science necessary — sanctity." For Solanus, there was no way one could know God or God's people and not appreciate them, and it was impossible to appreciate either God or humans without giving God thanks.

All spirituality involves God, self, and other. Hence, according to Wyschogrod, ethics constitutes "the sphere of transactions between 'self' and 'other,'"[5] whether that "other" is God or one's fellow humans and the world in general. What makes one a "saint" in those transactions is a recognized form of altruism toward those "others" that reveals how life can be lived with greater purity of heart or "singularity." Furthermore, this altruism or wholeheartedness is lived in such a way that it can be imitated; in other words, people are not saints unless others recognize them as worthy of imitation in their own lives. As the author notes:

> Saintly singularity *as seen from the standpoint of the saint's "flock" and addressees* takes as its starting point the visible manifestations of saintly desire for the Other, the saint's acts of generosity and compassion. From this perspective, saintly singularity is desire released from the bonds of a unifying consciousness, a desire that is unconstrained and excessive yet guided by the suffering of the Other. Despite the pain of saintly existence, the addressees of saintly discourse (if not always the saint) see the Other not as a weight or burden but as light.[6]

The rest of this volume will discuss the singularity that dominated the heart and actions of Solanus Casey, a man born in the United States of America. He offers people not only of that nation but of the world an example of virtue that can be imitated. In the process, it is hoped, the "other" — God and all people and creation itself — will be viewed as "light" because this Servant of God[7] let his own light shine for all to see in imitation of the One who said, "In the same way, let your light shine before others, so that they may see your good works and give glory to your Father in heaven" (Matt. 5:16).

For Solanus, "to know and appreciate is to advance in the one science necessary: sanctity." It is my hope that this book edited from the *Positio* submitted to the Congregation for the Causes of Saints detailing the life and virtues of Solanus Casey will serve to advance his cause for beatification and eventual canonization as well as, in its form here, make him better known for emulation.

Heroicity: An Outline of the Process for Canonization Used by the Vatican to Determine Whether and How Solanus Casey Practiced "Heroic Virtue"[8]

Solanus Casey died on July 31, 1957. At the beginning of 1958, Father Gerald Walker, minister provincial of the Province of St. Joseph of the Capuchin Order, sent to the general superior in Rome his report on the life and virtues of Father Solanus. At the end of this necrology on the Servant of God, Father Gerald wrote:

> As we attended his funeral, we could not help but think that there lies a man who lived almost eighty-seven years of life without tasting the good things of the world. It was not because he hated the good things God has made. It was not because he could not appreciate their beauty and desirability, but it was because he so loved Christ and souls that he could not allow anything else to come in between. Recognizing his utter poverty, his privation of everything, with scarcely enough flesh to cover his bones, one who does not love God would say: "Silly monk, crazy Capuchin." But it is my firm conviction that God will yet proclaim the truth about Father Solanus to the world.[9]

In response to Father Walker's report, the minister general of the Capuchin Order, Father Benignus, expressed great admiration for Father Solanus. He wrote:

> Father Solanus was certainly an extraordinary man, a replica of St. Francis, a real Capuchin. The wonderful spontaneous tribute paid to him by Catholic and non-Catholic alike is surely an ample proof that our traditional spirituality is still very much capable of winning

the people among whom we work to a realization of the primacy of the spiritual and Catholic outlook on life. May he still continue to do much good from heaven bringing many souls nearer to God and inspiring his own brethren with something of his own spirit.

By 1960 many reports from many places concerning the virtues of Father Solanus Casey began to be relayed to the friars at St. Bonaventure's Monastery in Detroit. Because so many people experienced Father Solanus's help either while he lived or since his death, an effort began to find some way to preserve his memory. On May 8, 1960, a group of lay friends met to discuss organizing a guild in his memory. On July 31, 1960, the third anniversary of Father Solanus's holy death, the Father Solanus Guild held its first membership meeting. It began with the approval of the minister provincial. The stated purpose of the guild is: "To keep alive the inspiring memory of Father Solanus Casey...to collect and disseminate information about the life and work of Father Solanus...to promote and support his Cause...and to uphold the inspiring ideals of Father Solanus Casey, especially his work on behalf of the poor and the missions." The guild now numbers over seventy thousand members in the United States and thirty-four foreign countries. Starting in 1970 the guild has published *The Father Solanus Guild News.* Four times a year, this official organ of the Cause keeps members informed about the progress of the Cause as well as promoting ongoing writings from and about Solanus Casey. It also includes reports of favors granted.

Beginning of the Cause for Canonization

In 1966, prompted by the continuous requests coming from the guild members and many people of Detroit — including clergy and religious — the minister provincial, Father Gerard Hesse, OFMCap., wrote to the minister general. He requested the appointment of a vice-postulator and directions on how to proceed with a Cause for Father Solanus Casey. A vice-postulator works at the local level with the postulator general at the Capuchin headquarters in Rome. He in turn is appointed as postulator by the Congregation for the Causes of Saints at the Vatican.

On October 4, 1966, Father Bernardine Romagnoli, the Capuchin postulator general, appointed Father Paschal Siler, OFMCap., as vice-postulator. Father Paschal then began to collect information about the life of Father Solanus, to gather statements from people who had known him personally, and to search for his writings. Throughout this time, the archbishop of Detroit, Cardinal John Dearden, was kept informed. On September 7, 1978, Cardinal Dearden granted the imprimatur for a prayer for the canonization of Solanus Casey. Well over a million copies have been printed and distributed. The text reads:

> Father, I adore You. I give myself to You. May I be the person You want me to be and may Your will be done in my life today.
>
> Thank You for the gifts You gave to Father Solanus. If it is Your will, glorify him on earth so that others will carry on his love for the poor, lonely and suffering of our world.
>
> In order that others will joyfully accept Your divine plan, I ask You to hear this prayer [*insert own prayer*] through Jesus Christ Our Lord. Amen.

In 1967, the vice-postulator began to compile the *Articuli* relating the life, work, and virtues of the Servant of God according to the instructions of the postulator general. Around this time James Patrick Derum of Detroit began work on a biography of Father Solanus. He had heard of Father Solanus several years before. He was so impressed that he felt he should be made better known. On his own accord he offered to write Solanus's story. This biography, *The Porter of St. Bonaventure's*, was published by the Father Solanus Guild in 1968. It has done much to popularize the story of this Servant of God. Since then two other full-length biographies have been written, *Thank God ahead of Time: The Life and Spirituality of Venerable Solanus Casey* by Michael H. Crosby, OFMCap.[10] and *Father Solanus* by Catherine M. Odell.[11]

On March 19, 1969, Pope Paul VI issued *Sanctitas Clarior.* It outlined new procedures for the Congregation for the Causes of Saints. The postulator general sent a brief outline of the new directives to Father Paschal on February 16, 1971. The revised procedures called for the obtaining of permission (a *Nihil Obstat*) from the National Episcopal Conference before initiating the Cause. On April 17, 1972, the National Conference of Catholic Bishops granted its *Nihil Obstat.*

The Provincial Chapter of 1973 made many changes in personnel. At this time, Father Paschal Siler was transferred to St. Labre Indian Mission at Ashland, Montana. This brought his work on the Cause of Father Solanus Casey to an end. A year later Brother Leo Wollenweber, OFMCap., was appointed as vice-postulator for the Cause.

Preparation for the Process

Leo met with Cardinal Dearden on June 24, 1976. After this meeting
he decided to pursue the Cause in the Archdiocese of Detroit. The first
step was to gather all the writings of Father Solanus. The following year
everyone in the dioceses where Father Solanus had lived and worked was
requested by Cardinal Dearden to submit to the archdiocesan chancery office any writings, letters, or other materials from Father Solanus By June
1980, these were organized into the Collected Writings of Father Solanus. In July 1980 they were all transcribed and bound into four volumes.
In September the NCCB again granted its *Nihil Obstat* for the Cause to
be opened. By the beginning of 1981, everything was ready for Cardinal
Dearden to petition the pope for permission to open the Cause in the
Archdiocese of Detroit. Included in the petition were the writings of Solanus, the *Articuli,* a list of fifty-four witnesses (lay people, priests, sisters,
and Capuchins, who had known Father Solanus over a period of years),
ten sworn and signed statements from people who had known Father
Solanus very well, and eighteen postulatory letters from bishops, religious
superiors, and prominent lay Catholics, along with the two letters of the
National Conference of Catholic Bishops with their *Nihil Obstat* of 1972
and of 1980. All these documents were sent to the postulator general to be
forwarded to the Congregation for the Causes of Saints.

The Investigative Process

On June 4, 1982, the Congregation for the Causes of Saints declared that
the Cause of Solanus rested upon a legitimate and solid foundation. It recommended that permission be given for the archbishop of Detroit to set up
the Investigative Process on the life, specific virtues, and outstanding signs
of the Servant of God. This decision of the Congregation was ratified and
confirmed by Pope John Paul II on June 19, 1982.

The instructions of the Congregation were sent to Cardinal Dearden's
successor, Archbishop Edmund C. Szoka. He, in turn, published the Decree to Introduce the Cause in the Archdiocese of Detroit on September 21,
1983. At the same time, he appointed the judge-delegate and the other
officials for the Investigative Process.

The Investigative Process involved testimonies of people who knew
Solanus well. Thirty single-spaced pages of questions prepared by the Congregation were asked of them by a tribunal of judges. The first session

was held on October 26, 1983, with twice-weekly sessions until September 1984. Fifty-three witnesses were examined, including priests, religious, and lay people. By the beginning of October 1984, the Investigative Process was completed. After Archbishop Szoka signed the decree to close the process on October 8, 1984, two sealed copies of the completed acts were then carried to Rome and presented on October 13, 1984, at the Congregation for the Causes of Saints. On November 7, 1986, the Congregation declared the acts of the process to be valid.

The Congregation then appointed a relator for the Cause in the person of Father Peter Gumpel, SJ.[12] Meeting with Father Paolino Rossi, the new Capuchin postulator general, Father Gumpel requested that an "external collaborator" be appointed from the Province of St. Joseph to prepare a *Positio*. The *Positio* would need to include three volumes: the collected testimonies of the witnesses noted above, a sociohistory of the time and biography of Solanus Casey, and an articulation of the way Solanus Casey exhibited heroicity in the practice of fifteen virtues (the latter two volumes summarized in this book). Michael Crosby was appointed to be the collaborator to the relator for the Cause in the summer of 1987.

As part of the process for beatification, following ancient procedures, it is necessary for the remains of a Servant of God to be exhumed and canonically examined. On July 8, 1987, in the presence of the archbishop and other officials and witnesses, the metal casket in which Solanus Casey was buried was raised from the ground. While the interior of the coffin was in poor condition, his body was found to be quite intact and recognizable although some decay had taken place.

After being cleansed and treated with chemical preservatives it was clothed in a new habit, sealed in a plastic body-pouch, and placed in a new steel coffin of plain design. Then the casket was carried into the church and to the side chapel where a crypt had been prepared. The casket was lowered into the new cement vault and then sealed with a heavy concrete lid. Another concrete slab closed the crypt, level with the floor. Later the entire floor was finished with tile, and a carved wood tablet with Father Solanus's name and the dates of his birth and death was placed over the crypt.

In 1988 two censors who had been appointed to examine the writings of Solanus Casey declared that they contained nothing contrary to faith or morals. Four years later, the three-volume *Positio* was finished and presented to the Congregation for the Causes of Saints. Upon its submission Father Peter Gumpel recommended an affirmative decision by the Congregation, noting:

While his example is relevant for all priests and religious, it would seem to be such in a particular manner for all Americans. They will be able to derive from his life an inspiration entirely based on faith and charity and at the same time, also deeply human: social, optimistic and cheerful, compassionate and active in trying to alleviate the spiritual and material sufferings of others.

On April 7, 1995, the Congregation's panel of theologians unanimously approved the *Positio*. When their findings were presented to the cardinal- and bishop-members of the Congregation, they gave it their unanimous approval on June 20, 1995. On July 11, 1995, Pope John Paul II promulgated the decree noting Solanus Casey's "heroic virtue" and bestowed on him the title "Venerable." This decree thus made Solanus Casey the first male born in the United States of America to be declared Venerable.

What is left before Solanus Casey can be beatified and then canonized is for the Congregation to recommend that the pope declare two "miraculous" occurrences attributed to the intercession of Solanus. One declared "miracle" generally is necessary for beatification and another for canonization.

Part One

THE BIOGRAPHY OF SOLANUS CASEY

Chapter 1

The Family Background of Bernard (Solanus) Casey

Parental Background

The dynamics of Irish history and the tensions between the Protestants and Catholics in Ireland were reflected as a microcosm in the backgrounds of the parents of Bernard Casey, later to become Solanus Casey.

Ellen Murphy was born January 9, 1844, in Camlough in County Armagh (now Northern Ireland). She was fourth in a family of five children born of Michael Murphy and Brigid Shields. Ellen followed Owen, Mary Ann, and Patrick, and preceded Maurice. All were born about two years apart. Her arrival coincided with the period of Ireland's potato famine (1845–49).

After Michael fell victim to the famine in 1849 his widow, Brigid, moved with her children to Dungooley. In 1852 she took her brood and journeyed to America from Liverpool on the ship *Western Star.* They arrived in Boston on June 21. Shortly after, the family moved to Portland, Maine. There Brigid and her two sons Owen and Patrick followed the pattern of most transplanted Irish subsistence farmers who came to the large urban areas: they went to work in the factories. Unprotected by labor laws, the three Murphys worked in a textile mill six days a week, twelve hours a day. The girls were supervised by a Portland woman in exchange for their help around the house. Little Maurice received the care of a family friend.

In 1859 Brigid moved to Hastings, Minnesota, to be closer to three of her children: Owen, Patrick, and Mary Ann. Mary Ann had married at sixteen and was now pregnant. Fifteen-year-old Ellen remained in Maine. Later Solanus Casey would write that this happenstance reflected "the wonderful designs of Divine Providence as revealed in the plans and strivings of these and similar 'children of St. Patrick.'" Part of this divine plan involved Bernard James Casey.

Born before the famine, on June 10, 1840, Bernard was raised in Castle-blayney in County Monaghan. Like Ellen, he suffered the premature death of his father, James. Like Ellen's father's death, Bernard's father's death also would be linked to British control of Ireland. On July 12, the day Protestants in Ireland commemorate Oliver Cromwell's invasion of the country, James and other Catholics were celebrating Forty Hours devotion in their local parish church. While he was there "Orangemen" (Protestants) attacked the church. In the ensuing battle, James was killed with a black thorn club. His grandson Bernard (to be Solanus) would later say he died a martyr in defense of the Blessed Sacrament.

Although times became better in County Monaghan after the famine, eighteen-year-old Bernard and his sixteen-year-old sister, Ellen, emigrated to the United States. The last thing his mother told him before leaving Ireland was: "Barney boy, keep the faith." Upon their arrival they joined their brother, Terrence, in the Boston area. Bernard went to work with his brother in a shoemaking and repair business.

The Irish had developed a pattern of marrying young. It was not unusual for boys to marry at sixteen, while girls were wed as early as fourteen. On the one hand it was "a form of reckless hopelessness. It led young people to conclude that the responsibilities of married life could not possibly make their condition worse." On the other hand, the priests encouraged early marriage so as to thwart sins against the Sixth Commandment.

On July 4, 1860, "Barney" Casey met Ellen Murphy at a picnic in Biddeford, Maine. Her face "beamed with kindness" in a way that attracted the serious Barney. After a short courtship, Barney proposed marriage. Ellen was sixteen. When Ellen wrote to her mother in Minnesota that Barney Casey had asked her to marry him, Brigid Murphy — now helping to take care of Mary Ann's twins — recalled that Mary Ann had married when she was sixteen. Consequently, her response was abrupt: Ellen was to leave Boston immediately and come to Hastings.

When Ellen arrived her mother explained that she wanted her to enjoy the years of her youth before being saddled with family responsibilities. Brigid arranged that Ellen would live with Mrs. Ignatius Donnelly, whom she had befriended in the choir at Guardian Angels Church in Hastings. True to the pattern at that time, this was the "Irish church." It stood a block from St. Boniface, the "German church." After Ellen had spent three years with the Donnellys, Mrs. Donnelly convinced Brigid Murphy to let her daughter marry Barney Casey. Thus, when the Donnellys made a trip to Boston, Ellen accompanied them.

On October 6, 1863, nineteen-year-old Ellen Elizabeth Murphy and twenty-three-year-old Bernard James Casey were married in a small church in Salem, Massachusetts. Because of the need of shoes for Union soldiers during the Civil War (1861–65), Ellen and Barney were able to spend but a half-day on their honeymoon.

When the war ended, the young couple moved to Germantown, Pennsylvania. There they sent for Terrence. Upon his arrival he helped Barney open a new store in New Castle, Pennsylvania, a mining town. However, due to a local depression and the Casey brothers' willingness to offer credit to parents of shoeless children, their business did not thrive.

If the shoe business was failing, Owen and Patrick Murphy were prospering at farming in Wisconsin. They had been urging Terrence and the young Caseys to come to Wisconsin, file a claim, and begin farming themselves. The fact that Ellen and Barney already had two children made the need for greater economic security offered by the homesteading more appealing. Little Ellen had been born on July 8, 1864, and James on August 14, 1865.

Terrence decided to stay in "the east." He went to Boston, graduated from law school, and later became a judge. However, in the autumn of 1865, the young Casey family took a train to "the west." Capitalizing on the Homestead Act passed by Congress in 1862, Barney Casey staked an eighty-acre claim in exchange for his promise to work the land for at least five years. There, while living with Owen and Pat, Barney, with the help of his brothers-in-law, constructed a log house beside the Mississippi River, just below Prescott on the Wisconsin side.

The Early Years of Barney Casey Jr.

While Barney worked the land, the family grew in the three-room log house with a lean-to shelter for oxen and a cow. Mary Ann was born on September 19, 1866, Maurice on November 7, 1867, and John on February 10, 1869. On November 25, 1870, a fourth son was born. Barney and Ellen Casey decided to give him the name of his father. Less than a month later, on December 18, their sixth child was baptized Bernard Francis Casey at St. Joseph's Church in Prescott. Soon the baby was called the same nickname as his father, "Barney."

The family lived at Prescott for eight years, until 1873. There, five children were born, including Barney. Years later the younger Barney (as Father Solanus) would recall:

> Here it was, smiling down on the "Father of Waters," that five of us were privileged to breathe our first morning air and "sing our first baby music." No doubt little Bernard must have been proficient in that music; because it was during his term of boyhood that Papa went blind with ague. For two weeks he had to be led by the hand, and his little namesake got a rupture from which he never completely recovered. Like in all other trials, however, the good God had His designs herein also, and we can say with fullest conviction and in all gratitude today: "The Lord knows best." May He be in all His plans eternally blessed!
>
> How we must have thrived there in real unworldliness and innocence. Dangers of course were not wanting, to keep dear Father and Mother "on edge" and often, no doubt, in anxiety. Wild beasts and rattlesnakes seem to have been the most common cause of such anxiety, though two of our little cousins were drowned together just below our little retreat near that River. Otherwise it was so generous, so noble, so majestic.

Meanwhile Barney Sr. continued working the land. Doing so in Wisconsin demanded learning a new way of agriculture different from that practiced in Ireland. Because manorialism and serfdom had not encouraged agrarian skills or knowledge, and because much of the land that was owned was small lots subdivided into even smaller lots for inheritance, Irish peasants were among the most inefficient farmers in Europe. Consequently they were not equipped for rural life in the United States. Farming in the Ireland of Barney's youth involved simple tools like the spade, the scythe, and the hoe. Now the larger plots of land, many covered with trees, demanded new techniques. But Barney prevailed and was a "quick read."

When Barney Jr. was three, Barney Sr. had proved so successful at farming that he was able to purchase another farm a few miles away at Big River, Wisconsin. Patrick had been born in 1872, and another baby was due in 1874. A larger place was needed; Barney's success enabled him to make the move. The new farm was part of an area called "The Trimbelle," after a nearby river. It was also closer to a Catholic church and school. Solanus later recalled the picturesque area teeming with a wide variety of wild flowers, fruits, nuts, and berries. In its pasture cattle grazed along with deer and other wild animals. It was here that his Irish Catholic identity was truly formed.

In Solanus's mind, he "had never seen a picture — in Bible history or elsewhere — so nearly like an earthly paradise," as he remembered the scenery at The Trimbelle to be — with deer in twos, threes, and more stopping on the hillside or in the valleys to gaze at what he might be doing. "No doubt," he wrote (in an allusion to sin), "what heightened the appreciation of those days was our innocence." Much of the time the older boys helped Barney Sr. in the fields and barn; young Barney's job was to help his mother in the kitchen. Now and then chores invited him into the fields, especially as he grew older. As he later recalled it:

> Those hills formed a great part of our pasture lands where we boys, especially Maurice and I (till he left for Stillwater to study), used to watch the cattle and study our catechism. Sometimes we'd roll rocks down the hillside ... or pick berries, or fish and swim till the cattle would stray away and get into mischief. Then we would have our own anxieties finding them. Sometimes we got our medicine for carelessness.

The Casey who would come to be known as "Solanus" often recalled vividly the years at The Trimbelle. He later described the "one story mansion about 12 x 30 feet" as having a public road that ran just past the "little log cabin." Below, a partition separated the bedroom of his parents from that of "Ellie and Mary Ann and little Mattie. In the loft above, the little boys slept." But little Barney and his brothers were typical boys. Consequently, as he recalled: "In the morning, they sometimes played till they quarreled as little boys are wont to do."

Besides quarreling with his brothers, young Barney also was not unaccustomed to fighting with his sisters. Once, when he was six years old, he threw a fork at one of them. "This is the first time you have ever done anything like this," Barney Sr. said. "So your punishment will only be three lashes. But if you do any such thing again, you'll receive six lashes. And if it should happen a third time, you'll get nine lashes." Although he was very emotional and could easily become angered at this early age, such stern discipline helped Barney Jr. realize his need to temper his anger.

Although the environment was idyllic, the family was often exposed to sickness and disease. In 1878 black diphtheria struck the neighborhood of the Caseys, taking the lives of twelve-year-old Mary Ann and three-year-old Martha. Several of the boys also contracted the disease. Barney Jr. had a particularly severe case which made his voice weak, wispy, and high-pitched for the rest of his life.

The Early Religious Formation of Barney within the Casey Family

Of the 1,925,000 Catholics migrating to the U.S. between 1830 and 1860, more than two-thirds (about 1,300,000) were Irish, one-fifth (400,000) were German, and just over 6 percent (120,000) were French. By 1860 the Irish-born constituted more than one-third of the total Catholic population in the country.[13] The United States Catholic community, especially the Irish and the Germans, was ripe for devotionalism. Evidence of this can be shown in the rapid rise of the devotional literature market. Ann Taves has shown that the publishing data suggest that the demand for devotional literature increased with the growth of the English-speaking Catholic population. Many of the Anglicized Irish immigrants who wanted to assert a distinctive cultural identity in the Protestant-dominated U.S. context found a Romanized form of Catholicism to be an effective vehicle.[14]

Two main forms of devotion existed at this time. The first involved those practices that were an extension of the celebration of the Mass and other sacraments, such as prayers before, during, and after Mass, exposition of the Blessed Sacrament, and scriptural or prayer devotions connected to the administration of the Sacrament of Penance. The second was to those devotions that might be prayed either privately or in a group, such as the rosary, the stations of the cross, litanies, novenas, and prayers to the Sacred Heart, the Blessed Virgin, and the saints, as well as prayers and practices to which indulgences were attached.[15]

A certain worldview pervaded the prayer books and devotional guides for the people. According to Taves, it helped create a kind of universal "Household of Faith" which united the church militant in an intimate, familial way with the saints in heaven.[16] Some common features of the devotions were that many were originally associated with religious orders, such as Forty Hours devotion with the Capuchins; all devotions were approved by some church authority; many of the most popular had not only ecclesiastical approval but even some kind of alleged supernatural foundation. Finally, they tended to be focused and specialized on some particular aspect of the Catholic faith (intercessory prayer and Our Lady of Perpetual Help) or some historical event (the apparition of the Sacred Heart to Margaret Mary).

Devotionalism rose in midcentury to such a point that it came to identify Roman Catholics of all ethnic groups and remained in the Catholic community for at least a century, overshadowing the Eucharist itself. In fact, for many Catholics, receiving Holy Communion was as good as attending Mass. Such attitudes must be kept in mind as we examine the prayer, piety, and practice of the theological virtues by the Caseys during the latter half of the nineteenth century and by Solanus Casey himself throughout his life.

One of Solanus Casey's earliest childhood memories was his family's regular night prayers during which everyone would pray "for a happy death and a favorable judgment." Every evening at seven o'clock Mr. Casey would ring a bell. It called all the children — and often the neighbor children as well — to the recitation of the rosary. This practice from his youth led Barney to recite the rosary each night, kneeling at his bedside even when he was away from home.

Daily prayers in the morning and at meals, as well as night prayers, were the staple of the Casey family. According to Catherine Odell:

> In the Casey cabin, there was prayer for rain, prayer to be spared from ravaging insects, blights, or molds, and prayer for dry days to harvest when the crops were ready. There were also prayers raised to avoid prairie fires and prayers offered for the protection of livestock — chickens, cows, the team of oxen, horses, and pigs. The Caseys prayed and never really got finished with praying.[17]

Whenever possible, after moving to The Trimbelle, the family traveled six miles to the local parish church on Sundays. Fasting since midnight, those going to the ten o'clock Mass would start out at eight. Because the family had only one horse and wagon, not all could go. So they took turns. One Sunday half of the children would go with one parent, and the next Sunday the other half would go with the other parent. Those staying home had their own service. Precisely at ten the parent staying home would gather the remaining children and read the prayers of the Mass for that day. When Mr. Casey led the services at home, he would talk at length on the text of the day's Epistle or Gospel. On one such Sunday when Barney Sr. was away, a fire descended across the fields toward the Caseys' farm. The reaction of those at home characterizes the quality of faith in action and word which its members lived. As Solanus later recalled:

The wind was pretty strong too and poor dear Mother seemed quite anxious. She was giving instructions what to do and getting ready for what must have looked like a probable burnout.

Ellie scratched a little "hoe-mark" out in front of the house and sprinkled holy water in it about half way down to the barn. By this time the fire was crackling through the grass and brush...and the smoke rolled over our heads in thick, dark clouds. Then the barn took fire, some ten rods east of the house, and we all went down, carrying some bedclothes, to the lone tree that for a long time stood in the middle of the original, four-acre field....As we huddled together under said lone tree...I heard mother saying in accents of relief: "Thanks be to God! Some of the neighbors have come and let the pig out."

At The Trimbelle Barney and Ellen Casey made sure that their Boston-Irish culture would help shape their environment. Though both left Ireland as teenagers, they carried with them its folk songs and stories. On many evenings they shared these around the table in the log cabin. Sometimes the children played indoor games, especially on cold winter nights. The cabin had been made warmer by the fact that Barney Sr. had made banks around the house to prepare for the winter. On winter nights, as well as at other times, Barney Sr. would read the poems of the great Irish poets and writers. He would also narrate Cooper's *The Deerslayer*, fascinating the children for hours. At other times, Barney Sr. would encourage the playing of the fiddle in the house. Barney Jr. tried to perfect it. Although his brothers urged him to practice in the barn, he kept at it, even throughout his later years.

The Trimbelle, like Prescott, proved financially successful for Barney and Ellen Casey and their ever-increasing "Casey Clan." So in 1882 they made another move, to Burkhardt, Wisconsin, in St. Croix County. Their 345-acre farm there housed a six-room, clapboard house, two barns, a large ice house, and a deep root cellar for preserving food. It stood near the Willow River and bordered the Dry Dam Lake, an excellent place for fishing and swimming.

By the time the family moved from The Trimbelle to Burkhardt, eleven-year-old Barney was in the older half of the Casey Clan, preceded by eighteen-year-old Ellen, seventeen-year-old Jim, fourteen-year-old Maurice, and thirteen-year-old John. Those following him were Pat (ten years), Tom (eight years), Gus (six years), Leo (four years), Ed (three years), and Owen (one year) — whom Solanus would later call "The Kid." Another girl, Margaret, was born on September 23, 1882, at Trimbelle. She would be followed by Grace in 1885 and Genevieve in 1888, both born at Burkhardt.

After the family moved to Burkhardt, Catholic magazines and devotional books abounded in the house, and Barney Jr. became well-read in things Catholic. A railroad ran though the farm. This made St. Paul, Minnesota, less than an hour's ride away. The railroad's presence also offered another way for Barney Sr. to meet the needs of his ever-expanding family. By this time he had already started selling subscriptions for the *Irish Standard* and *Extension* magazine, the latter dedicated to the promotion of expanding the home missions of the Catholic Church in the United States. With the railroad's proximity, Barney could now serve as a distributor for religious articles and catechetical materials.

After buying books at the religious goods store in St. Paul, he would return with them on the train. As the train neared the farm, he would lug the book-filled canvas bag to the train's rear platform. From there he'd heave the bag to the boys who waited to pick up the new supply. Then he would get off the train at Burkhardt and walk back. Barney Sr. encouraged the family to read the books before they were sold — as long as they remained unsoiled. In this way he could make sure his family was abreast of all the latest in religious thought.

Sundays not only enabled the family to spend extra time at prayer; they provided the family with time to be together and observe the Sabbath rest. Consequently Sundays were special for the Caseys. Barney Jr. soon learned how special Sundays were when he went rabbit-hunting on one of them. He never forgot being punished by his father, who viewed such an activity as a violation of the Sabbath.

When Barney Jr. would watch the cattle he carried his catechism and studied the truths of the faith. Two weeks before his First Communion, at the age of thirteen, Barney Jr. went nine miles to Hudson and stayed in the house of fellow parishioners from St. Patrick's. From there he joined other communicants at morning and afternoon instructions meant to assure the pastor, Father Thomas Kelly, that they were able to defend clearly the church's teachings. Following his First Communion, Barney Jr. "took the pledge," a promise not to drink alcoholic beverages until one's twenty-first birthday. Later that year in 1883, Barney and his brother John received the Sacrament of Confirmation.

In 1883 Maurice entered the German-speaking seminary of St. Francis in Milwaukee. His entrance into the seminary was an answer to a dream Bernard and Ellen Casey had nourished for years. Ellen's brother, Father Maurice Murphy, was a Catholic pastor in nearby Stillwater, Minnesota. She had rowed up and down the St. Croix River soliciting money and pledges for the church he was building there. Somehow, it was just assumed that her brother's namesake, Maurice Casey, would be the one to become the priest. Not only was this the case within the immediate Casey family; it was an assumption shared by relatives and friends as well as neighbors. When Maurice left the seminary after three years because of neurosis, the family was greatly disappointed.

By 1885, when he was fifteen, Barney was nearing the end of his elementary education. It took that long because of the need for his help on the farm. The last two crops had failed, and the winter of 1886 would prove to be bleak. As family necessity demanded that Barney Jr. take some more time from school to augment the dwindling family finances, the family turned even more to prayer. Now, in addition to the usual fifteen-minute evening family prayer shared by the entire Casey family, another petition was added: "that the harvest not fail totally."

By now Barney had been praying the rosary nightly before retiring. One night after a hard day's work with chores, he felt like skipping it just to get more sleep. While he had an inclination to forget about saying the rosary, he sensed a drive deeper than his need for rest. It would not let him get into bed. So he knelt down, determined to recite at least one of the five decades. He knelt upright, without support, following the example of his mother and Ellen. To his surprise, he was able to stay awake until the rosary was completed.

That night he dreamed he was suspended over a huge pit of flames and was about to fall into them. Looking around for something to grasp, he saw a huge rosary hanging just above him. He reached out for it firmly. Now he felt secure. Later he recalled that this dream reinforced in him a special relationship with the Blessed Virgin.

The family was close and supportive during those days and remained so for the rest of the lives of its immediate members. They not only worked hard and prayed fervently; they played well also. Dry Dam Lake afforded the family the chance to fish and swim, and the fields provided space for competitive sports, especially racing and baseball. Barney Jr. generally was the catcher for the "Casey Nine." His brother Edward recalled that young Barney played hard, but always with an air of playing largely for the fun of the game. Winning or losing, he remained good natured. He was never known to find fault with another player, never argued a point as if the world depended on it, and never got "huffy." He had no enemies. He participated in all sports except boxing. When asked why he refused to box he turned the question aside with a whimsical quip. His brothers thought it was because he just did not want to hurt anyone.

While nonviolent in this way, Barney did not lack courage to protect himself and others in the face of danger. When he was fifteen years old, as he and three younger brothers returned home after weeding an onion field, their dog, Rover, who had gone ahead, tangled with a wildcat near the Willow River. The dog's barking led them to where bloody Rover was bounding up against a tree as the wildcat lay on the tree's lowest limb. As they drew nearer the cat descended and another fight ensued. As Patrick struck the wildcat with a stick and the dog kept lashing out, Barney ordered little Leo and Ed to stay on the upper bank while he proceeded to circle the cat holding a heavy stone. When he got within two feet he threw the stone, which struck the wildcat's skull with a dull thud. He killed the animal.

As they carried the dead wildcat home in triumph, Barney suggested they play a trick on the family. They set it on the side lawn in a crouching position and then Leo rushed into the kitchen shouting, "There's a wildcat outside." As the family ran outside they found not only the cat but the four boys eagerly recalling their exploits near the river. Killing a wildcat brought a ten-dollar bounty — a small fortune in those days. Barney and Pat insisted that their father keep their prize.

The Early Education and Occupations
of Young Barney Casey

Barney Casey Jr.'s first education took place in the home. Any subsequent education he received was nourished by the faith-filled approach to life that characterized the family. However, little, if anything, is known of where and how Barney's formal education took place.

Rural schooling at that time revolved around the seasons for planting and harvesting. Furthermore, students such as Barney realized that family survival preceded formal education, so the latter was often deferred to insure the former. When the farm market became depressed in the mid-1880s, and with Maurice returned from the seminary, Barney Jr. searched for a way to help increase the family's dwindling income. If he could find work elsewhere, he personally felt free to leave home if he could obtain his parents' consent.

Although only sixteen years old, he received permission to go the twenty miles to Stillwater, Minnesota, to seek employment. There he worked during the days on the log booms, unjamming the felled trees that choked the St. Croix River. Barney's job was to feed logs into the Stillwater mills. At night he stayed with his uncle, Father Maurice Murphy, at St. Michael's. With winter approaching, the St. Croix waters would freeze the logs, so Barney would be out of a job.

His devotion to the Blessed Virgin was reinforced again later when he was seventeen years old and working at a brick kiln near Stillwater. His sister Ellen had given him a Brown Scapular of our Lady of Mount Carmel. As Solanus later recalled, it proved to be a most providential gift:

> Outside next to the building there was a large, deep pit filled with water. I saw a man fall in, and I dove into the water with all my clothes on and grabbed hold of him. He struggled with me and was pulling me down among the weeds so that I couldn't free myself.
>
> Suddenly I grabbed at the scapular I was wearing and with it I was somehow pulled up. Then another man who saw us dove into the water and pulled the man away from me. However, the drowning man struggled so hard that the would-be rescuer had to let him go, and so he drowned. I think I could have saved him. I know the Scapular of our Lady saved me.

He returned home to finish school and help on the farm. Although the wheat had failed, the other summer crops had been good. Barney's help from the Stillwater work and the money from the good crops made it possible for the family to pay off its debts. When all debts were paid, the first surplus in a long time was realized.

During his final year of grade school, at the age of seventeen, Barney pursued the debating skills he had begun to learn a year before. His keen insights and sharp wit, as well as his Irish background, made him eager to discuss facts and to perfect his argumentative skills. While he refused to participate in boxing matches, he often went out of his way to provoke a debate. One of the debates which involved him at this time dealt with the issue of prohibition of alcohol, which, in time, was to become a law of the United States: "Resolved: that the intemperate consumption of alcohol has been a greater evil than war." Barney, his older brother John, and their father constituted one team. While the outcome of the debate is not known, people recalled that it became quite heated, and it generated many comments among the audience who had come from the surrounding area for this public event.

This willingness to help the family financially led Barney to leave home at seventeen. After finishing eighth grade he began a series of jobs that would help the ever-growing family to make ends meet. He returned to Stillwater and began working there at the state prison as a handyman and relief guard. Among the prisoners were several notorious outlaws, including Jim and Cole Younger, whose crimes were well known throughout the nation. With his engaging personality and quick wit, Barney was able to befriend them to such a degree that one of the Cole brothers gave him a wooden chest, which Barney kept for many years.

The next summer he took a job as a part-time motorman on Stillwater's new electric street railway. Enjoying this new work, he then applied for a full-time motorman's position in Appleton, Wisconsin, about 230 miles to the southeast of his home. While waiting for an answer he earned money coloring photographs. When a job in Appleton opened for him, he moved there, thus beginning his permanent separation from his family. He kept this job about a year until the late spring of 1890, when he moved to the rapidly growing port city of Superior to work as a streetcar motorman there.

While his short time as a prison guard and his change of places from Stillwater to Appleton to Superior as a motorman — all in three years — might indicate a certain instability, Barney Jr. seems to have made these moves not because he felt they might provide permanent work for him but because they provided more money with which he could help his family. This money was especially needed because drought and cinch bugs in 1887 and 1888 had caused two successive years of crop failures. The money he sent home became very important for the family welfare.

Barney Jr.'s Developing Intimacy and Friendships beyond His Family

Besides being a house of faith, hope, and love for its members, the Casey home welcomed all who came. Somehow, ethnic differences which elsewhere brought clashes between Irish and Germans and Germans and French and all of these with the English had no place there. The neighbors liked to visit because the Casey spirit was expansive, gay, and welcoming.

There was good talk, singing, and political discussions, as well as farm-talk. Many of the neighbors were Irish, Germans, or French-Canadians whom political or religious discrimination had driven from their countries. Here, in the Casey home, such discrimination was absent. The family members learned what it meant to be open to all people.

Among the neighbors of the Caseys was the Tobin family. Andy Tobin was the last person with whom Barney Jr. was known to have become violently angry. This occurred when Barney learned that Andy was the likely culprit who poisoned Rover, the Casey dog that had previously battled the wildcat. Barney's brother Edward recalled: "When Barney first saw the dog's stiffened body, he paled with anger. Andy, he threatened, would pay for the crime. Grief-stricken, he went to his room. When he came down again, he was calm. He never uttered another word about punishing Andy."

Andy and his sister Rebecca went to school with Barney and the rest of the Caseys. In their midteens Rebecca and Barney developed a mutual attraction. They began to spend time together at school, and later. With her dark hair and eyes and her sweet and pleasant personality, she held a special attraction for Barney. At fifteen years of age she was the kind of young woman other girls admire. When Barney left home for Stillwater, he stayed in communication with her. She also wrote to him. Through their visits and correspondence their attraction became more serious, as was evidenced in a letter which nine-year-old Gus discovered in Barney's half-open valise while Barney was visiting home. In the letter, which Gus read to Leo and Ed, Rebecca informed Barney that she had told her mother of his desire to become engaged to her and that her mother had refused approval. Because she was only sixteen, the Tobins sent her to a boarding school in St. Paul, about forty miles away. The romance was nipped in the bud.

Although frustrated in his proposal to Rebecca, Barney Jr. lost no time in developing other relationships with young women. One of the attractive young women in whom he later admitted having "an interest" was "a modest school friend of cousin Tess" by the name of Nellie O'Brien (who later became his brother John's wife). However, realizing he was quite emotional, Barney kept his distance and did not allow himself to develop a relationship with Nellie in the pattern that had happened with Rebecca.

With small groups of young men and women of his own age, as well as in crowds, Barney was an excellent mixer. People felt his genuine care for them and enjoyed having him at their parties, especially when he brought his violin. Practice had made him able to carry a recognizable tune, and he knew the latest dance numbers. Although his music was only passable, it was free and open-hearted and added to the liveliness of the parties that took place at that time.

Barney's Initial Vocation:
Sensing a Need to Make the World Better

In 1891, after Barney had moved to Superior as a motorman, he urged his family to join him there. After three successive years of crop failures (1887–89), Barney Casey Sr. did not need much prodding. He moved to Superior the same year. There he added 160 acres to the 40 acres already owned by the three oldest brothers. Highlighting the complex was a ten-room house.

In Superior Barney Jr. began more seriously to think about something that had been developing in his mind for many years: he might be called to be a priest. Even before Maurice went to the seminary, Barney, at thirteen, "began to wonder if possibly there couldn't be two priests in a family," thinking "he would be the other." Although his father had been very disappointed when Maurice left the seminary, even muttering, "If I were to start life over, I'd be a priest," Barney had not been known to articulate his own thinking about this particular vocation.

On a late afternoon in the fall of 1891, as he worked at his conductor's job on the trolley cars, something happened which proved to be the kind of jarring experience many people need to begin a conversion process. On this cold, dreary evening, as the trolley rounded a corner in an area of Superior known for its poverty and crime, it came to a halt. There a crowd surrounded a drunken sailor standing over a woman on the track. As he stood with a knife in his hand, the sailor was drunkenly cursing the woman. In a few moments two policemen arrived and disarmed him at gunpoint. This experience shook young Barney Casey quite like nothing before.

He realized that this was not just an isolated incident, but revelatory of the wider violence and anger in the world beyond Superior. As he prayed for the woman and her assailant, Barney began to feel that he could not just pray to bring about change in the world. He, too, had to help make the world change. At this point he came to realize he had to redirect his life more radically.

After two more days of thinking and praying, he visited his pastor at

Sacred Heart rectory in Superior. He told him that he wanted to serve God as a priest. Father Sturm recommended the diocesan seminary in Milwaukee, St. Francis de Sales. The fact that he was twenty-one years old and had finished only eight grades of school meant he would be starting seminary high school with boys five or six years younger than himself. However, he accepted the suggestion of Father Sturm, and thus began the separation from his family for religious reasons. This would keep him separated from them geographically, but not emotionally or spiritually, for the rest of his life, except for rare occasions.

Remaining Connected to His Family throughout His Life

Once he left home for the seminary in Milwaukee, except for his home visits before entering the Capuchins, Barney [Solanus] Casey returned to visit his family only three times: in 1911, when Maurice (who had decided to return to the seminary around the time of Solanus's ordination in 1904) celebrated his First Mass; in 1913, when his parents celebrated their golden jubilee of marriage; and in 1945, when his newly ordained nephew, John McCluskey, SJ, offered his First Mass.

However, after he entered the Capuchin Order in 1896, Solanus by no means lost contact with his family. Throughout his life he kept up an active correspondence with them and, after the death of his parents, especially with his brothers and sisters and their children. Many of these visited him when they "came East" from Seattle and were near the places where he was stationed. His niece, Mary Casey Molloy (the daughter of his oldest brother, James), worked for the Campfire Girls organization. It transferred her to Detroit in January 1930. Solanus had been transferred there in 1924. She recalled:

> I lived on the West side of Detroit, but worked on the East Side so I could often drop into the monastery on my way home from work. I would take my place with other visitors at the monastery office, sometimes waiting half an hour or more. As he stood up to say good-bye to the person he was speaking with, he might glance up and spot me. Then he would beckon to me to step inside his small inner office. I would feel guilty to thus get ahead of others waiting before me. When he would get a chance to come in and talk to me, he always

wanted the news of the family, especially my dad and mother. He also asked news of all my uncles and aunts in the Casey family.

Sometimes if I hadn't stopped to see him for several weeks, he would call me by phone. In his wispy voice he would say, "This is your old uncle just calling to hear how you are and what's the news from Seattle."

This special care for his family as well as the extra time he gave them on the rare occasions when they visited him is evidenced in the testimony of his Jesuit nephew, Father John McCluskey. In 1953 or 1954, when he was studying in Chicago, Father McCluskey visited Solanus at Huntington, Indiana. When he arrived, several people were waiting to speak to Solanus. Despite this fact, Solanus spent three hours talking with Father McCluskey. When the latter began feeling uneasy that the others needed attention, Solanus merely said, "Oh, I think it is God's will that I should be talking to you. It has been so long since I have seen you, I think I should talk to you. They will be taken care of. God will take care of them."

One of the recollections repeated regularly among those who either waited to speak to Solanus or who observed others waiting for a chance to talk with him was the tranquility of the people who waited, no matter how long. Somehow the sense was that Solanus would take as much time with everybody as was needed, and that somehow this was all part of God's plan.

On this visit, Father McCluskey came to know how much Solanus believed in God's loving providence. As he noted:

Just prior to my going down to Huntington to visit Father Solanus, I purchased an airplane ticket for my return to Seattle. On the morning that we left for Huntington, there was a report in the daily papers of an airplane crash in New York in which three people were killed. I...canceled my reservation and then proceeded to the train depot and bought a ticket for the train. When we got to Huntington, in the course of our conversation, Father Solanus revealed that he had just flown to Huntington from Detroit that morning. I asked him: "Were you not afraid?" and he just said, "Oh no, we're all in the hands of God; He takes care of everything." I was so impressed that when I returned to Chicago I returned my train ticket and bought the airline ticket for Seattle.

Solanus evidenced a special bonding with Maurice, who became a priest in 1911, and with Edward (later to become a monsignor), who was ordained in 1912. In 1904 Maurice had come from Chicago, where he worked for the Railroad Mail Service, to Appleton, Wisconsin (the Capuchin parish closest to his parents' home), for Solanus's First Mass. Maurice served the Mass. Later in the day, as the two strolled together in the monastery garden, Maurice "brought a tear" to Solanus's eye when he told him something that he had been thinking about for more than two years: "By George, Barney, I think I'll have to try it over again. I'm getting tired of this blamed rail-roading!" He did try again for the priesthood.

Although he told Solanus that he would never become a diocesan priest, Maurice entered a seminary in Berlin (now Kitchener), Ontario. From there he wrote Solanus, "I have found the grace again I looked for so long." He was ordained in 1911 for the Archdiocese of St. Paul, Minnesota, and spent his first years as a priest ministering in mission parishes in "the West." Gradually growing more melancholic and disillusioned, he used the occasion of a 1928 visit with Solanus in Detroit to discuss with him and the Capuchin superiors his desire to join their Order. He returned to Detroit again for Solanus's silver jubilee of ordination on July 28, 1929. On August 10, 1929, he entered the new novitiate of the Province of St. Joseph at Huntington, Indiana. He received the name Joachim. In April 1930, Solanus wrote his sister Margaret: "Thanks be to God, he seems well and hopeful of making profession in September."

Not being with his brother, Solanus knew only what his brother would share with him or what he heard from others. The superiors, however, sensed something amiss. They decided not to accept the sixty-two-year old's request for vows. Instead they offered him the possibility of remaining part of the province as a Third Order member. He would be able to keep his own money but be under obedience to the local superior where he would live. His first assignment was Yonkers, New York. From there he went to Our Lady of Sorrows in Manhattan. While there he celebrated his priestly silver jubilee in 1936. Solanus went to Manhattan to celebrate with Maurice. He noted an increased agitation and depression in his brother. It was not long before Maurice's neurosis increased to such a degree that the superiors decided to send him to Marathon, Wisconsin, to the Capuchin theologate built there in 1917.

By the following year, 1938, Maurice had become dissatisfied at Marathon and, even more so, with Capuchin life. He declared he wanted to return to the St. Paul Archdiocese. Solanus forcefully and clearly disagreed with the thinking of his brother. On December 15, 1938, he wrote to him of his prayerful concern. He told him that he had offered his "rosary this morning... for your intentions and your guidance." He reminded him of his increasing age and appealed to him to be concerned only about the salvation of his soul. The letter is written tenderly and is full of recollections of happier times. As to Maurice's thoughts about rejoining the St. Paul Archdiocese after an absence of almost a decade, Solanus argued:

> But dear Father Maurice Joachim, I hardly know what to say or to think of your present proposition to write back to your old diocese, to a prelate you've probably never met and who has possibly never heard of Father Joachim. Naturally you would hope to be received with open arms, dreaming as you probably do, of some cozy little place just smiling across the Wisconsin hills at you. Ah, dear Father Maurice Joachim! You may be sure, such would be only dreaming. Your age and your experience should rather exclude such dreams as belonging to the long ago. This we might think especially, considering your years of dreaming when and how you might get away from the world to a monastery. Think of it, Father Joachim....

At Marathon the local doctor who cared for the friars wanted to have Father Joachim committed to a mental institution but would not do so because he did not have the permission from an immediate family member. Before this could be received, a very painful carbuncle on the back of his neck necessitated that Maurice receive special treatment at St. Agnes Hospital in Fond du Lac, Wisconsin, twelve miles from Mount Calvary. When medical personnel there did not know how to treat him, he left for Detroit. However, he was so hostile toward the community at this time that he would not come to the headquarters except for a visit with the provincial. This resulted in Maurice's being asked to leave the Order.

After leaving Detroit, Maurice wandered around the East Coast. Finally, it was discovered that he was a "guest" at Mt. Hope Sanitarium in Baltimore, Maryland, a broken-down, embittered old man. In an effort to support him emotionally and spiritually, Solanus visited his brother there from July 20 to August 5, 1940. However, Maurice's debilitated psyche and emotions affected Solanus to such an extent that the following January 1 he noted with truly fraternal concern that he was "inclined to be discouraged in regard to Fr. M. Joachim's condition" and, thus, rededicated himself to prayerful reflection.

In 1945, when it came time to attend the ordination of their Jesuit nephew in Seattle, Solanus made it clear that he would not go unless Maurice went as well. Consequently Owen, Patrick, and Edward traveled to Baltimore to pick up their brother. Solanus met them in Chicago and continued with them to Seattle. The reunion did much to buoy the spirits of Maurice. He died four years later on January 12, 1949, after a peaceful retirement at the Benedictine Sisters Hospital in Graceville, Minnesota. The fact that he could go to Maurice Joachim's funeral in Graceville brought Solanus much peace. Upon his return to Huntington he remarked what a joyful occasion the funeral had been.

Solanus's relationship with his priest-brother Maurice was one of solicitude, but the bonds he established with Edward involved deep respect and mutual concern about the promotion of faith among God's people. Even before Edward's ordination, the priest and poet in him sensed the unique fact that Solanus's priesthood would revolve around the Eucharist. Since Solanus's first assignment in Yonkers (1904) involved being sacristan as well as porter, Edward authored a poem, "The Brother Sacristan." He sent it to Solanus, who often shared it with others.

Edward was ordained a priest in 1912. After various assignments in the Archdiocese of St. Paul, including a professorship at St. Thomas College, he volunteered to serve in the missions of the Philippines, where he became a monsignor. Whenever he returned home he made it a point to visit Solanus. During the Second World War he was interned by the Japanese in a prison camp and released in 1945. During his life, Solanus often shared poems written by Edward and quoted passages from Edward's letters, including one that he used often: "God condescends to use our powers if we don't spoil His plans by ours." Edward, along with Martha Casey, their deceased brother Owen's widow, was with Solanus in his dying days and celebrated his funeral Mass in Detroit.

During their life the two brothers kept up an active correspondence. Solanus saved the letters from Edward and wanted to make sure he would be sent them when he moved from Detroit to Brooklyn in 1945. However, Solanus's letter-writing was not limited to just Edward. It extended to his entire family — especially his sister Margaret LeDoux and his brother James, to whom he wrote a particularly long letter (fourteen pages) dated July 18, 1938, recalling many events from their childhood — and to his nieces and nephews. While most of the time his letters were in response to theirs, often he would write a short note on the occasion of one of their birthdays or other days of significance to them or their family.

Family Celebrations

Solanus's few visits to his family afforded him many fond recollections. Maurice's First Mass occasioned a trip from Yonkers, New York, to Superior, Wisconsin; the other two took him to Seattle, Washington. In the autumn of 1913 all four daughters and ten sons joined together to celebrate the fifty years of marriage of their "dear parents." They had moved to Seattle in 1905 or 1906 to be nearer their children, most of whom had settled in that area. Edward presided at the Mass and Maurice was deacon. Solanus was subdeacon and preacher. His sermon stressed gratitude to God for the past fifty years of union as husband and wife blessed with each other, the blessings of their many children, gratitude for their present health, and prayerful thanks for their holy and happy future. Years later Solanus recalled some of the reminiscing that took place in the week the family had together:

> ...at the Golden Wedding in 1913, we were all musing over scenes and events on the River Bank and in Old Trimbelle. Someone remarked, "Wouldn't it be nice if we could go back there again!" Dear mother, gently sighing as if revisioning the trials of those days which outweighed their beauties and pleasures, half-whispered an exclamation: "Thanks be to God, I'm glad it's over."
>
> Many a time since I've thought, how beautiful was that little exclamation. It was really Christian!

The last time Solanus visited his family was in 1945, for the occasion of the First Mass of his nephew, John McCluskey, SJ, in Seattle. Solanus went to his nephew's First Mass in the same old black suit he had when he entered the Order almost fifty years before. The First Mass in Seattle was Father McCluskey's first recollection of meeting Solanus. What impressed him was Solanus's "very intense person, absorbed in whatever he was doing at the moment. In regard to his spirituality, what impressed me was his complete trust in God."

Experiencing the death of his sisters Mary Ann and Martha in 1878, Solanus got used to the death of loved ones at an early age. Barney Casey Sr. died a slow and painful death in 1915. Three years later Ellen had a "beautiful death...at the second ringing of the Angelus." Obedience kept Solanus from being with the family for their funerals. In time, one by one, his siblings passed over to the Lord. The first to die after the two little girls was the eldest, Ellen. She succumbed to cancer in 1928. The next two died quickly and tragically. In January 1929, on their way home to Seattle from Tacoma, where they had been trying a lawsuit, Solanus's two lawyer brothers John and Thomas were killed in a car accident. Owen died in 1955 and Patrick in 1956. These deaths were particularly hard for Solanus since he was so close to these brothers. However, his natural sorrow was cushioned by his faith-filled grief. He could weep for the passing members of his family and yet thank God for having taken them to their eternal reward.

When Solanus died in 1957 the only siblings still living were Margaret (LeDoux), Genevieve (McCluskey), and Edward.

Chapter 2

Barney Casey Jr.'s Response to His Call: Failure in the Diocesan Seminary; Acceptance by the Capuchins

Catholicism in Wisconsin: The German Influence

Possibly one reason why Barney Jr. did not seem terribly concerned when Rebecca Tobin was not allowed to accept his proposal of marriage when he was seventeen was his recollection of something that had happened more than a decade earlier. It had made him sense he might be called to the priesthood. When he was about seven years old, at a time when it was assumed that Maurice would be the priest in the family, Barney had a feeling that he, too, might be called to the priesthood. In a fragment of a letter he drafted for a member of the family around 1949, Solanus noted that when he "was in his seventh year... and perhaps earlier, [he] began to wonder if possibly there couldn't be two priests in a family — hardly hesitating that [he] would be the other [himself]."

Thus, when Barney Casey Jr. experienced the incident of violence on the motorcar tracks in Superior and began to perceive a wider world of violence around him which demanded a personal response, Barney made the appropriate decision: to consult with a spiritual guide.

Father Edmund Sturm was pastor of Sacred Heart, Barney's parish in Superior. Aware of his family background as well as his piety, Father Sturm recognized in Barney a certain steadiness and self-respect. If Barney was willing to enter a high school seminary with younger students, his pastor saw no reason why he should not recommend the twenty-one-year-old for the seminary.

It would have been much closer and much easier academically if Solanus would have been born on the other side of the Mississippi or lived in Duluth rather than Superior. The seminary serving Minnesota was in St. Paul

35

and everything there was in English. However, the seminary Father Sturm had in mind was St. Francis de Sales Seminary in Milwaukee, where Maurice had attended for three years sometime around 1883–86. Maurice had left there, a broken young man. The texts were mostly in Latin and the courses were taught in German. If Barney could face the obvious comparisons with his brother, no moral or spiritual encumbrances would hinder him. Or so he thought. There would be another challenge that would be even greater: the culture he would be entering by going to Milwaukee's seminary.

In 1843 Milwaukee became a diocese, with John Martin Henni as its first bishop. He became archbishop of Milwaukee in 1875 with two suffragan sees, Green Bay and LaCrosse. The Caseys lived in the diocese of LaCrosse. It had been established as a diocese in 1868, two years before Barney Jr.'s birth. At that time it had eighteen priests and forty-seven small churches. Its first bishop was Michael Heiss.

Believing that the life and development of the Catholic Church in the Midwest and Northwest depended on priest-graduates of a seminary, Archbishop Henni founded St. Francis Seminary in Milwaukee.[18] Thus, if any man within his overall jurisdiction (including LaCrosse) desired to go to seminary, it would be in Milwaukee.

If one made a triangle with Cincinnati and St. Louis as two of the points and Milwaukee the third, within this triangle (excluding Chicago) German language and culture dominated in the Catholic Church. In the U.S.A., every other diocese or archdiocese was Irish American. Although English-speaking Catholics were in the majority in the Archdiocese of Milwaukee and almost all the others understood English, only two of the thirteen professors at St. Francis Seminary spoke English when Barney Casey arrived there.

Life at St. Francis Seminary

St. Francis Seminary had a full schedule. The students were awakened by a bell at 5:30. Morning prayers and an hour of meditation preceded Mass which was celebrated at 6:45 a.m. Breakfast was at 7:30 and the first class started at 8:00. After a full day of classes, prayers, meals, and a little free time, they retired at 9:30 p.m.

Being five to seven years older than his classmates, Barney would automatically be a natural model for them. However, their emulation of him was reinforced by more than a simple age difference. Although associating with what he considered "children" was quite embarrassing and difficult for him, he modeled a solid spirituality and a fraternal charity. When the students might develop difficulties with each other or have an incident that led to an altercation, he would come between the combatants, saying, "Now, boys, take it easy!" The warring parties, who considered Barney to be like an older brother, would soon be friends again.

To help meet his expenses, Barney cut the other seminarians' hair. He also found time to recreate. In winter he skated on a big rink the students had made. In spring he played baseball, although demands of time allowed him only to be a relief catcher. Possibly used to the way he played at home with his brothers on the "Casey-All-Brothers-Nine" team, he refused to wear a catcher's mask. Despite warnings about his safety from stray balls hitting him in the face, he made the sign of the cross, crouched as close to the batter as he could, and carried on.

While he was never injured by a baseball, Barney seemed to have more than usual attacks of "quinsy sore throat," the common name for peritonsillar abscess. The disease caused throat swelling, penetrating pain, and fever. These regular incidents were bound to undermine his efforts to apply himself to his studies.

The Growing Academic Problems of Barney Casey Jr.

The seminary had three areas for grading a seminarian's work: academics, application, and conduct. During Barney's first year of high school he generally received marks of "Excellent" for all three. His lowest mark was in "vocal music," quite possibly due to his soft, wispy voice that developed with the black diphtheria when he was eight years old. During the fall and winter of 1892–93 his averages showed a slight falling off, but his marks remained in the 80s and 90s.

On his return home for the summer vacation of 1893, he joined the family in working the farm. But he also made time to organize a small literary society among his brothers and friends. For the 1893–94 school year, his grades slipped again, but were still sufficient to move on. In his final year of high school (1894–95) he was able to raise his marks sufficiently to be allowed entrance into "Class Five," the equivalent of a first year in college.

In the first semester of his "Fifth Year" (1895), he received good grades in Christian doctrine and English (as well as excellence in application and conduct). However, after the second semester, his grades fell considerably. They ranged from 70 to 77 percent in Latin, algebra, geometry, and history, and from 77 to 85 in German. His highest scores, 85 to 93, were in vocal music, U.S. history, and natural philosophy. These grades were not exactly failing marks, but they were low in courses critical for his future, particularly Latin.

At this point the seminary superiors informed Barney that he would not be able to manage his studies if he continued in the diocesan seminary. Despite his efforts and the amount of time he gave to better his grades, he lacked "the basics" needed to pursue serious studies. The seminary superiors decided that he did not have a vocation to the priesthood.

While Barney accepted their decision without a challenge, at this point one can rightly ask what might have happened (allowing for God's providence that had it happen this way) had Barney been in an environment that better nourished him as an English-speaking person. On the one hand there were personal issues that got in the way. First, Barney did not seem to have developed regular study habits as a youngster. Second, he had been away from studies for a long time. Third, his highly intuitive nature made details and long hours at study extra burdensome. The result was that, at this time, he found that his "brain just didn't seem to want to work." On the other hand, despite such realities that contributed to his lower grades and the superiors' decision, there may have been institutional obstacles as well.

In the same year that the superiors said he could not continue for the diocesan priesthood an editorial appeared in the *Milwaukee Catholic Citizen* noting that other state and Catholic colleges had graduated large numbers of Irish Americans that June, but not one Irish American could be found in the graduation class at St. Francis de Sales Seminary — only German- and Polish-Americans. The *Citizen* challenged: "What is the explanation of the situation? Is there a dearth of vocations for the priesthood among the Irish Americans of Wisconsin? Or is there something inhospitable about the atmosphere of St. Francis? We pause for meditation."[19] That the English-language Catholic paper would ask such a question in a predominantly Germanic church indicates that "Irish need not apply" might refer not only to jobs in the wider society but to the seminary as well.

Introduction to the Capuchins

While determining that Barney had no future at St. Francis, the seminary superiors were sensitive enough to the work of God in people's lives that they sensed Barney might have a vocation to religious life. Hence, they suggested he visit the Capuchins in Milwaukee, whose seminary was near the city's downtown area.

Traveling the five miles from St. Francis de Sales Seminary on the shores of Lake Michigan to the Capuchins' St. Francis (of Assisi) Seminary, Barney was not impressed by what he saw. When he was a teenager, Barney had thought he might have a vocation to the religious life, but he did not know to which Order he wanted to go. Academically, what he found at St. Francis Seminary downtown was like that at St. Francis Seminary at the Lake. The Germanic environment was *déjà vu*. Here again, course work invariably would be in Latin and explained in German. On the emotional level he did not like what he saw, either. The Province of St. Joseph, founded by two German-Swiss diocesan priests, was noted for its austerity. The beards of the friars — often untrimmed — did not present a positive image to someone as concerned about appearances as Barney seems to have been. He could not imagine himself going through life encumbered by a beard. It may have been the strict Rule and way of life they observed, or perhaps the more urban setting of the seminary. Whatever happened during that visit, the impression that Barney carried with him when he left was not favorable toward the Capuchins.

Barney returned home for his summer vacation of 1896 very uncertain and quite unsettled. Furthermore his throat seemed to get worse. He confided in his mother and his now-married sister Ellen, who often visited the family home. He prayed to know God's will. He found himself wondering what God wanted of him, especially if God wanted him to continue in the seminary. His chief question was: "Does God want me to be a priest?"

At this point Barney went for counsel to a priest well-known in the Superior area for his wise and prudent advice. He was a Franciscan of the St. Louis province, Father Eustace Vollmer. He sometimes assisted at Sacred Heart. In a most positive way he alleviated Barney's concerns and assured him that he felt he did have a religious vocation, as well as a priestly one. He encouraged him to apply to his own Franciscan Order and not to reject the possibility of joining the Capuchins. Responding to Barney's repulsion by the Capuchins' beards, the Franciscan remarked jokingly: "You above all, Barney, should value the Capuchin beard! Those big beards protect the throat and chest. With that troublesome quinsy of yours, a heavy beard is precisely what you need!"

Given the advice of Eustace Vollmer, Barney decided to send a letter of application to the provincial of the Capuchins, Father Bonaventure Frey. He also sent a letter to the Franciscans, asking how he could be admitted to the Sacred Heart Province. Another group that Barney seems to have considered was the Jesuits, even though his academics would seem to indicate that this interest could not have been serious.

To help him discern God's will, Barney decided to make a novena to the Blessed Virgin, to end on the Feast of the Immaculate Conception. He asked his mother and Ellen to join him. On the last day of the novena he felt the call to celibacy. Consequently he made a "vow of chastity and at once" experienced a call to go to Detroit. The words "go to Detroit" he considered a "favor of Our Lady." While the meaning of the revelation was clear (that he would be going to the Capuchins, whose novitiate was in Detroit), the source of this revelation is unclear.

In Solanus's own written words the revelation seems to have been given as a strong conviction. However, others have said that he told them it came in a dream and a vision. Given these various interpretations, the phenomenon (or, more properly, people's recollection of what he said happened) deserves more examination.

James Maher first met Solanus when the latter was stationed at Huntington, Indiana, between 1950 and 1954. One of his visits included driving Solanus from Detroit to Huntington, a trip that took about four hours. In response to Maher's questioning about some kind of "sign" for a particular vocation, Solanus told him that while he was still in doubt about which Order to join he had a dream. In this dream he found himself at a railroad station in Chicago. He had no idea what he was doing there or where he was going. Then suddenly he had in his hand a ticket, and on this ticket was printed the word *Detroit.* He realized then that his vocation was to the Capuchins, since the headquarters of the Capuchins was in Detroit.

A more dramatic interpretation makes the "Detroit revelation" an actual "vision" of the Blessed Virgin Mary. This has been recalled in official testimony by the one Capuchin who, during Solanus's lifetime, proved to be his greatest critic, Father Elmer Stoffel, and by a lay couple, the Ryans, who told slightly different versions. Mrs. Daniel Ryan said, "On the last day of the novena he said the Blessed Mother appeared to him and told him to go to Detroit. He said when the Blessed Mother appeared to him, she appeared on the wall of the church." Daniel Ryan simply testified: "He told us that he came to the Capuchins because he had a vision of the Blessed Mother telling him to come to Detroit."

The most detailed vision interpretation can be found in the writings of Capuchin Cuthbert Gumbinger. He lived with Solanus while he was in Huntington and later became archbishop of Smyrna, Turkey. Cuthbert recalled:

Bernard continued to pray to Our Blessed Mother for the whole time of the novena before the feast of the Immaculate Conception in 1896. On the feast itself, as he related to the writer, he went to Mass and Holy Communion and felt very happy and at peace. As he knelt in prayer after Holy Communion Our Blessed Mother appeared to him in a clear, external vision and told him simply: "Go to Detroit." Our Lady did not hold the Divine Child but seemed rather like our pictures of her as the Immaculate Conception. For Bernard it was a never-forgotten day, and the experience gave him a wonderfully beautiful and tender love, devotion, and confidence in the All-Holy and All-Powerful Mother of God.[20]

While the interpretations differ between the two other versions and Solanus's own words recalled in 1908 twelve years after the incident, they have one common element: recognition that the message was "Go to Detroit." Since the Capuchin novitiate was in Detroit, the meaning was clear: Barney Casey Jr. should go to the Capuchins. Although he did not want to give up everything to enter religious life, his reluctance was overcome by prayer, as well as the sense that God's will had been made clear.

When Barney announced to the Caseys that he would be joining the Capuchins, they were extremely pleased. In deference to the position of his local bishop, he had earlier consulted his ordinary and received clearance from Bishop James Schwebach of La Crosse, Wisconsin, who assured him: "No doubt you will become a good religious." He had received clearance also from the Capuchins earlier, assured by Father Bonaventure that, if his father and brothers offered the procurator of the seminary "half of the amount of your debt, I have no doubt it will be accepted. I know neither the Most Reverend Archbishop nor the Reverend Rector will object to it." Having been assured his debts would be paid, the provincial also wrote Barney: "I will make no objection now to your application of joining our novitiate, as the Rev. Rector of the Salesianum thinks you have a vocation for monastic life. You may therefore come to Detroit, as soon as circumstances will allow you, or the sooner the better for yourself."

Within thirteen days of hearing the message "Go to Detroit," Barney was ready to leave. His family, realizing that once he entered the Order he probably would never be home for the holidays again, urged him to stay until after Christmas. But Barney's mind was made up. With his strong will power, he was determined and even quite enthusiastic to begin. He packed his bags and left Superior on the 11:00 p.m. train, December 21, 1896.

Chapter 3

Solanus Casey's Novitiate, Studies, and Ordination in the Province of St. Joseph (1896–1904)

Novitiate

After the train battled snow much of the way from St. Paul to Milwaukee, Barney Casey Jr. took advantage of the layover there to visit the Capuchin seminary a mile from the depot. The next day he left for Chicago. There he transferred to a Detroit-bound train pulled by two locomotives. Averaging twelve miles an hour through the heavy snow, the train arrived at Detroit at dusk. From the depot he went to St. Bonaventure's, arriving at "the privileged novitiate" on Christmas eve.

Barney was greeted warmly by the porter, by the superior of the community, and by his future novice-master, Gabriel Messmer. Although they offered him a meal, Barney was too exhausted to eat. He wanted only to go to his room and get some sleep before Midnight Mass. As he walked up the stairs to the room designated for him, he noticed the starkness of the architecture, which reflected the Capuchins' poverty and austerity. Opening the wooden latch of his "cell," he saw a 9 x 12 foot room with a single curtainless window overlooking the large grounds behind the friary. Opposite the narrow iron bed stood a one-drawered wooden desk with a straightback chair. Two clothes hooks on the wall would hold all his clothes, if not then, at least once he became a Capuchin.

With the Capuchins gone and the door closed, Barney looked around in anxiety and wonder: what had he gotten himself into? Recalling the December 8 experience, he asked in confusion: "Why did our Blessed Lady send me here?" Suddenly all the former negative feelings and prejudices against the Capuchins seemed to envelop him; his fatigue only added to the sweeping depression that came upon him. Taking off his coat, he lay on the bed with a blanket thrown over him. Only a deep sleep quieted his misgivings.

Although his fears and anxieties about the future were dissipated by the Christmas celebrations, they surfaced again as he anticipated his investiture with the habit and entrance into the novitiate slated for January 14, 1897. By the 13th, Barney's doubts had reached a peak. In the small book of the Rule of Francis and the Constitutions of the Capuchins that had been given him, he noted that it was a "day of anxiety," "dark indeed." Despite his fears, which seemed to have remained with him, his resolve to "go to Detroit" seemed to be strong enough for him to proceed with his investiture in the Capuchin habit. Upon receiving it, he also received a new name: Francis Solanus, in honor of the violin-playing Spanish Franciscan who worked in South America in the seventeenth century. Somehow, in receiving the habit and the name, he received also a peace and a conviction about the rightness of his decision that would remain with him for the rest of his life.

Within the tightly regimented horarium, which began with 4:45 rising, "Frater" (Brother, the title all men received until they were ordained if they were on the "clerical" track) Solanus adapted quite easily to the routine of prayer and play, classes and "clericalia" (household chores). Frater Solanus began writing in a notebook various personal reflections and admonitions to himself as well as sayings (mainly in English, though some in German) from saints like St. Augustine, St. Gregory, St. Theresa, and various Franciscan saints. The notebook also contained addresses, retreat notes, and recollections of past events. The first page had three entries:

> "You are afraid to suffer here & unwilling to go hence; what shall I do with you?" — Our Lord to a sick bishop. "If I must die once, why not now?" — St. Augustine. "Can one do better than humble that and overcome it which God has given us to master, & which a loving Providence has ordained should be humbled?" — i.e. the flesh.

During the novitiate, Solanus became increasingly aware that his initial enthusiasm and efforts might be colored as much by a desire for a good reputation and to be respected as for the honor of God. Having this realization, he copied a quotation in his notebook:

> As for desiring to do things which may deserve glory, though it is what magnanimity desires, yet the magnanimous man desires it not for the glory that arises therefrom but only that he may deserve the

glory without possessing it. On the contrary he has raised himself so high above the opinion of the world, that finding nothing estimable but virtue and looking with the same eye on the praise and scorn of man, he does nothing for love of the one or through fear of the others; his flight is higher. It is for love of God and virtue that he is moved to perform great actions; all other motives have no influence on him. Virtue is so excellent a thing that men cannot either reward or recompense it sufficiently. God alone can do this.

God alone was what Solanus was beginning to desire; his heart was becoming purified. This purification began with the eradication of cupidity, the enemy of charity. Quoting Bonaventure (in Latin), he noted: "Hinc sicut radix omnium malorum est cupiditas, sic radix et principium perfectionis est altissima paupertas" (Since the root of all evil is avarice, so the root and principle of perfection is most high poverty).

One could not reach the goal of perfection (which principally consists in charity), he noted from Bonaventure, without certain steps or practices. In particular, Solanus decided, he would begin to practice in the noviatiate, and try to develop, controls which would make these steps part of his permanent approach to the spiritual life. Thus, immediately before the quotation from Bonaventure he entered the following:

MEANS FOR ACQUIRING THE LOVE OF GOD

I. Detachment of oneself from earthly affections. Singleness of purpose!

II. Meditation on the Passion of Jesus Christ.

III. Uniformity of will with the Divine Will.

IV. Mental Prayer-meditation & contemplation.

V. Prayer — Ask & it shall be given to you (Matth. VII-7).

Immediately following the Bonaventure quotation he noted:

TO PRESERVE GOD'S PRESENCE

I. Raise your heart to Him by frequent ejaculations.

II. Make a good intention at the beginning of each work & frequently during its execution.

Gradually, by purifying his natural inclinations and by becoming more centered in God and abandoned to God, he learned to be free from both excessive rigidity and the anxious scrupulosity that earlier seems to have been a problem. This problem could be overcome, he believed, the more he became abandoned to God.

Solanus's spirituality during the novitiate was not just inner-directed; it extended in charity to his confreres, especially his fellow novices, who were not allowed to speak to professed members except their superiors and confessors. Realizing his charity might be hindered by his single-mindedness and/or his perfectionistic tendencies, he knew he might be quite judgmental. Consequently he wrote in his novitiate notebook the following quotation, without noting its source:

> If a fault of anyone disturbs you, know that it is more a weakness for him than for you, and that he suffers more from it. Perhaps, however, it is but "a mote in thy brother's eye" which on account of "the beam in thy own," appears so great. At all events have the charity to pray the Lord to deliver thy brother and if the latter be the case, it will prove a double blessing.

Seeing that Solanus built his life around such intentions, the solemnly professed Capuchins in the novitiate came to consider him a good candidate for first vows. He passed his first two "scrutinies" (evaluations) with nine positive votes. The last scrutiny took place November 17, 1897. There he and another novice received eight positive votes and one negative vote. It is not known why the negative votes were cast, although the vote against Solanus could have had to do with his poor German and Latin.

Whether or not the negative vote dealt with his questionable academic skills, the Capuchin superiors later approached Solanus about their own concerns in the matter. They feared he would not have the necessary grasp of his course work in the seminary ahead. With first vows coming soon, they also wanted to discover his motivation for entry into the Order. Was it to be a Capuchin or to be a priest? In those days, many people came to the Capuchins to become priests, since Capuchins were the only priests they knew. Solanus had been told that he could not become a diocesan priest. While he had come to the novitiate not excluding the idea of being a priest, he came to be a Capuchin. If one day he might become a priest in the process, fine.

To satisfy their concerns, the Capuchin superiors asked Solanus to state his intentions clearly on this point. To allay any fear they might have about his future abilities at the seminary and its effect on his vows and possible ordination, Solanus made an "Attestation" on July 20, 1898, the day before he would make his first vows:

> I, Fr[ater] Solanus Casey, declare that I joined the Order of the Capu-
> chins in the Province of St. Joseph with the pure intention to follow
> thus my religious vocation. Although I would wish and should be
> thankful, being admitted to the ordination of a priest, considering
> the lack of my talents, I leave it to my superiors to judge on my
> faculties and to dispose of me as they think best.
>
> I therefore will lay no claim whatsoever if they should think me
> not worthy or not able for the priesthood and I always will humbly
> submit to their appointments.

Living more than fifty-nine years after making this "attestation" indicated that Solanus remained true to his promises to "lay no claim
whatsoever if they should think me not worthy or not able for the priesthood" and always to "humbly submit to their appointments."

Studies

Having made his "attestation," Solanus was accepted for first vows. On
July 21, 1898, he knelt before Father Bonaventure, the provincial who also
had accepted him into the novitiate twenty months earlier. He declared: "I,
Frater Solanus,... vow and promise to... live in obedience, without property, and in chastity." Immediately after this, he and his newly professed
classmates took the train to Milwaukee. There they would continue their
studies at St. Francis Capuchin Seminary.

As in the novitiate, Solanus quickly adapted to the new regime. Although the schedule here revolved mainly around studies, Father Anthony
Rottensteiner, the Director of Studies, insisted that the cleric seminarians
also have other outlets for some external ministry. Consequently, Frater
Solanus was given charge of the friary chapel and the altar boys for the
parish church of St. Francis which was connected to the U-shaped monastery at its northern side. In his assignment, Solanus was conscientious
to the point of perfectionism. According to a classmate, Father Boniface
Goldhausen:

> As far as his work is concerned, he was always on time. I do not re-
> member that he ever came late for religious exercises or for the work

to be done. It was always perfect.... He was very exact and painstaking. At times I would go down to the choir when he was busy there. I would observe him. I was highly edified. On feast days he would put perhaps three candles and three bouquets out. Then he would put candles one on each side and he would go way back and look at it. If it wasn't exactly perfect he would go back and move one candle until they were just where he wanted them. It was the same thing with the bouquets.... It took him at least a half hour to trim that simple choir altar. But at the same time he seemed so recollected. When he was finished, he made his adoration. One would notice that he was deeply absorbed spiritually. That's one thing I cannot forget.

That Solanus made such an impression on a fellow classmate that he would remember it seventy years later indicates that Solanus's behavior appeared to be edifying even then. However, while classmates like Boniface might consider Solanus quite exacting in the spiritual journey, he himself was aware of his own deficiencies and his tendency to be overly impatient with them (and himself). In his notebook he reminded himself: "Patience, therefore, *with* your faults." Solanus learned then that he needed to be patient not only with himself and his failings, but also with his classmates. His impatience, while not vocalized, led him to pass judgments on them. Aware of this undesirable tendency, he cautioned himself: "Beware of silent criticism."

College-level days found Solanus increasingly concerned about human beings beyond the cloister walls, as well as about his own inner life, motivations, and efforts at fraternal charity. In his notebook he reminded himself that the "Traits of Saintly Characters" consisted of three things: "(1) Eagerness for the glory of God; (2) Touchiness about the interests of Jesus; and (3) Anxiety for the salvation of souls." Since some of those "souls" were "interests of Jesus" in a particular way, Solanus realized at this early stage of religious life that they must become his interests as well. One of the first quotations he had noted in his little book came from Pope Clement XIV, while he was still a cardinal. It addressed the need to be concerned about the poor and one's neighbor:

Be not contented with giving, but also lend to him that is in need, according to the precept of the Scriptures. I do not know a more contemptible object than money if it be not employed to assist our neighbor. Can the insipid pleasure of heaping up crowns be compared with the satisfaction of conferring happiness and the felicity of attaining heaven?

In communications to others at this time, he seems to have urged them to do what they could for the poor, as well. In one extant letter from that period he reminded his sister Ella to "admonish" their brother Owen "not to neglect the most salutary [deed] — almsgiving for the poor and orphans."

While Solanus might have felt obliged to do what he could for the marginal of society, his position as a student demanded that he spend the majority of his time in studies. However, given his past problems at the diocesan seminary and Anthony Rottensteiner's stress on excellence, combined with the fact that the whole context for his studies was the German language, which was a second language for him, Solanus began to manifest some of the same difficulties as before. In his final semesters of philosophy he was just below average in his class of six. His records show that he found philosophy itself the most difficult subject.

Textbooks were in Latin and lectures and discussions took place in German. According to his classmate Father Boniface Goldhausen, Solanus could handle himself "very well" in German and gave "good answers in German at the classes." However, these had been two of his most difficult subjects in his first year of philosophy at the other St. Francis Seminary in Milwaukee, a few years before.

In spite of having courses taught in a language not native to him and lectors who did not understand his need for other learning methods, Solanus, as well as the province, placed the onus for his difficulties squarely on his own shoulders. When he began his first semester of formal theology in the fall of 1899, the superiors voiced their serious concern whether Frater Solanus would be able to succeed within the prescribed academic system. Although their general impression was that the educational problem rested in Solanus's own academic deficiencies, the professors did not deal with him severely in any way. This was especially true of Anthony Rottensteiner. Despite his reputed severity, Anthony sensed something special about Frater Solanus that was expressed in the way he related to his confreres — even to wanting them to win at chess — and the way he meticulously and devotedly performed his tasks as sacristan. The director of studies did whatever he could to coax answers from him, especially when he realized any stumbling on Solanus's part might not be from want of understanding, but because of the nuances of the German language and Latin texts.

A report card of his first year of theology shows that he was having great difficulty. The difficulty was compounded by the fact that small numbers of theologians necessitated a rotation system wherein courses were taught on a four-year cycle. Thus, upon entering theology, Solanus would be with others who had three years of theology more than he. Six months into his second year, there was no change. By now, the superiors had become very concerned. Solanus was to make solemn vows on July 21, and it seemed certain that he would not be able to complete successfully his academic courses. If he took solemn vows, he would have to realize that this did not mean he would be ordained. Furthermore, if he were to be ordained, that did not mean he would be allowed to function fully as a priest.

Although Solanus was aware of his situation and had indicated at the time of his simple vows that he would accede to whatever decision his superiors decided about his possible future as a priest, the superiors again demanded that he put this understanding in writing. Thus, on July 5, 1901, Solanus signed a statement that declared his intentions. Ironically, the statement was drafted in German:

> I, Fr[ater] Solanus Casey, having entered the Order with a pure intention and of my own free choice, wish to remain in the Order, and I therefore humbly ask for admission to solemn profession. However, since I do not know whether as a result of my meager talents and defective studies, I am fit to assume the many-sided duties and serious responsibilities of the priesthood, I hereby declare (1) that I do not want to become a priest if my legitimate superiors consider me unqualified; (2) that I still wish to be able to receive one or other of the orders, but will be satisfied if they exclude me entirely from the higher orders. I have offered myself to God without reservation; for that reason I leave it without anxiety to the superiors to decide about me as they may judge best before God.

The next school year (1901–02) witnessed Solanus's grades slipping slightly. Possibly thinking that this slippage was quite insignificant, the superiors allowed Solanus to receive tonsure, the first step into the clerical state. The following year, despite minimally lower grades again, he received the subdiaconate, his inauguration into major orders. A deciding factor seems to have been the intervention of Anthony Rottensteiner. "We shall ordain Frater Solanus," the Director of Studies had said, "and as a priest, he will be to the people something like the Curé of Ars."

In February 1904, Solanus's first semester grades indicated that something serious had happened with his academic performance. He received no marks at all for Sacred Scripture and Liturgy — two courses essential for effective priestly functioning. The superiors were raising even more questions. That same month Solanus indicated that there were questions regarding his reception of the other orders, although the odds indicated the decision would be made in his favor. Nevertheless, he sought to be open to whatever resolution the superiors might make. He wrote his sister that he would "probably be ordained deacon and priest before August. May the Holy Ghost direct my superiors in their decision in this regard and may His Holy Will in all things be done." This time, under his signature, Solanus added *"Resignation+,"* one of the few times he would sign his name this way.

Ordination

Despite his efforts, the next months showed no significant improvement. While his combined grades in Dogma, Morals, and Canon Law were the best average he had yet achieved, no marks were awarded for Sacred Scripture and Liturgy. Of six in his class, three clerics had received mostly all "good" and "very good" and "average" marks. The other three, including Solanus, received almost all "average" and "passing" grades. Solanus came just behind Frater John O'Donovan and quite a bit ahead of Frater Damasus Wickland. Because these three had such poor grades, it was decided that they would be ordained with their classmates but that they would remain "simplex" priests. This meant that they would be ordained but never given permission to "hear confessions" or preach formal sermons (which are contained in "preacher's patents").

Solanus and his five classmates were ordained in the parish church of St. Francis on Sunday, July 24, 1904. The ordaining prelate was the ordinary of the Archdiocese of Milwaukee, Sebastian Messmer, the brother of Solanus's former novice master. It was one of the happiest days of Solanus's life. Two days later, in Rome, the head of the Capuchin Order, Bernard of Andermatt, signed the letter giving Solanus his "preacher's patents"[21] contingent on the decision of his immediate superiors. John O'Donovan later convinced his superiors that he could receive them; Solanus never tried to change their mind. He and Damasus would remain simplex priests — able to offer Mass but never to hear confessions or to preach formal sermons — for the rest of their lives.

A week later, on July 31, 1904, Solanus celebrated his First Mass at St. Joseph's Church in Appleton. The province had a policy that First Masses must be offered in the Capuchin parish closest to one's home, so Solanus's family came the two hundred miles from Superior to join in the celebration. It was the first time he had seen his mother since joining the Order eight years before. She had come with Barney Casey Sr., and Maurice had come from Chicago, where he worked with the Railroad Mail Service. As Solanus recalled it, the day was momentous not only for him but for all in the family, especially Barney Sr., who "wept all during the Services at the thought that God had finally blessed his family with a priest." Later in the day, as they walked through the monastery garden, Maurice told Solanus that he had decided to try the priesthood again.

Shortly after ordination, Solanus received his "obedience" assigning him to Sacred Heart parish in Yonkers, New York. He was to be there by August 4, 1904, four days after his First Mass.

Chapter 4

Yonkers, New York, 1904–18

National and Parochial Life during the Period

Having achieved its overseas ambitions by the defeat of the Spanish in 1899 and having declared the same year that there would be an "Open Door" policy for China, the United States now was successfully exerting international influence. With William McKinley's assassination in 1901, Theodore Roosevelt became president. In the year Solanus Casey arrived in Yonkers, the "Roosevelt Corollary" was added to the Monroe Doctrine, unilaterally asserting U.S. police power in the Americas.

Roosevelt was succeeded by William Howard Taft in 1909. Although Taft was less flamboyant than Roosevelt, his one term (1909–12) was more effective in stabilizing the nation. In a notebook which covered that period and dealt mainly with altar boys, the young Father Solanus indicated that national and world events were not beyond the monastery doors only. An entry for September 29, 1911, noted: "*WAR* between Italy and Tripoli." The first notation for 1912 (after "In the Holy Name of Jesus Let Us Begin the Year 1912") was: "The old year closed with a dreary day-rain, snow and fog — as though mourning at prospects it had to leave for the new year of trouble and promises of war on all sides and directions." On page 12 Solanus noted that the "giant steamer *Titanic,* a $6,000,000 ship 'bumpt' against an iceberg and the pride of naval equipment was buried in a watery grave with 1200 passengers. Nearly 1000 souls were rescued." On the next page, an entry, "July 2nd, Feast of Visitation," noted that the "Democratic convention decided on W. Wilson as candidate by a 46th ballot" after various machinations. Three pages later the notation stated: "Nov. 5th. Woodrow Wilson elected President of U.S. by Democratic 'landslide' — congratulated by opponents." It was under Wilson that the United States entered the First World War.

As noted earlier, much of Catholic life revolved around devotional piety, especially that related to Mary and the saints. The rosary and Tuesday devotions to Our Lady of Perpetual Help were regular mainstays. Capuchin parishes followed the tradition of having Forty Hours devotions and Tuesday prayers to St. Anthony, as well as Lenten stations of the cross. The Provincial Chapter of 1885 had "stressed with great emphasis the devotion to the Sacred Heart in all monasteries and parishes, ordaining that a Holy Hour be held at midnight before every first Friday of the month, although no friar should be strictly obligated to attend."[22] Marian apparitions such as those at Lourdes were unquestioned; private revelations of Jesus, the Blessed Virgin, and the saints were considered part of the mystical life of holy people who, in turn, communicated the revelations to ready recipients.

The parish served as the focal point of social life for Catholics. In addition, a multiplicity of groups, such as sodalities for young women and athletic groups for young men, were formed beyond the parish to promote Catholic social teaching and other Catholic values. These groups had a "Father Moderator" or "Priest in Charge." Thus, besides Catholic forms of worship and Catholic schools, there were Catholic Boy Scouts and Girl Scouts, Catholic lawyers' guilds and doctors' guilds, Catholic summer camps, Catholic societies to promote agriculture, poetry, economics, and journalism — all of which were copies of identical societies in the secular world.[23]

Sacred Heart in Yonkers had been founded in 1891 by the Capuchins. Into this setting came Solanus Casey on his first assignment.

First Assignments for a Simplex Priest

In Solanus's eyes, the "monastery of the Sacred Heart in picturesque Yonkers" was "ideal." However, in a clerically controlled church that was sacramentally oriented, Father Bonaventure, the pastor, did not have an easy assignment for the new resident who only recently had been ordained a "simplex priest." Seemingly at a loss to come up with anything else, he assigned Solanus the care of the sacristy and the overseeing of the altar boys. In the eyes of many people this might seem demeaning for a priest; in the eyes of Solanus, the care of the sacristy was a special privilege. Referring to his sacristy work, he wrote: "Something came to mind of our ineffable privilege in doing the little things we are able to do for the general welfare — most especially in a religious community. Each one is in his own place without thought or distinction as to what the work may be. To whatever office or service one may turn, it is not easy to say just which is more privileged, possibly excepting that of a sacristan."

In his function as sacristan, Solanus regularly served the Masses of the other friars and also served as chaplain of the Altar Society. In his role as chaplain to the altar boys, Solanus did not always find the task pleasurable.

Since he was conscientious to the point of being pedantic, Solanus did not tolerate sloppiness or mischief among the servers. His notebook is filled with entries about altar boys who were late, who misbehaved, and who "spilled burning censer on carpet." However, other entries speak of more serious matters, including various tragedies suffered by the servers. One of these is of Martin Kennedy, who was mentioned in a notation of December 31, 1911: "Happy death of altar-boy Martin Kennedy at 3 a.m. Had served 93 times during 1911 A.D. A dear good boy of eleven years. R.I.P."

Although he was very strict with the altar boys, Solanus knew how to reward their fidelity. His notebook speaks of elections and of prizes — including gold and silver medals and a pearl knife — for those who served the most times (B. Landy served 560 times), as well as of subway trips to Manhattan and of baseball games. An entry for December 25 noted: "Feast of Nativity — a happy day for the altar boys — and for all the parish — though very busy for the former. All received Holy Comm[union]. A few of the boys served as much as five times. They enjoyed the privilege but seemed tired when all was over in the P.M. Aloysius McCarthy to serve for the first time arrived for duty and rang door-bell at 3:45 a.m."

The altar boys did not like to serve Mass when Solanus celebrated it (often at 5:30 a.m.) because they thought it took too long. However, when the time for outings came, they wanted to make sure they were in his good graces. James Lawless was one of the many boys who were altar servers for Solanus. He recalled:

I have fond memories of the good times we had under his super-vision, such as the yearly outings for the altar boys. I remember on these occasions that we had to attend Mass and pray for a safe journey to and from our destination. These visits were to Rockaway Beach, to St. Patrick's Cathedral, and other places.

Before heading home, Father always treated us to an ice cream soda. After that we would stop at the nearest church and say a few prayers for a safe return home.

Father Solanus was the personification of patience when it came to teaching us our Latin for serving Mass. He was a patient, dedicated, and devoted servant of God.

When the altar boys misbehaved or did not seem to have correct demeanor, Solanus would firmly reprimand them. Any insensitivity and lethargy in face of the sacred mysteries troubled him. One time their inattentiveness reached such a degree and his corrections had fallen on deaf ears to such a point that Solanus began a novena to Our Lady of Perpetual Help in the hopes that his anxieties and fears about the servers might be resolved. Quite soon, before he "thought how it came, every one showed new zeal."

When a new superior ("guardian") and pastor, Father Aloysius Blonigen, came to Sacred Heart in 1906, one of the first things he did was to give Solanus another job. Solanus would be the doorkeeper, or porter, of the monastery and church offices.

Beginning the Ministry of Porter

As porter at Sacred Heart, Solanus quickly learned about the problems people faced in ways that went beyond the theories he had learned in theology. In the early days after the Capuchin with the dark black beard appeared at the desk in the front office on Shonnard Street, people came and asked to talk to a priest. Solanus would tell them that he was a priest, but when they asked him to hear their confessions they became confused when he said he could not. They had observed him celebrating Mass at the side altars, so why could he not hear their confessions? "I'm not able to," is all Solanus would usually reply.

As word began to spread about his compassion, sensitivity, and gentleness with the many people who started to come to see him, the parishioners developed their own reasons why he did not hear confession. One of these was that, because he loved God so much, hearing the sins of others might be too difficult for him to bear. One woman recalled: "Father Solanus loved God so much that he could not hear confessions because he might not be able to take it if he discovered how many people were hurting God!"

His humility and concern were evident to people who came to see him. One person recalled: "He never acted as though he was what he wasn't. He accepted people wherever they were. If you were sick, he hurt with you. He was very compassionate. He could say a few words to you and you would be perfectly at ease." Regularly each morning the people in the neighborhood would see Solanus sweeping the sidewalks and talking with those who passed by. Other times they would see people going into the office and coming out with food; Solanus had seen to it that they would not go away hungry. The story circulated in the parish that Solanus gave away his dinner, fasting instead of keeping the food for himself.

People with troubles unable to visit Solanus in the office often asked him to come to their homes. These included not only the Germans and the Irish who constituted the core of the parish, but the newly arrived Italians as well. As an eight- or nine-year-old, Carmella Petrosino acted as Solanus's interpreter for many in the Italian community. "If anything went wrong in the neighborhood, the people would say, 'Go, get the Holy Priest.'" She recalled:

> We lived in the neighborhood where there were all Italians who had just landed from Italy. Our parents couldn't speak English. We lived three blocks below the monastery. In between there were lots of woods. My father went to St. Anthony, the Italian church, but my mother went to Sacred Heart. I was in the third or fourth grade there.
>
> I went from house to house, acting as Father Solanus's interpreter. My first experience happened with Mrs. Maria De Santo in our neighborhood. She had come from Italy with her three or four children, and was about to deliver another. In those days instead of doctors, they had midwives, so my mother went over to help. In the process of delivering the baby, the woman got very, very sick. As the days went on infection set in. The doctor came, very concerned about her failing health. My mother said, "I don't think Maria is going to get over this; she's going to die."
>
> So right away I suggested that I go and get "the Holy Priest." To the Italians, they wouldn't say, "Father Solanus," they would just say, "The Holy Priest." So I went to Father Solanus and told him that one of the ladies who just had a baby was going to die. So we started down the hill into the valley where we lived.
>
> As soon as Father came in, he asked for holy water. But they had no holy water. Father Solanus said, "Oh, poor, poor, poor." I ran over to our house and got some. When I came back he prayed over her, blessed her and from then on the woman got over her infection and lived a long time afterward.

From the beginning, Solanus used the sacramentals of the church and various prayer forms as instruments for the healings that were requested. He believed deeply that these church-given means were the vehicles that were divinely appointed to bring about healing. Thus, any favorable response coming to those in need reinforced his faith in the efficacy of the church's rituals and the acts of mercy practiced by the petitioners. While people would credit "The Holy Priest," he would credit the sacramentals or the works of mercy the people promised to perform as their part in the divine transaction.

During their walks to the various houses in the neighborhood, Solanus and Carmella would often have good talks. "Carmella, what are you going to do when you grow up?" he asked her one day. "I'd like to be a Sister of St. Agnes," she replied, thinking of the Sisters from Wisconsin who staffed the school and had taught her. "You will be a Sister of St. Agnes," is all that she recalled him saying. Years later Carmella became Sr. Agrippina Petrosino, CSA.

In this first account of extraordinary gifts that people identified in Father Solanus, two stand out: the gift of healing and the gift of prophecy. In the use of both gifts, Solanus communicated to others his belief that his insights came from God alone. He merely cooperated with God.

Most of the people with whom Solanus related belonged to the parish. Whether receiving them in the office, visiting them in their homes or on the street, or mingling with them on social occasions such as "field days" for the school or Labor Day picnics for the parish, Solanus seemed to be the one friar at Sacred Heart with whom they felt most at ease. Solanus genuinely enjoyed being with the people, especially at their celebrations. His notebook has regular references to his participation in the Yonkers annual Labor Day picnics and the customary parish festivals. Even though he might be there to enjoy himself, the people did not find it amiss to use the occasion to bring him their problems. One of these was a young Agnesian sister whose father had stopped going to church:

> She approached him one day during a parish festival. When she went up to him, she told us that he was eating a hot dog that had mustard and sauerkraut on it. She said she couldn't help but laugh when she first saw him, but she told him that she wanted a favor of him. She said he continued to eat his hot dog, and she told him what she wanted, that her father was [re]married out of the church and not going to church. He told her not to worry, that everything was going to be all right. Shortly after that, she received a letter from her brother stating that her father had had his marriage validated and was returning to the practice of his faith.

Such humanness combined with holiness endeared Solanus to the parishioners at Sacred Heart. His popularity proved financially beneficial for the parish, as well. In 1915 it was decided to build a new church. With Solanus at Sacred Heart and his classmate John O'Donovan at the Capuchins' Queen of Angels parish in Harlem, the two parishes vied with each other to raise money for construction at Sacred Heart. According to Cosmas Niedhammer, the "success of the drive seemingly depended upon the popularity of the two priests. As it turned out, Father Solanus at the last moment produced more tickets that had been sold, than did Father O'Donovan." From Solanus's own notebook, it seems he also stood to benefit personally. The opening notation for 1915 mentioned a "contest for set of Vestments between Rev. John O'Donovan, OFMCap. of Harlem and his classmate Rev. Father Solanus OFMCap. of Yonkers in February to conclude May 26th."

Beginning Efforts at Ecumenism

Solanus's connection to the laity was not limited to Sacred Heart parishioners nor even to Catholics. He was always concerned about Protestants and sought to communicate a positive message about Catholicism to them. His first entry for January 1, 1911, in his notebook at Sacred Heart describes two funerals of infants and how "many Protestants [were] impressed." However, Solanus did not limit his relationships with Protestants to the times they might come to Sacred Heart; he sought them out in their homes as well. At times he would visit them for simple reasons of friendship; at other times he went to them because many of them were wealthy and could provide jobs for people who came to him looking for work. Later he recalled:

> Non-Catholic neighbors over on Hudson Terrace, especially where the more wealthy and the "millionaires" lived, were wont to employ Catholic girls and young men.
> ... I found that many of these dear good people would feel slighted if we failed to see them too. It just seemed sufficient to ensure employment if a Capuchin father sent anyone over where there was work to do.

Another aspect of Solanus's ecumenism was his supportive ties to the Atonement Friars and Sisters in Graymoor, New York. He had become a friend of the well-known Anglican convert Paul Francis Wattson, who had brought his Anglican community of religious men into the Roman Catholic Church. Solanus was present at Paul Francis's ordination and preached for his First Mass on July 3, 1910.

If Paul Francis was "Francis" to the Atonement Friars, Sister Lurana was "Clare" to the Atonement Sisters who had entered the Catholic Church at the same time. Upon entry into Roman Catholicism, the sisters discovered that a benefactor who had deeded their convent to them now wanted to take it back, saying it had been given to them because they were Anglican sisters. The whole matter created quite a legal scandal at the time. Even though the sisters resisted the man's effort, Solanus complimented them at the "Franciscan" way they presented their case. He wrote to Sr. Lurana:

> I take this occasion also, Dear Sister, to assure you that I thanked Almighty God — and do thank him — for having inspired someone with such truly Franciscan sentiments as were manifest in your gentle protest to the plaintiff attorneys of that Graymoor church property case.
>
> I am fully confident that there are too many upright lovers of justice, even among our separated brothers and sisters, who read *The Lamp* [the Graymoor magazine] and paused at that letter ever to hold their peace while an act of such injustice were perpetrated as would be perpetrated should your community be ejected from Graymoor. In my opinion there is no sane man who has a spark of Christianity who will hesitate (when he knows the facts and the present circumstances at and around Graymoor) to second these sentiments, and acknowledge your sentiments as really Christian. Continue, Dear Sister, in your determination never to quarrel, as our Holy Rule enjoins us, and be sure you will have more powerful patrons on your side than intrigue with irreligion and silver and gold can ever procure.

After a lengthy battle, the sisters lost their appeal in 1917. They were evicted from the property. True to his personality, which could be adamant on matters of justice, Solanus was tenacious in his belief that the sisters had morality and right on their side. He felt their eviction represented "the killing letter of the law." It enabled unscrupulous people to triumph. Yet he believed firmly that "the majority of our separated brethren will condemn it as done in their name and will regret it." Furthermore, he tried to help the sisters put their loss in the context of the pattern of Jesus Christ.

"Needless to say, we all hoped that things would never come to such a farce against common justice and charity." He continued:

> However, the victories of the world are short-lived: "Man proposes but God disposes." We may be sure that Almighty God has not permitted things to take such a course without some good design of his own—to turn evil into good.
>
> At all events the words of our Divine Master, "Blessed are you when they revile you and persecute you...," should be a consolation to you and an encouragement. The sisters will hardly be able to do anything better than pray earnestly for their persecutors, according to the same divine authority: "Do good to those who hate you, and pray for those who persecute and calumniate you."

In concluding his supportive letter, Solanus enclosed a "little donation ...to help you in your present need." It came from the superior of Sacred Heart, a very human response to some friends and co-workers facing a very difficult situation.

Developing Devotion to the Blessed Virgin through Devotion to Mary of Agreda and *The Mystical City of God*

From his youth Barney Casey had had a strong devotion to the Blessed Virgin. In his mind she had been instrumental in saving his life from drowning as well as in leading him to the Capuchins. As a Capuchin he made it a daily practice to pray the Little Office of the Blessed Virgin. When he missed it, he would correct himself as being ungrateful and insensitive. After all, had not the Blessed Virgin Mary been solicitous of him throughout his life? Had she not been at the heart of some of the unique religious encounters he had experienced?

From the middle of the nineteenth century, popular piety was replete with accounts of private revelations and devotions. These had the blessing of various local ordinaries or the support of the major religious orders, especially those of men. While at Yonkers, Solanus heard from a woman about one of these private revelations. From being an initial skeptic he grew into one of the best known devotees of the mysteries connected to the accounts narrated by Mary of Agreda, a Spanish mystic (1602–65):

> Shortly after my ordination to the holy priesthood, I heard of a "Life of the Blessed Virgin." I was skeptical. "Who could think of presum-

ing to write the life of the Blessed Virgin these days?" So I thought, erroneously taking it for generally understood that it had never been written. However, I was determined to see if it possibly might be more than a compilation of favors, etc., like the "Glories of Mary" which my Father used to peddle in the wintertime and give away.

We found an abridged copy of *The Mystical City of God*. WHAT A REVELATION! What a treasure!

From that first perusal of the simple but masterly introduction by the humble secretary, the actual writer..., my conviction has grown that the same *Mystical City of God*... is not only a genuine "Life" of the same Blessed Mother Mary, but, having studied it for more than forty years and on my knees having prayed the whole four volumes, I am convinced that the work has been rightly referred to as the most opportune and authentic autobiography of the Blessed Virgin herself, the Queen of all Creation and chosen by the Divine Creator himself to be his own Spouse and our Mother. Glory be to God!

If today Solanus's largesse about this work might be considered extreme, it was far from uncommon at that time. Solanus was aware of the controversy surrounding Mary of Agreda's work, but he knew that kings and popes, universities and theologians had fought about its merits as well. He was satisfied to know that the Spanish Inquisition had approved it after studying it thoroughly for fourteen years. While others might argue its worth, Solanus had experienced its value for himself and his own spiritual life. According to a theologian and confrere of Solanus who later became archbishop of Smyrna, "the constant meditation of this Life of Mary brought Father Solanus to the realms of the mystics in his contemplation. A volume of this work and the rosary were ever close at hand for Father Solanus."[24] Solanus knew *The Mystical City of God* inside and out. He marked key passages which he found helpful in understanding Mary's role in salvation, noting how these passages might apply to the church and have relevance for issues that touched people's lives.

Solanus approached the work in the way that the author of the article on Mary of Agreda in *The Dictionnaire de Spiritualité* suggests all should do: "In order to understand the work, one must, we believe, approach it with an openness of mind and simplicity of heart similar to that of the author; equally as helpful are the testimonies of those who knew Marie d'Agreda and witnessed her mystical states."[25] This author makes it clear, from its narrative genre, that the work is not intended to be a doctrinal or theological exposition, although both doctrine and theology can be found within it. This "narration surpasses the category of history and ventures into a realm which transcends both time and space to the eternal plan of God."

Today the controversy about Mary of Agreda and *The Mystical City* may not be as critical as it was during Solanus's life; however, it is evident from the *Dictionnaire de Spiritualité* that the debate about the work continues. The conclusions of the author of the article offer a proper context for understanding the four volumes, which cover the order of the life of the Virgin Mary in three parts, (1) Mary's predestination until the Incarnation; (2) the Incarnation to Christ's Ascension; (3) the Ascension to Mary's Coronation in heaven:

> Undoubtedly, it is sometimes difficult to distinguish between what surfaces as private revelation and what is the fruit of knowledge. It may be that Mary of Agreda is not able to discern the one from the other. But she is very conscious of the more or less great clarity of illuminations which she receives. The church has not given a definitive opinion on this major work nor on the proceedings for the beatification of Mary of Agreda. After all, the church does not authenticate private revelations. Perhaps *The Mystical City* possesses fruits for yet a more opportune time. In any case, its numerous editions and translations are a sign of the influence it has exercised for three centuries in spreading this so very singular reading of the mysteries of Mary.

Preaching the Word of God

As Solanus continued at Sacred Heart he was assigned chaplaincies with the Children of Mary (a sodality of young women) and the Sacred Heart League. He also usually conducted the First Friday services at which he gave short reflections, which Cosmas Niedhammer remembers as "most inspiring." While these duties took much of his time, preparing and preaching simple sermons and "fervorinos" took even more. One of his notebooks has fifteen pages of reflections he shared with the people. Instead of the "hell and brimstone" genre of many preachers of the day, Solanus's themes stressed unity, God's love, the roles of the Sacred Heart and the Blessed Virgin in people's lives, the nature of the church and its teachings, and the need to cooperate with God's graces.

Solanus's second notebook contains handwritten reflections for sermons encompassing the relationship of discontentment to sin, the Eucharist and unity, marriage and the disruption of divorce, the need to receive the sacraments frequently, concern for the Poor Souls, the desires of the Sacred Heart, the "Triumph of the Church," Marian devotion, First Communion, and the need for a strong Catholic press.

Solanus grounded these sermons, which tended to be theological and exhortatory, in contemporary exegesis, homespun examples, and quotations from the popes. A good example can be found in the sermon he gave on November 11, 1917, at the 10:15 a.m. Mass.

The final entry in his Yonkers notebook is a quotation from Pope Leo XIII, addressed to the clergy, about the demands of citizenship which Solanus himself had tried to inculcate in his own sermonizing: "Let those of the clergy who are occupied with the instruction of the multitude, treat plainly this topic of the duties of citizens; so that all may understand and feel the necessity of conscientiousness in political life, and of self-restraint and integrity; for that cannot be lawful in public which is unlawful in private affairs."

In July 1918, the province had its triennial Chapter. At that time, the superiors decided that Solanus Casey had been at Sacred Heart long enough. He was transferred to Our Lady of Sorrows on the Lower East Side of Manhattan. Hearing of his new assignment, Solanus penned a note to his sister Margaret, giving her his new address. It would not be easy to leave his first assignment, his "first love," but obedience invited him to a new area of ministry. He wrote:

> Am just about to leave Yonkers for a new field, down in the very heart of the metropolis. In a way I almost feel sad to leave the Sacred Heart Monastery and Parish where I've been laboring (if laboring is the right word) for close to fourteen years. We had a provincial Chapter in Detroit last week (July 11–14) and we just learned today (July 16) of the changes made.... Well now, "Good-bye" for the present from Yonkers. My new address will be 213 Stanton Street, New York City, New York.

Solanus Casey left his first assignment and began his new one on that same day.

Chapter 5

Manhattan and the Expanding Concern of Solanus for Justice in the World (1918–24)

Our Lady of Sorrows, Manhattan (1918–21)

Little is known about Solanus's activities during his time at Our Lady of Sorrows in Manhattan. However his journal entries indicate a deepening of his internal life, especially of humility, and a deepening social concern, especially for the poor. One journal entry seems to be a chastisement for having acted as though he were "little conscious of the beauty or success of [the] sermon" he preached the day before. Solanus reproached himself also for refusing to give a nickel on one occasion and for rejecting a request for two cents another time. Two entries below this notation about refusing help to the poor, he jotted a reminder of what the author of Deuteronomy says about the way the poor are to be treated: "Therefore I command thee to open thy hand to thy needy and poor that live with thee in the land" (Deut. 15:11).

The only known eyewitness to that period recalled Solanus's making a deep impression by his gentleness with children as well as by his manner of speaking and his friendliness. Solanus's retreat notes for 1919 indicate an intense desire to be involved in the struggles faced by humans. Most of the references to this fact can be found under the heading "Zeal for Souls." Solanus copied the Lukan Gospel's words of Jesus, underlining the first words: "*I am come* to cast fire on the earth and what will I do, but that it be kindled" (Luke 12:49). Solanus then linked union with God achieved in ecstatic prayer with the desire to bring others into a similar union. He quoted approvingly St. Catherine of Siena's words after she woke from an ecstasy which had afforded her a vision of heaven: "Oh wonder! Oh wonder! How can I begin to describe the ineffable and the indescribable?" As a result of that religious experience, he commented, Catherine "was ready to give her life a thousand times to save even one sinner for such glory."

While Solanus was at Our Lady of Sorrows, the ecstatic experience of Catherine had a parallel in a brush with death which brought him to his own out-of-body experience. He had gone to the hospital, diagnosed as having a gangrenous infection. There he was approached by the doctors with an anaesthetic. He related:

> After some joking with the doctors...they took off their "long faces" although they kept on their white caps and gauze-covered mouths. Dr. Edgerton concluded: "Well, roll him in here now, head first." With my sixth breath of gas, and with effort, I called out: "All right!" (after the first couple of breaths, I almost doubted if the stuff was any good).
>
> Life and light were going by fast when beautiful bells began to ring (from St. Joseph's Hospital for Consumptives across the street). A voice gently and piously reminded: "There's the Angelus." Oh, how sweet was the music to my soul and the announcement, how confidence-inspiring!
>
> Then I realized that consciousness had come to the very end. The description of Mother's beautiful death...at the second ringing of the Angelus flashed on my memory and my heart was only able to respond: "Behold be it done to me according to your holy will."
>
> I can realize now as never before how beautiful in the sight of heaven Mother's death must have been. With the above act of resignation, I came to "perfect *darkness* and *death.*" A shorter instant, however, than that death lasted could not be imagined. With electric quickness the bubble broke. What peace! What solemnity!!! The very breath of my experience seemed to be principles of wisdom and truth, such as "To the pure, everything is pure." "Charity knows no evil...is not suspicious," etc.
>
> At about 12:15 p.m., I heard Dr. Kirchen urge Dr. Edgerton: "Hurry up! Hurry up!" I seemed to see the latter cutting away the last fleshrags as I actually felt him do it without the slightest pain. I could only weep out with joyous wonder: "Deo Gratias! Deo Gratias! Thanks be to God!"

This hospital experience enabled Solanus to identify more closely with others who were ill and infirm. As the pain receded, he thanked God over and over. He left the hospital thankful that he had been able to celebrate the Mass each day, despite the severe pain he had endured.

Our Lady Queen of Angels, Manhattan (1921–24), and the Irish Cause

From the Lower East Side, Solanus was transferred to Our Lady Queen of Angels Parish in Harlem on October 25, 1921. Since many of the parishioners were Irish, this transfer enabled him to minister among the largest concentration of Irish immigrants in the world during the peak of Ireland's "Troubles."

The victory of the United States in the First World War was a bittersweet triumph for many Irish Americans because it meant that Ireland's colonizer, England, also had been victorious. England had been the ally of the United States, whose president was hardly pro-Irish. In fact, when Woodrow Wilson was approached on the issue of Irish independence, his reply was quite clear: "My first impulse was to tell the Irish to go to hell, but, feeling this would not be the act of a statesman, I denied myself this personal satisfaction."[26] Such sentiments could not have failed to have some influence on Solanus Casey, sixth child of Irish immigrants and grandson of an Irishman killed by the English.

Former Capuchin Benedict Joseph Groeschel, who lived with Solanus during the former's novitiate, has noted that Solanus "was conversant with all respects of this uprising and was in great sympathy with it. I must say though that I never heard him make any negative or scurrilous observations about the occupying power [the British], which was often the case of people who had an interest in the Irish Revolution."

The Casey family was raised on newspapers, including the *Irish Standard*. Ever loyal to his Irish background, Solanus made the Irish cause his own crusade. Much of his involvement took the form of correspondence with the press. His notes indicate that he had connections with significant people in the media. A March 21, 1912, entry in his notebook indicated: "Met Mr. Ford of the *Freeman's Journal* and *Irish World* in N.Y. City. Pleasant interview. Manager, 28 years, goes to communion every day and to two Masses." The former Barney Casey Jr.'s press connections increased when he moved to Manhattan. As his various letters indicate, his patriotic passion for the Irish cause was based on justice and, grounded in

Catholic teaching. He challenged any — including churchmen — who were reluctant to stand on the side of the oppressed Irish.

Solanus's own notes indicate an extensive correspondence with various editors about events in Ireland and reactions which were duly noted in their respective publications. Two extant letters have been uncovered thus far. Both seem to have been written a few weeks apart in 1922; both are signed "Homo Simplex" (Simple Man). One adds "A.A.R.I.R." (American Association for the Recognition of the Irish Republic); the other, "F.S.C." As a preface to the latter, written July 29 and published August 19, 1922, the editor commented: "The writer of the subjoined letter to the editor of *Brann's Iconoclast* is a Capuchin priest personally known to us. An Irish American by birth, he is zealously devoted heart and soul to the Irish Republican cause. He frequently expressed to us the view that that cause cannot fail because it has arrayed on its side God's justice which must prevail in the end."[27]

Solanus's letter makes it clear that the "heroes of the 1916 Easter Rising and their martyred comrades" gave their lives for a just cause. Challenging the skewed reporting of the press, Solanus warned of "a day of retribution coming":

> Bear in mind what the words may mean to each one of us: "What you have done to the least of my brethren you have done to me." And again: "I am Jesus whom thou persecutest" (Acts IX). Do you ever try to realize that "every lie, inasmuch as it is a lie, is in the last instance nothing less than a denial of God's existence"? Have you ever fathomed the fact that every crime against justice is at once an outrage on truth and an act of idolatry? I ask you to think it over and to realize, if you can, something of the awful avalanche of inequity now calling down the wrath of Heaven on civilization through a God-less press — blasphemy against truth and justice, not by individuals, but nation-wide and international blasphemy.

Another letter of equal passion was penned to the *Catholic News* of New York in response to two editorials which Solanus considered overly "one-sided." With an opening reference to the late Pope Pius X's call for an "efficient Catholic press," Solanus scored the *News* for its dependence on sources of information that were "positively atheistic" and docilely servile to the interpretations of the secular press, which he considered controlled by "news Agencies":

With the above-referred-to Agencies you seem to espouse views of the situation in Ireland, which Britain would like very much to "believe personally" to be the only proper views. Please just glance it over, and ask yourself if such an article might not be expected rather in a London Daily, or in any of our Metropolitan Yellow Jackets — every one of them heart and soul in sympathy, not with a crucified Nation or with Catholic Principle, but with Brazen Brutal Britain.[28]

After elaborating at greater length on press misinterpretations, Solanus turned his eyes to bishops. He noted how even these could be duped into being used by the forces for wrong and injustice. Recalling that "it was a bishop that condemned St. Joan of Arc for witchery and that a little later, duressed as he was by the British (and at that time supposed to be Catholic), exposed her to unmentionable cruelties and finally burned her at the stake as a heretic." He makes the connection that, if reports would be true, "there are one or two prelates in America who would do the like for a number of Irish Joans, even without British duress." He found these prelates in Buffalo and Baltimore:

> May the Good God deliver us from scandals! But I would ask his Lordship from Buffalo and his Grace from Baltimore if "Eamon De Valera [the Sinn Fein leader and proclaimed head of the Irish Republic] seems to have completely lost his reason," who is to blame, if not the despicable power his own Grace and his Lordship seem to be now espousing and that De Valera has frustrated, escaped and withstood these four years — so long and so bitter for poor Ireland, and for De Valera? What is to blame after British hypocrisy more than the above mentioned international silence? More than the already referred to leaders and guides? May God in his mercy overlook the crimes of it all and pity such leaders and their responsibility. Your correspondent prays for them without exception.[29]

Whether because of the sheer length of the letter's five pages or because of the tenor of its writer's passion, the *Catholic News* refused to run it. Solanus realized the intensity of his feelings. Yet he wanted to be sure that he would not be controlled by acrimony. Thus he wrote: "If your correspondent seems acrimonious... may the Lord help us to see clearly! For bitterness like falsity and exaggeration is to no purpose in an honest cause."[30] Undaunted by the rejection from the *Catholic News*, Solanus sent the letter to the *Irish World*, which ran it *in toto*.

From the strength of his arguments, Solanus seems to have fully believed in the innocence of the Irish vis-à-vis England. Consequently, he would have been the first to insist that he was not prejudiced against the British. He would have distinguished between the British as a people and as a government. But Solanus Casey *was* prejudiced nonetheless. Prejudice is an inherited social sin. It is not necessarily *willed,* but it is part of one's constitution, received as it is from one's social environment. Because it is so deeply rooted in the psyche, it is not something that can be extricated from one's emotions overnight. He was raised in a republican home, and so it is small wonder that Solanus was not even more anti-British, given the atrocities that were part of Britain's colonization of Ireland, including those affecting both sides of his family.

If Solanus was critical of some bishops, it was not to attack their function, but only what he perceived to be their inability to read the situation correctly. On the contrary, in promoting the Irish cause he was concerned that his Ordinary understand his position and be informed about it. For instance, the day after Solanus spoke at the convention of the A.A.R.I.R. he had an "audience with his Eminence, Cardinal Hayes" and mentioned his involvement. He asked, "Am I doing right?" "It's all right, Father," the cardinal responded. "Encourage the people and console them in every way you can," was the cardinal's reply. This time, Solanus underlined his trademark response: *"Deo Gratias!"*

Solanus and the Seraphic Mass Association: The Beginning of "Favors Reported"

Solanus's letter-writing on behalf of Irish republicanism was merely a footnote to what was becoming more and more identified with him: his promotion of the foreign missions. Since his seminary days Solanus had been inspired by the devotion to the missions of the cloistered nun, Therese Martin, whose cause for beatification was in process.[31] For his part, he encouraged enrollments in the Seraphic Mass Association (SMA, now more properly entitled the Capuchin Mission Association).

The SMA was the original inspiration of a Swiss laywoman who wanted to help financially the Capuchin foreign missions. She convinced the Capuchin superiors that if she could get people to make contributions to the missions, the Capuchins ought to promise those people a remembrance in their Masses and other community prayers. Their contributions would benefit the Capuchin missions; the Capuchins' prayers and Masses would benefit the contributors. The superiors accepted the idea; the SMA was launched. As Solanus explained it later: "The members of this Association are asked to pray for our foreign missions and their work and for one another — those members, of course, who can pray. And those who can afford to do so are asked to help with an offering of some kind (for the missions) besides by prayer and Masses."

Each major Capuchin friary offered SMA memberships. Thus, when people came to see Solanus in the front office asking for favors, he would often suggest that, as their way of showing thanks to God for the gift they requested, they support the missions through membership in the SMA. As Solanus envisioned it, enrollees would benefit from all the Masses, prayers, and good works of the worldwide Capuchins; in turn, the memberships would facilitate the functioning of the Capuchin missions. When people understood that they were helping the Capuchin foreign missions as well as receiving spiritual benefits for those enrolled, they did not perceive the requested fifty cents for an annual enrollment as too extravagant. If some could not afford that amount, Solanus would enroll them without cost. In being named an official "promoter" of the SMA for the Capuchin Order by the superior in Rome, Solanus was at liberty to give a certain amount of free memberships to those he determined to be in need.

Many of those who came to Queen of Angels asking for favors began to notice that their requests were being answered. Soon the word began to spread about the phenomena taking place in Harlem. Personal problems were being resolved; marriages were achieving peace; people with sicknesses were saying they were healed. As the word spread, more and more people came. Before very long, Solanus was busy all day counseling people, praying with them and for them, getting them involved in doing some charitable work or in joining the SMA. Whereas people's faith was oriented to Solanus, Solanus's faith was based in the efficacy of the sacramentals he used when blessing them or in the promises of the church and of the Order as these connected with the SMA.

Because so many persons were coming to Queen of Angels and reports of favors received were multiplying, the minister of the province, Father Benno Aichinger, became quite intrigued. During his annual visitation to the parish and the friars in 1923, Benno talked with Solanus about his portering and what was happening in his front-office ministry. Solanus told him about the various favors being granted, never identifying them with himself but always attributing them to the sacramentals used or to the

fruits connected to membership in the SMA. Touched by Solanus's simplicity and humility in narrating the many wonderful things being done,
Father Benno told Solanus to start keeping better records of what was
occurring.

That same day Solanus obtained a twelve-by-ten-inch letter-type book
with heavy covers and lined pages. The first notation under "NOTES ABOUT
SPECIAL CASES — November 1923," referred to Benno's request: "Nov. 8th,
1923. Today Visitation closed. Father Provincial wishes notes to be made
of special favors reported as through the Seraphic Mass Association."
The choice of words Solanus used for his notebook — "favors reported
as through the Seraphic Mass Association" — reflects an attitude of humility he had noted many years before in another notebook: "Beware of
congratulating thyself on the blessing wrought through thy medium." His
comments at the opening of the notebook also reflect his conviction that
any favor people might receive could be attributed to two factors: (1) They
had witnessed to their faith and confidence in God by doing some good
work for their neighbor, such as supporting the missions; and (2) God
alone had answered their prayers.

The "secret" of the healing of the person or the happy resolution of the
problem rested not in Solanus but in the blessing that came from membership in the SMA or whatever other good deed each was asked to perform,
from "going to confession" to helping the poor and needy. In Solanus's
mind, great results could be attributed to people's membership in the
SMA. To one person who asked a favor Solanus noted that efficacious results could come to anyone who enrolled in the SMA at any Capuchin
office. "Other Capuchins," he said, "can enroll you in the Seraphic Mass
Association as well as I can, and that is a big feature in the 'secret' of the
many notable favors reported. Thanks be to God."

Solanus's first entry in the notebook opened with the phrase that,
by now had become a constant utterance on his lips and from his pen:
"Deo Gratias!" Then it continued, using Solanus's unique method of
abbreviations:

> This P.M. Marg. Quinn — who enrolled her neighbor Mr. Maughan
> against drink and consequent anger [on] October 26, as also her
> sister, E. Remy of Philadelphia against severe inflammatory rheuma-
> tism, reports wonderful improvement in former and letter this a.m.
> from [her] sister [writing]: "Thank God and the good prayer society,
> I'm feeling fine."

The first page has notes about people in many stages of life and death. It refers to someone praying for "the grace of a religious calling and strength and grace to accept it." It mentions a hitchhiker who had been "terribly beaten-up." Someone (whose husband drank) had "two partial strokes." A woman's "16-year-old had vanished a week before" and was "found next day in Jamaica." Another woman "had a nervous breakdown." Someone else whose brother had "been drinking for five years" and was "very careless about church" had lost sight in one eye. The period for these entries on page one covered the days between the book's inception on November 8 and December 9.

About every third or fourth entry is a notation written in such a way as to indicate that a positive resolution of the problem has taken place. Page after page outlines the "pathetic stories" (as Solanus was wont to refer to many of the cases). About half of the cases reported in the first pages give full names and addresses. The places of residence range from a few blocks from the church to Danbury, Connecticut, and to places in New Jersey. Slowly Solanus's reputation was growing. His increasing popularity was evidenced at his silver jubilee celebration on January 14, 1922. The house Chronicle notes that it attracted "a great multitude of the population of New York."[32]

The first extended entry in Solanus's notebook came on St. Valentine's Day, February 14, 1924. Under the heading "Use of glasses restored," Solanus detailed the account of a seventy-three-year-old woman from East Eighty-Eighth Street:

> Extremely anxious lest operation for double cataract be necessary. Promises to do all in her power for missions if use of glasses be restored without operation. This was November 1. She returned on January 20th, wearing her glasses but not yet satisfied. She renewed her promise that day. Today she returned jubilant and perfectly cured. In fulfillment of her promise, she joined herself [to the SMA] perpetually, and reenrolled her parents and brother besides paying for a heathen child [five dollars].[33]

Between his years at Queen of Angels and the time of his death Solanus filled seven such notebooks (extant). As far as he was concerned, the records were just a matter of obedience. From the superiors' perspective, it was a matter of having a kind of insurance. They needed Solanus's comments about what actually was happening in face of the inevitable rumors which were beginning to create for Solanus the reputation of being a "miracle worker."

Solanus's Prison Ministry

From February 1922 until shortly before his departure from Harlem in June 1924, Solanus ministered to the needs of the prisoners in a nearby Harlem prison. Until he came, it seemed that the prisoners had had to suffice with recitation of the rosary and a "little sermon" from the chaplain. With Solanus's presence on the scene, a more personalized approach seems to have developed. For instance, for Christmas and the New Year of 1924 he gave "Xmas cards for all."

This was Solanus's first extensive experience with nonwhites, especially African Americans. In his notebook, besides noting the numbers who came for services, Solanus often noted how many nonwhites were there. As was typical for that period among well-meaning but uninformed white people, he referred to African Americans as mulattoes or "darkies." Occasionally he would refer to them as "black." However, nowhere in these notes — nor anywhere else in his corpus of writings — did he ever give African Americans a negative label.

While the vast majority of entries merely note the number of participants for the "Rosary and Sermon," some entries indicate that he was able to be with people as they took "the pledge," a promise not to drink for a certain period of time, or to share newspapers with them.

At various times during this period, besides visiting the Harlem prison, Solanus also celebrated Mass in a local home for wayward children, going from there to the prison, as an entry for March 30, 1924, notes: "(40 Communions in delinquent's Home. First Mass at 7:30). Full house at prison, mostly black. Four or five answered Rosary. Edward Walsh took pledge for year and promised to go to church again." Because of a lack of interest, it seems that the prison ministry was dropped by St. Paul's Parish, its original sponsor, where Solanus often offered supply help.

At the July Provincial Chapter, Father Benno was reelected provincial. At that time it was decided that Solanus should come to the headquarters of the province, St. Bonaventure's in Detroit. Solanus noted that the word of his transfer came at 1:15 p.m. July 30. He was to be in Detroit by August 1. Although he went joyfully and freely, something about New York, where he had so many positive experiences, always kept Yonkers and Manhattan close to his heart. As he later noted: "While I never long to go back to any old place from which Divine Providence has seen good to remove me, yet I must acknowledge that I have a natural inclination that way — like the Israelites in the desert naturally yearned (many of them) to go back to Egypt. No doubt, we are all naturally inclined that way." The uprooting was made easier for Solanus by his conviction that the move was simply one more step in the journey God had outlined for him.

Chapter 6

The First Time in Detroit: 1924–45

The Rapid Increase of People in the Front Office upon Solanus's Arrival

The Detroit Solanus Casey arrived at in 1924 was one of the largest cities in the United States. One of the most Catholic cities of the nation, it had its own cardinal. Not far from the bustling downtown, St. Bonaventure's large friary housed the novitiate and the provincialate of the Province of St. Joseph. Immediately, Solanus fit into the regular daily routine.

The friars' day began at 4:45 a.m. Lauds at 5:15 was followed by the Litany of the Saints and meditation in common. At 6:00 Prime and Terce were chanted, followed by the "conventual," or community, Mass at 6:15. If he had not celebrated Mass privately beforehand, Solanus would do so after the conventual Mass. This would be followed by breakfast, usually in silence. At noon two more "hours" of the Divine Office were chanted, Sext and None. The midday hours were followed by the main meal. Afterward the friars usually repaired to the recreation room. The recitation of Vespers and Matins at 5:15 or 5:30 was followed by supper. Before the friars retired, they recited the Litany of the Blessed Virgin and shared other prayers in common. Between the common prayers and other spiritual exercises the friars attended to their individual assignments.

Upon his arrival, Solanus was assigned as porter. However, while he had been the main porter in New York, he now was named assistant to the head porter, Brother Francis Spruck. The fact that a priest would be taking orders from a lay brother did not seem to Solanus to be anything out of the ordinary. He accepted his secondary position with his usual thanksgiving. Previous to Solanus's arrival, the portering job at St. Bonaventure's had been minimal enough that Francis was able to function also as tailor and habit-maker for the rapidly growing province, which now numbered 176 solemnly professed friars. The tailor shop was on the right side of the entrance to the monastery and the porter's office was on the left. This arrangement made it easy to hear the doorbell no matter where Francis might be.

To the surprise of Francis, within a few weeks of Solanus's arrival more and more people were coming to see the new porter. Meanwhile Solanus continued adding references to his notebook as ordered by the provincial. The majority of the sixty-four entries for his first months at St. Bonaventure's — the period from August 1 to December 31, 1924 — contain no follow-up notations indicating what, if anything, happened to people after visiting Solanus. Yet among the entries there are enough significant notations to explain why the front office was becoming increasingly crowded. Short references to what the people considered healings were noted, as evidenced in the entry about a woman who came during the first months:

(August 30) Mrs. Clara Kowalski (23, of 3392 Palmer Ave.) on August 18, extremely anxious lest X-ray examination demands [an] operation for dead bone in [her] ear. Joins Mass Association. Today [says] nothing was found yet in photo X-ray.

(Sept. 1) Danger disappearing, good color returning.

(Nov. 1, 1925) Perfectly cured. Deo Gratias.

With the passing of the months at St. Bonaventure's the notebook shows more and more problems, many with happy resolutions. Soon the increasing numbers of people coming to the front office demanded that the office space be enlarged. In the rearrangement Solanus's desk was placed at the right of the entrance, and additional chairs were placed along the wall. Francis's desk was a few feet behind. The chairs were necessary not only because of the numbers of people coming, but also because of the extended time Solanus gave to each supplicant. Whoever had a problem would receive Solanus's full attention for as long as they wanted.

It surprised Brother Francis that nobody seemed to get impatient at having to wait. When people were asked why they were willing to wait so long with so much patience, they merely replied that they knew they also would receive Solanus's undivided attention when their turn came. When he was reminded that people were waiting, Solanus would reply simply, "Yes, we'll get to them, we'll take care of all of them."

"I have plenty to keep myself busy for at least eighteen hours a day," he wrote to one of his sisters. Brother Gabriel recalled:

He would be in the office from 7:00 in the morning until 10:00 at night. He was porter as long as he was at St. Bonaventure's. I would say that he performed this office with great fruits. He saw thousands of people. He saw people all day from seven in the morning until night. He was most patient with them. He never hurried them, and he tried to help them.

Solanus graciously made himself available to those in need. He would meet the people, respond to their phone calls, and answer their letters. Over time, so many people asked for his attention that he worked three-fourths of the day and, even then, was not able to attend to a quarter of the letters addressed to him. While the rest of the community might rise at 4:45, Solanus often was up long before, praying in chapel, communing with God.[34] In the evening, after the last person left he would mop the office and then repair to the chapel to be with God again. There he'd intercede for the needs of those who had communicated with him that day. Finally he would go to bed.

Accounts of Those Helped through Solanus's Enrollments in the SMA

As more people believed they were helped by Solanus, more began coming from places farther away. One of these was Earl Eagen from Smiths Creek, about forty miles northeast of Detroit. Believing he had little time to live, he visited Solanus. Years later, Solanus recalled what happened in a letter to Eagen's daughter, Dorothy:

> It was Saturday morning, January 10, 1925, that a neighbor-friend of theirs from Port Huron, brought your dear parents to St. Bonaventure Monastery in Detroit. Your poor father was hardly able to talk. He tried, however, to tell briefly how he felt and that the doctors said he had "ulcers of the stomach." Later on I learned that they had sent him home as a hopeless case of cancer. I told him quite a little about the Seraphic Mass Association and suggested that he do something for the missions.
>
> "Now I have your name, Mr. Eagen," I said. "And you can enroll perpetually if you wish. If you are anyway short, however, I would advise that you enroll for just a year now and promise perpetual enrollment as soon as convenient, if things go favorably."

I took him to be seventy-five years old or upward. Your poor mother looked old too. Sunday morning, eight days later, your father drove his own car down to keep his promise. From their appearance alone I could hardly have known them; but the moment he spoke I thought, "This is the fellow from Port Huron!" He looked thirty years younger. He was only thirty-nine at the time.

"But, Father," he said, "the doctors in Port Huron want to take an X-ray. What do you think?" I asked him, "How much is it going to cost you?" He said, "Twenty-five dollars."

"What do *you* think?" I asked your smiling mother. They were both smiling all over. "Father, he doesn't need it. Look at him," she exclaimed.

"Listen," I said. "You make a promise to the poor souls in purgatory that, if you are able to forget that appointment tomorrow, you'll enroll them for a part of it." "Gee," he said. "I'll give them half of it. I'll go fifty-fifty!"

After that he drove down every week for several months. On February 29, I believe he had the whole family down. After enrolling some other member, as he nearly always did, he concluded about as follows: "Now, Father, I want to enroll the Poor Souls as I promised them I would do. Put them down for a good half of that twenty-five dollars. Enroll them for fourteen dollars."

The above letter, which was sent by Solanus to Sister Cecilia Eagen, was written in response to her simple request for an enrollment in the SMA. She had not mentioned her baptismal name, Dorothy, when she wrote. Yet, twenty-two years later Solanus was vividly recalling the event, as well as his first visit to the Eagen farm.

On that occasion, Solanus asked to meet the family. All but little Dorothy were introduced; she was too embarrassed to come downstairs because she did not have any shoes. At her mother's urging, however, Dorothy was coaxed to come to greet Solanus. In the way he responded to her, the self-conscious eleven-year-old immediately felt at ease. Solanus noted in his letter to Sister Cecilia: "And just incidentally, it was on that occasion that I remember seeing little Dorothy as a possible candidate for a convent or a missionary."

On March 12, 1925, a few months after the incident with Earl Eagen, Solanus's notebook contains an entry: "Big Company Enrolled." As with the Eagen story, a subsequent letter of Solanus indicates a fuller background that also points to the kind of theological reasoning that guided his faith-life. His account also indicates that in the pre-Depression days, not everything was well in Detroit:

I hardly think I ever told you about our enrolling companies and projects in the Seraphic Mass Association. The following, first of several similar to it since, I am sure will please you.

The slump of the 1925–26 winter was a tough one on Detroiters. Every auto factory in the city shut down for at least a week at Christmas, without a word when they would start up again. Only a day or two before New Years it was announced that Ford would start up again, on such and such a day after New Year's Day and would continue at three days a week till further notice. That was quite a "beam of hope" for perhaps millions. The other auto companies followed lingeringly, but most of them just worked one and two days each week. One of the slowest seemingly was Chevrolet. As we learned only a year or two later, it had already started negotiations toward bankruptcy.

On the 12th of February, Thursday after 9:00 p.m. John McKenna, who had become enthusiastic about the SMA the first months after my arrival back from New York, August 1, 1924, came to the Office. He was evidently discouraged, notwithstanding his otherwise wonderful faith.

"Father," he began, "I don't know what to do. I can't support a wife and family with the hours I've been working. I haven't had a full day now in two weeks. Today I had only two hours. They're always finding an alibi to send the men home." All at once, as though by inspiration, he said, "Father! Enroll the Company!"

"That's new," thought I. Twenty times quicker than I could tell it, however, so that it seemed absurd to hesitate, [something] flashed on my mind: "If a single Holy Mass must help any legitimate cause, why should not five hundred Masses daily in connection with the holy foreign Missions help?" "All right, John," I answered. "Yes, Father; I'll give them fifty cents" [for an annual membership in the SMA].

That same night the company received an astounding order. Two nights later McKenna waved triumphantly: "Father! We had overtime yesterday and today and we heard this afternoon that the company has an order for 45,000 machines, wanted in thirty days." It was believed that order also saved Detroit itself from bankruptcy.

Some friars and others who operated from a highly restrictive interpretation of the law might have disagreed with Solanus's enrolling a company in the SMA. But Solanus did not enroll a company; he enrolled the people who constituted the company. This was but one of many things Solanus did intuitively ("something flashed on my mind"), from the gift of wisdom, that his confreres found somewhat unorthodox. However, what in those days may have seemed out of the ordinary, the Spirit has led to become ordinary today. Solanus seemed to have been ahead of his time because he tried to be in tune with the Spirit.

Accounts of Those Helped by Solanus's Blessing of St. Maurus

Besides promoting the SMA for those who came requesting help at St. Bonaventure's, Solanus made use of many sacramentals. On Wednesdays, the front office was busier than usual because it was the day of the "St. Maurus Blessing of the Sick." The Blessing allegedly derived from a Benedictine by the name of Maurus (510–84). He had become noted during his lifetime for the gift of healing. After he died, the Benedictines continued to bless the sick and gradually developed a formula, which was approved on May 4, 1882, for a blessing with the relic of the True Cross. Although they were Capuchins, the friars at St. Bonaventure's had received permission to use the blessing.

Although it had long been a regular service offered on Wednesdays, after Solanus's arrival and his celebration of the blessing the numbers of people increased rapidly.[35] For instance, the friary chronicle on February 19, 1928, generously noted: "A very large crowd at the blessing at 3:00 p.m. Father Herman Buss acted as traffic cop, while Father Solanus offered the relic of the True Cross to the people."

Unlike other Capuchins who gave no sermons at the Wednesday service, when Solanus presided, he always included a simple homily. He would often mention examples from his "Notebook of Special Cases," or other incidents where people said they were delivered from their afflictions through the Wednesday blessing. Father Marion Roessler, who lived at St. Bonaventure's at this time, recalled:

His simple discourses in connection with this weekly devotion consisted in admonishing the people to strive to come closer to God through the frequent reception of the sacraments, prayer, and conformity to God's Holy Will in all the events of their lives. He insisted that penance was very necessary to make up for sin and for the salvation of their souls.

Because Solanus's "quinsy sore throat" forced him speak in a quiet, high-pitched voice, many people came early to get front seats. At times scores would stand immediately in front of the pulpit from which he spoke. Invariably, his theme would be trust in God and the need to manifest that trust in service to others and in gratitude. After his reflections, he would offer the prescribed prayers, incense the relic of the True Cross, take it from its reliquary at the altar, and give the general blessing of the sick. Then the people would process to the communion rail for an individual blessing with the relic.

Often Solanus would get so personally involved with the people in the office that he came late for the Wednesday service. As a result, Francis Spruck developed a routine to get him to the chapel on time. Fifteen minutes before the beginning of the service he would call out loudly: "2:45!" At five-minute intervals, he would reiterate the warning more insistently until the very time the service should have begun. Then he would say sternly: "Casey!" Sometimes, in a low boiling anger, he would say sarcastically, "It's time." Solanus then would get up and go sheepishly into the chapel for the service, leaving the people in the front office until he returned. On one such occasion, one of the people left to remain was Bernadette Nowak. She recalled:

> My sister, Geraldine Bieke, took me to Father Solanus. However, before I could talk to him, he rose and said it was time to go to the church for the blessing. I was disappointed, but went to church. As he passed before the people kneeling, he paused before me, gently touched my cheek and said softly, "Stop worrying now. You're going to be all right now," or words to that effect. I had not seen him stop to talk to anyone else and was surprised. That night I had the first sound good night sleep in over a month. From then on I was better.

Not all people who came to the monastery chapel for the Wednesday service were Catholics. Jews and Protestants were among the faithful as well. Besides the believers of various faiths and races, there also were skeptics. One skeptic was Casimera Scott. She had come to the devotions for thirteen weeks "not believing that he could heal others." However, she noted that on one Wednesday: "I saw a rabbi with his cap, long beard and a heavy cane. He used to come every week, too. Now he had faith and I was full of doubts. But when I saw him walk away *without* the use of his cane, then I believed."

When people attributed healing power to Solanus, he immediately let them know that the source of any healing was the power of God. A Protestant minister had been bringing his son to the Wednesday afternoon services. The son was seriously ill, and the minister asked Solanus if he would pray for the boy. When Solanus said that of course he would, "the minister said that he had hesitated coming in before because he didn't know whether Father Solanus would be willing to cure his son because he was not a Catholic. Father Solanus said, 'Only God can cure your son, but I will pray for him.'"

Accounts of Healings Attributed to Solanus through Use of Other Means

Besides inviting people to help the missions through enrollments in the SMA and blessing them with the St. Maurus Blessing and the relic of the True Cross, Solanus almost always would bless people with the sign of the cross or with holy water or some other sacramental. Clare Ryan testified that she personally had experiences of healing in which Solanus used sacramentals:

> I was suffering from cancer of the stomach. I had been diagnosed by a Dr. Reiger who was at Harper Hospital [in Detroit]. He is now deceased. He told me that there was nothing that they could do for me. He did not think that an operation would be successful. At my sister's suggestion I went to see Father Solanus. Father Solanus blessed me with a relic of the True Cross and I was cured. I did not go back to see any doctor after that. There was no need for it. After that I visited Father Solanus perhaps once every two or three weeks for about a year. I didn't see much of Father Solanus after that until 1941. I came down with a severe case of arthritis and was in bed for nine months. Finally, my husband drove me over to the monastery. I was not able to get out of the car. Father Solanus came out to see me. He went back to the monastery and got a stole and some holy water and he prayed over me for about fifteen minutes and told me that I

would be all right. When I went home, with the help of my husband I was able to walk up the stairs of my home for the first time in nine months. My condition improved to the point that I was able to do my own housework and cook and it remained that way for a long time. It is now coming back upon me though [1984].

The summaries of the testimonies that were made for the Vatican to determine the heroicity of Solanus's virtues are filled with many accounts of people who narrated what they perceived to be healings identified with Solanus. Clare Ryan's is but one. However, her conviction about Solanus's holiness was enough that she would be one of the founders of what is now known as the Father Solanus Guild.

Marie O'Reilly was another such witness. She told of a dentist with staphylococcus septicemia who was not expected to live through the night. The sister at the hospital suggested to his wife that they call Father Solanus to come and give him a blessing. When he came, "Father Solanus told Mrs. Kean that her husband would recover and he did." Ms. O'Reilly also recalled the incident of a blind man who visited Solanus and received his blessing: "I'm not sure how long afterward but at the consecration of the Mass, Marion's father regained his sight."

Mrs. Martha Houlihan testified to events that she believed indicated that Solanus was twice involved in the healing of her son James, once for whooping cough when he was two weeks old, and again when he was four with such a severe case of "strep" infection that they feared he would die.

After completing his medical training, Dr. Lawrence Kroha, M.D., became seriously ill. He attributed his recovery from being "unconscious for 16 days with [a] high temperature of close to 106" to the blessing he received from Solanus: "An hour after Father Solanus left me, my temperature was down to normal."

James Derum, the first biographer of Solanus, included in his book account after account of physical and spiritual healings attributed to him. These often involved a kind of prophetic indication of whether the one in need would be healed or not. He noted:

In 1935, while Sister Mary Joseph was on duty in St. Joseph Mercy Hospital in Detroit, a severe streptococcus infection of the right side of her throat sent her temperature to 105 degrees, and her neck became rigid. She began to slide into a coma, with heavy choking spells. Her doctor informed Sister Mary Philippa, a hospital supervisor, that the infection was spreading to the other side of the patient's throat. He ordered a tray set up, preparatory to doing a quick tracheotomy if needed.

At this point, Sister Mary Philippa telephoned Father Solanus. He said he would come at once. When he entered the sick sister's room he went directly to a stand at her bedside, seemingly oblivious of others. Taking a book from his pocket, he started reading prayers, slowly and quietly, though the sister was in the midst of a choking spell. Almost immediately, Sister Mary Joseph's choking stopped.

While reading the passion and death of Christ from the Gospels, he several times blessed the sister with a relic of the True Cross and placed it to her lips and throat. Thus for two hours he read and prayed, while three sisters, kneeling, joined their prayers to his.

Then he closed the book and said, "Sisters, it won't be necessary for me to return. Sister Mary Joseph will soon recover and join her community."

As he was walking down the corridor toward the elevator, ac-companied by the hospital chauffeur who was to drive him back to the monastery [Solanus did not drive], a man who seemed well ac-quainted stopped him. He asked Father Solanus to come to his wife's room and give her his blessing.

After he had done so, the man walked with him to the elevator. Calling him by his first name, Father Solanus counseled him to be resigned. His wife, he told him, would not recover.

Shocked, the husband exclaimed, "Father, her operation wasn't serious — why do you say this?"

In answer, the friar talked to him as the chauffeur stood by, urg-ing him to place his wife's soul in the arms of God, and to pray for strength to accept his cross.

On the way to the monastery, he did not speak, and seemed to the driver to be praying.

When the driver returned to the hospital, he went at once to Sis-ter Mary Philippa, and repeated the conversation between Father Solanus and the man who had stopped him in the corridor.

"The man's wife died," the sister informed him, "shortly after you left the hospital."

Sister Mary Philippa is one of the few who, telling of cures, was able to describe them in professional terms. In recounting attributed recoveries most of those people quoted merely repeated in their own way what they had been told, or thought they had been told, by physicians.[36]

Solanus's Expression of the Prophetic Gift

As both Derum's account and Solanus's prediction of Sister Agrippina Petrosino's and Sister Cecilia Eagen's entrance into the convent indicate, Solanus had some deeply intuitive sense or prophetic gift. It enabled him to tell people what would happen to them or to their loved ones. From the way he communicated the anticipated result, people were able to sense it as God's will and to be more easily resigned to accept it, if negative, or to realize God's special gift to them, if positive. From Solanus's reply to their requests, people gradually learned to tell whether or not the requests would be answered as they desired. Brother Ignatius Milne, who later worked with Solanus, "noticed a pattern in these replies. To those people for whom he gave... specific and detailed instructions, their problems were solved whatever they might have been. For those for whom Father merely said 'I will pray for them,' they were not." More simply, Marguerite Baker, remembers, "One had a way of knowing by the way Father Solanus spoke whether he would promise a cure, or whether he just asked us to accept God's will."

Solanus used his gift in relation not only to physical healing but also to spiritual healing. His ability to read people's hearts was narrated well by James Derum, who recalled the incident of a young man who came to the monastery with the couple with whom he lived:

> The young man was asking for prayers for his parents. The couple with whom this young man came were practicing Catholics. They thought this young man also practiced his faith. Father Solanus looked at him and said: "But you do not go to Mass on Sundays." The couple began to disagree with Father Solanus because they thought that the young man had practiced his religion. Father Solanus insisted that this young man had not been to Mass in five years. Finally the young man agreed to this fact. As a result of this, he reformed his ways.[37]

A mother went to the monastery to have a Mass offered for the intention of her son in the military. She asked Solanus to pray for him. But Solanus said, "Do not worry about that son, but worry about the one who lives at home. He is going to get a divorce." The mother knew nothing about this and confronted her son about it when she got home. He was amazed that she knew, because he had not said anything to her about his plans. Another woman went to the monastery to get an enrollment in the SMA for a friend's hospitalized mother. Solanus said, "Do not enroll her in the Seraphic Mass Association; have a Mass said for her instead. She'll never live through the night." The woman died at 11:55 that evening.

Although Solanus's gift of prophecy was expressed in many ways that touched people's hearts, the best remembered are those prophecies relating to whether or not people would experience healing. These might well be summarized in the testimony of the former chancellor of the Archdiocese of Detroit:

> He heard more of the ills, or the sufferings, or the worries and fears of people of our city, perhaps more than all the priests in any one parish or more than two or three parishes combined. From morning to night he would be listening to persons with worries and cares and disturbances and with all the humility and all the patience in the world he would give them fatherly advice and often enkindle their courage and hope and reassure them in a brief time their troubles would be finished or counsel them to be resigned to suffer with Christ. "Tomorrow at 9 o'clock," "in two days at 3 o'clock," or "within a short time," "if you have faith these troubles will disappear." It is my conviction that after reading his biography [by Derum] and the records of cures which seemed to have resulted from his prayers, perhaps there were more cures reported in these notes, which he kept by order of his superior, than were reported in the Gospels, than were reported perhaps at Lourdes, at St. Anne de Beaupré or at Fatima, in the same length of time. Now that would be a very surprising record if the dear Lord was working more supernatural cures through the prayers and faith inspired by Father Solanus here in our city on Mt. Elliott Avenue than in all the notable shrines of Christendom combined.

Solanus's Way of Approaching Lay People

Probably the most common characteristic of Solanus described by people who knew him was his approachability. In all situations, whether with

Catholics or non-Catholics, he honored people's integrity, their freedom, and their conscience. Invariably, Solanus's approach to others arose from a deep sense of compassion for them in their situation. Realizing many people were in very embarrassing situations, he never seemed to "talk down" to them but made them feel very specially loved by God — and by Solanus himself. He spoke with people very quietly and calmly. He had no pretensions of education or formality or aloofness. He treated everyone the same way, whether a Mayor Frank Murphy of Detroit or an unemployed person needing food. When Brother André (now Blessed André Bessette) of St. Joseph's Oratory in Montreal visited him and asked for a blessing, Solanus asked for a blessing from André in return. He did not relate to people to win their favor. Protestants and Catholics, women and men, rich and poor, whites and blacks, educated and illiterate, Capuchins and non-believers — all found him simply himself. The inner freedom which came from his sense of abandonment to God made him a brother to all others, even to the most fearful. Many people recall that even crying babies seemed to relax when Solanus would get up from his desk and take them from their perplexed parents' arms.

When people approached Solanus for a favor, his response always seemed suited to the occasion. He would not allow people to remain passive in their relationship with God, merely asking for help. He always invited them to further growth in God's life and grace. After listening to people, he would build on some positive thing he discovered in what they said. Then he would embellish that point with references to God's goodness and to God's love for them. After that, he would invite them to grow in their relationship with God by deepening their prayer life or by doing some good work for others.

If someone did not believe in God, he would try other approaches. To a man who was a professed atheist and whose son had drowned, Solanus evoked the example of the man's wife, Kathleen. Solanus tried to help him remember her "example of never-failing Christian virtues." It was "just six weeks after the son's death" that "his wife, Kathleen, also was taken, leaving him three children to mother by himself as best he might." Yet Solanus was not afraid to invoke *her* faith to encourage her grieving husband. With other atheists he might be stronger or more firm. Given his own radical faith, he was shocked when people said they did not believe in God. To a man who said, "Father Solanus, I am an atheist," he immediately retorted, "You are a damned fool." At first glance this response might seem insensitive to an extreme; Solanus, however, was merely responding in light of the

scriptural declaration: "Only fools say in their heart, 'There is no God'"
(Ps. 13:1; 52:1).

With non-Catholics, Solanus often asked them to investigate the differences between their own religion and Catholicism. He often invited them
to consider the "claims of the Mother Church." He stressed that people
should be faithful to their own beliefs, whatever they are. They should be
open to the beliefs of other people and, above all, should act on their beliefs. In his mind, all people were called to be faithful to true religion, as he
defined it, despite their different religions. He wrote:

> If religion is the greatest science of all ages — "The science of our
> happy dependence on God and our neighbor," which no one seems
> to question — then there can be but one religion. In like manner, if
> "We are Christians only inasmuch as we believe in Jesus Christ and
> keep his words" — his doctrine — so there can be but one Christian-
> ity. Therefore, it is up to each one of us individually to examine our
> own conscience whether we be Christians in reality or only in name.
> Too, it ought to be our happy privilege to perfect ourselves in the
> faith more and more, and to find out its infallible Guide on earth.

To nonpracticing Catholics he often was more direct than he was to
Protestants and to Jews. Invariably he would ask Catholics about the fre-
quency with which they celebrated the various sacraments. If they were lax,
he would invite them to greater fidelity. If people did not go regularly to
Mass on Sundays, he would challenge them to their obligation; if they went
to Sunday Mass but did not communicate he would get very concerned.

Solanus did not approach the sacraments lightly. He realized that the
sacraments were made for humans, and he deeply desired that people participate in them. When people shared with him their failings and sins he
would tell them firmly but gently that he could not give absolution. However, because of the embarrassment many would have in narrating their
sins again, Solanus developed a humane and practical approach with the
help of his confrere, Father Herman Buss. According to Father Herman
(who started working with Solanus in 1926):

> A person would come in [to Solanus] and talk and talk. Father Sola-
> nus got the story. Then he would say to the man or woman, "Now
> go over to the church and I'll call Father Herman and he'll go over to
> hear your confession." Father Solanus could not give absolution, but
> many, many persons told him of their lives. Father Solanus would

say, "Now you told the whole story. Just give a résumé to Father Herman. He will understand that you talked to me and he'll give you absolution." Then Father Herman heard their confessions.

The arrangement between Solanus and Herman might have created problems for some casuists, but for these priests it was no problem. For the people seeking reconciliation, it was a humane and deeply spiritual way to meet their needs.

Solanus served people also through correspondence and the telephone. In time the number of those writing to him increased to such a degree that he had to have a secretary. Phone calls also increased so much that more telephone lines had to be installed. In the beginning, there was but one line into St. Bonaventure's, which came through the front office. Since Solanus had to answer the phone while on duty in the front office it often happened that a call would interrupt him when he was in the midst of counseling people.

Solanus's Relationship with His Fellow Capuchins

Given his increasing popularity, it might seem that Solanus would incur varying degrees of jealousy and/or hostility from his fellow Capuchins. On the contrary, most — like Herman Buss — sensed something special about him. Thus they were willing to bear the various inconveniences caused by the numbers of people coming to St. Bonaventure's. At this time, probably the harshest criticism he received came from Brother Francis Spruck, and that was not very severe. At times, half in frustration and half in jest, Francis would call Solanus "that old fraud"; at other times he would chide Solanus for taking so much time with people that he would be late for meals. When this happened, Francis would come into the refectory muttering that Solanus was "still talking, still talking."

Bernard Burke, who sat at table with Solanus in his later years at St. Bonaventure's, bet him a rosary for every time Solanus would be on time for meals. Father Bernard insisted that he never had to pray a rosary. There were just too many people to see; Solanus felt their needs were more important than his need for food. Sometimes his meal would be cut short because people were waiting. His sister-in-law Martha recalled that on a visit to New York in 1940 she stopped in Detroit to see Solanus:

I was admitted to the reception room and was astonished to find only standing room, all waiting for a word with Father, who was returning from a quick lunch. I found out that as a rule, he didn't bother about lunch or [would] leave it half eaten rather than have anyone wait. Later, when I spoke to him about it he said, "The food is not as important as trying to help others."

From accounts of friars who lived with Solanus, Martha Casey's recollection does not do justice to the times that he would join them after the noon meal for a period of recreation. Often this recreation included responding to another friar who wanted to play billiards. Father Blase Gitzen recalled: "I liked to play billiards, and most of the other priests in the house did not care for it. I don't think Father Solanus particularly cared for it, and he wasn't a good billiard player either, but he would play a game with me because I wanted to play a game." Father Cosmas Niedhammer recalled that no matter how involved Solanus might be in the game, "when he was called to the front office, he would leave immediately, without any expression of impatience. It was remarkable. And it meant that when he was called, he would be in the office until supper time."

Some friars did not like the way Solanus tended, especially at breakfast, to mix everything he was going to eat and drink into the one bowl. The practice had become his trademark. Some friars would half-seriously chide Solanus about his high-pitched, low-volumed voice: "Nobody understands you; open your mouth," they would say. He would respond quietly: "Well, God understands me." And he would leave it at that. While such comments must have cut him, no friar recalls him showing impatience toward those who uttered the remarks.

Sunday nights in Capuchin friaries in those days were evenings of relaxation and recreation. Cosmas Niedhammer recalled:

When I was with him in Detroit, I recall that he would come into the recreation room on Sunday nights. He would draw himself a glass of wine from the gallon jug by holding it over his shoulder and then he'd tell some humorous incidents. Father Solanus was very gifted in that way. He could spin out a story just like that, and become personally involved in it. He was always very simple as though he had no context of uncharitableness. Sometimes he spoke of some incident that happened in their family of 10 brothers and six sisters. And Father Theodosius would poke fun at him about when he used to be a streetcar conductor. He would say that Father Solanus was now doing penance for all the nickels he had taken and didn't ring up. Father Solanus would laugh and have another anecdote ready. He was really quite human in that way.

It can be said quite safely that during this period in Detroit except for periodic incidents such as those that frustrated Francis Spruck or for annoying idiosyncrasies in eating, none of the friars had anything but admiration for Solanus Casey. Although they knew he was considered a saint by the lay people, his fraternal camaraderie made Solanus seem not really different from any of the other friars who lived in the community. His demeanor never indicated that he thought he was special nor that he should be treated by the friars as anyone special.

As did all the other friars who were able, Solanus accepted assignments for weekend supply at several Detroit parishes, beginning in 1925. He had a regular summer "helpout" for a week or two at Brighton from 1933 to 1940. After 1938, he supplied on weekends at only one parish, St. Paul's Maltese Church, where Michael Z. Cefai was the pastor. Father Cefai recalled how this extended helpout began:

> I needed a priest to help at the parish and went to Father Marion, the superior at St. Bonaventure's Monastery, asking for this kind of help. He told me he had no one that he could send. All the priests already were assigned. He said he had some old priests. He also said, "We have Father Solanus, but he is not allowed to go out. He does not hear confessions; he can't speak Maltese."
>
> At that moment Father Solanus came in. He fell on his knees... and asked for his [Father Marion's] blessing. I told Father Solanus why I was there and asked him if he would be willing to come if his superiors approved. He said, in his high-pitched voice, "Father Superior, can I go?" Thus, it worked out that Father Solanus came to my parish weekends.

The relationship between Solanus, Father Cefai, and his sister, who worked as his housekeeper, proved beneficial for all. Father Cefai was indebted to Solanus not only because he proved to be so popular with his parishioners, but also because he believed that Solanus had been instrumental in the healing of his father. Mr. Cefai and Solanus got along very well, swapping stories and telling jokes. Solanus loved recalling events of the past, and Father Cefai was a ready audience for these recollections. He remembered how Solanus regularly brought a faith perspective to them.

The Depression Years and the Foundation of
the Capuchin Soup Kitchen

On October 29, 1929, the stock market crashed. Although periodic reces-
sions and economic downturns had been experienced before, especially
in a highly industrialized city like Detroit, the Great Depression left few
people or few areas unscathed. Detroit was especially hard hit. If before this
time the friary office needed to be expanded because of increased numbers
of people, the Depression brought an even greater segment of all strata of
humanity in need.

For as long as people like Herman Buss could remember, the Capuchins
shared their food with those who came to the monastery door. This food
was sometimes from the friars' regular meals, but most of the time it consisted of coffee, a bowl of soup, and bread. As many as 150 people came
daily for such help.

As the numbers of poor people coming for food increased, so did the
imposition on the friars. With expected food not there, the complaints and
criticisms of the friars rose. They came to believe that they might not have
any food themselves. When the numbers reached more than two hundred
and three hundred daily, the superior of the house concluded that it was
becoming impossible for the porters to continue giving out bread in addition to their other work. He asked Father Herman, the spiritual director
of the Third Order of St. Francis, if the fraternity might help. On November 1, 1929, Father Herman bought the first pound of coffee and began
serving the people in the Third Order Hall, down the street from the monastery. The area of the hall serving as a kind of restaurant became known
as "The Soup Kitchen" after its chief meal, a large bowl of soup.

According to Herman, "The soup kitchen was a continuation of the
work of Father Solanus in the monastery.... Even though he wasn't there
all the time or directing the thing, through his holiness I believe he is the
one who helped us to get the help from Divine Providence." Besides as-
sisting when he could, Solanus tried also to get others involved, reminding
them that to feed the hungry is a corporal work of mercy. He persuaded
even rich and powerful people, including Mayor Frank Murphy, to cooperate in the project as well. Besides helping directly in the soup kitchen,
the mayor once arranged that a blue-ribbon steer from the Michigan State
Fair be donated to the soup kitchen.

On the very rare occasions when benefactors like Murphy were not
available and the food ran out, Herman would appeal to Solanus. "One

day," when the soup kitchen was serving up to three thousand people daily, Father Herman recounted:

> I said, "Father Solanus, we have no more bread and two or three hundred men are waiting for something to eat."
>
> He went over to the hall and told the men who were waiting in line, "Just wait and God will provide." Father Solanus said an "Our Father" after inviting the men to join him in the prayer. We just turned around and opened the front door to go out, and there was a bakery man coming with a big basket full of food. He had his whole truck full of stuff, and he proceeded to unload it. When the men saw this they started to cry and tears were running down their cheeks. Father Solanus, in his simple way, said, "See, God provides. Nobody will starve as long as you put your confidence in God, in Divine Providence."

At the height of the Depression, with more food needed, Solanus increased the requests he made of those coming to visit him. He also contacted bakeries for day-old bread and asked butchers to donate meat bones. At times he joined farmers, helping to pick and load apples, or vegetables for use in the stew. One trip to the rural area which Solanus made each year was to the Eagen Farm in Smiths Creek. Solanus helped load the truck, pitching gunny-sacks of vegetables, especially potatoes. Heaving the big bags on the truck revealed a strength that lay hidden in his scrawny frame. On such excursions, the driver would have to pray at least one rosary with Solanus.

Solanus believed that the concerns of poor people should be handled with the same courtesy and care as the concerns of the rich and powerful. This belief was evidenced in the case of a woman guest at the soup kitchen who wanted jelly doughnuts instead of the sugared ones that were being served. The man in charge of supervising the distribution of food had had a trying day and was not ready to debate her demands. Exasperated, he came to the front office, complaining to Solanus about her insistence. In a manner that in no way made the man feel he was being insensitive, Solanus merely responded: "If we have jelly doughnuts, then why don't you give them to her?" It was as simple as that. The poor have a right to this food; it has been donated for them, not for us. This was the message of the Gospel; Solanus wanted to make sure that it would be lived out in all the activities of the soup kitchen. When persons in need would come to the door after the soup kitchen was closed for the day, Solanus would go to the friary kitchen and prepare food for them.

The soup kitchen, as well as the front-door ministry, brought Solanus into contact with people of all religions and races, of all kinds of backgrounds and predicaments. He received them all with compassion and sensitivity, as evidenced in his notebook regarding African Americans. After noting that he had dinner with "a colored family" in Mount Vernon on October 20, 1931, he wrote: "Too bad someone cannot go to them for service — a good field."

In 1937, to thank the Capuchins for their work among the poor during the Depression, the City of Detroit and others sponsored a benefit party at the Naval Armory on East Jefferson Avenue near the monastery. To thank the people of Detroit and its neighboring city, Windsor, Ontario, for their help in sustaining the soup kitchen, Solanus was chosen to give an afternoon radio talk over Station CKLW. He noted that "we have tried to be of service to the poorest of the poor, but must add that it was our simple duty." That evening, at the armory, Solanus again seems to have spoken the thanks of the province in a simple but profound speech which he entitled "Capuchin-Franciscan Appreciation."

The "New Deal" of Roosevelt and Solanus's Growing Disenchantment

In addressing the day-to-day needs of the people coming to the front office and the soup kitchen, Solanus was cognizant of the wider social issues that had created not only the Depression but also the sociopolitical and economic problems that needed to be addressed if things were to change. Like many other people in the United States, Solanus had become a regular follower of a priest who addressed the social issues of the city and of the nation, Father Charles Coughlin. The two priests had come to respect each other and to care deeply for each other.

On October 17, 1926, Father Coughlin initiated a Sunday radio broadcast, which gradually built to an audience estimated at twenty million listeners. In November 1934, he announced the formation of the National Union for Social Justice as a way of implementing Catholic social teachings. At first Coughlin enthusiastically supported President Roosevelt. Furthermore, his support was welcomed by the administration. In April 1935, a few Capuchins were Coughlin's guests at a large rally for the national Union for Social Justice in the Olympia Stadium in Detroit. When they arrived and the fifteen thousand people present recognized Solanus among them, they gave him "quite an ovation."

During the ensuing year, Coughlin's relationship with Roosevelt began to sour. He started charging the administration with communist tendencies which Roosevelt was forced to deny. As his attacks increased, Coughlin seemed to galvanize a heretofore passive Catholic electorate. During Roosevelt's campaign for a second term, in 1936, Coughlin's attacks became more vicious and notorious. While the majority of the Catholic community sided with Roosevelt, a strong minority stood with Coughlin. In the general election, 70–80 percent of the Catholics were reported to have supported Roosevelt. According to George Q. Flynn:

> Coughlin's personal attacks against the president had boomeranged. Roosevelt was a popular figure, and the intemperate language used against him by Coughlin only served to alienate many Catholics from the priest's cause. Others, perhaps neutral about the entire affair, became greatly embarrassed by the spectacle of a Catholic priest's attacking the president of the United States.[38]

While Solanus did not share Coughlin's vindictiveness and never exhibited any of the anti-Semitism that had become evident in Coughlin's speeches and comments, he did believe passionately that the poor were not being helped by Roosevelt's programs and that, on the contrary, the rich were the beneficiaries. Even after Roosevelt's landslide victory in 1936, Solanus considered Coughlin a "prophet" and wrote to his sister:

> As for being for Roosevelt: Well, I say God bless him, too, though my enthusiasm for him is almost, or fast becoming ancient history. If he were a practical friend of the laborer or of the poor, considering the billions he's been demanding and having spent, you and your class would hardly need worry for a decent employment. It seems to me he is simply of the bankers.

In early 1939 Father Coughlin housed Solanus's priest-brother, Maurice, when Maurice was becoming increasingly afflicted by psychological problems, which included an unwillingness to get help offered by the province. Despite Coughlin's kindness to his brother, by this time, when the Radio Priest had become even more radical in his views as well as more racist and anti-Semitic, there is no further record of Solanus being associated with Coughlin in public or in private.

Growing Controversy over Solanus's Promotion of
The Mystical City of God

The only other area of Solanus's life that might be considered controversial involves the way his enthusiasm for *The Mystical City of God* led him to recommend it so highly to many of the people who came to him. To Mrs. Elvera Clair he recommended praying to the Holy Spirit for guidance, then reading from the book for fifteen minutes and meditating upon it. In time Solanus increased his suggestions that people begin reading the four volumes. In Mrs. Regina Devlin's copy of the work, Solanus inscribed:

> Dear Reader: God bless you. To know is to appreciate. God Himself is loved, is appreciated, only inasmuch as He is known. The following pages offer a beautiful introduction to God's masterpiece of all creation — an introduction to Mary, ever virgin, Mother of God. Let us learn to know the same — our own blessed Mother Mary.
>
> *Fr. Solanus, OFMCap.*

With Solanus's promotion of the volumes, more concerns arose about his prudence in doing this. Some criticism revolved around the price of the volumes; other criticism noted that the average person visiting Solanus for help was not ready for such spirituality; still others rejected the authenticity of Mary of Agreda's work itself.

For every charge against the book, Solanus offered a countercharge. Aware of the criticisms, he made every effort to explain the rationale for devotion to the work. Always ready to defend what he considered to be issues of truth and justice, he argued that the book had been endorsed by popes and theologians and saints of the holiest reputation. In 1938 he wrote his brother, Monsignor Edward Casey:

> It ought to be self understood that no simple reading of any book is going to move the Heart of Heaven in our favor. Only inasmuch as any book can serve to raise the heart to God and thus draw His blessings to us can it be said to have any quality or prayer about it.... Now in my opinion, there is hardly another book written, outside the Bible itself, more inspired-like and more inspiring than this wonderful work, *The Mystical City of God*. Its introduction alone, if read with prayerful attention, will hardly leave a doubt as to its supernatural origin.

Father Elmer Stoffel, who later was known as a critic of Solanus, chastised Solanus for his attachment to *The Mystical City.* However, he added, "before we were finished he had me reading it myself!"

Even though people like Elmer had seriously questioned the merits of the four volumes, Solanus was convinced such people were plainly misinformed. After all, did not amazing signs often occur when people read the works devoutly? He himself could attest to a very important sign in his own life that came upon reading the work:

> About New Year's Day, 1941, inclined to be discouraged in regard to [his brother] Fr. M. Joachim's condition, I made up my mind, notwithstanding the fact that it had taken me nearly eight years to finish the four books before — the *Conception,* 610 pages, the *Incarnation,* 608 pages, the *Transfixion,* 790 pages and the *Coronation,* 610 pages — that I'd pray them this time on my knees.
>
> I had hardly started when Fr. M. J. wrote the letter to Fr. Edward which I received back from the Philippine Islands with his comment: "This is the best letter I've received from him in years." And before I was half through with the first book, he was saying Holy Mass... Deo Gratias! On October 16th, I finished the second book and that day I received about the most encouraging letter from him of any yet.

Any controversy surrounding Solanus's enthusiastic promotion of *The Mystical City of God* was compounded by the activities of his friend Ray Garland. The two had met a few years after Solanus's arrival in Detroit. Since then Ray often visited Solanus asking for help and counsel. In turn, Solanus enlisted Ray for drives into the country to get vegetables for the soup kitchen and other tasks. When Ray was "dropped from the employ" of a certain Charles H. Chisholm, Solanus described in a letter why he wanted to defend him: "I have known Mr. Garland for about ten years, and I can honestly say that I doubt if I have ever met a person more solicitous to do a labor or more practical in suggesting remedies in time of difficulties."

About five years after first meeting Ray, Solanus urged him to write to the publisher of the four volumes, asking for the right to represent the books in Michigan. Ray received the position. For fourteen years he devoted his leisure time to promoting the volumes, selling a little over two hundred books a year. Whether and to what degree Ray Garland benefitted financially is not known. His widow has stated that the publisher always got the full amount. Neither Solanus nor the Capuchins received any remuneration.

When Solanus began his Sunday helpout at St. Paul's Maltese Parish, not only Ray Garland but a whole band of devotees of Solanus and of Mary of Agreda began coming to the parish for the Mass he celebrated. According to the testimony of Father Marion Roessler, Father Cefai seems to have allowed these people to have a breakfast meeting in the church basement after Sunday Mass, as long as Father Solanus attended. Father Cefai insisted that Solanus be present because he sensed an excessive piety in some of the group's members. His insights were concretized when he received reports that some members of the group were taking petals from flowers in the church to have them blessed by Father Solanus. After his blessing, some insisted, they recognized images of Christ in the petals.

In September 1942, Solanus tried to get relief from the chronic eczema on his legs by using other people's remedies.[39] Following the recommendation that he place his legs under an electric light, he burned them and had to be hospitalized for what he called "a novena of weeks." His illness prevented Solanus from being present at St. Paul's during this time. Despite this, the group continued to hold their meetings there. Father Cefai stated later (in 1968) that he gave them no permission to meet. Upset with their failure to keep the agreement to meet only when Father Solanus was present, the pastor told the group to leave the parish. The meetings then moved to Ray Garland's home. From there they would phone Solanus in the hospital asking for his prayers, his comments, and his blessing upon their various concerns and causes.

When the Capuchin superiors discovered what Garland and his group had been doing, they sensed Solanus might be being exploited. They told Ray not to come to the monastery once Solanus returned from the hospital. Garland complied literally. He stopped coming; yet he maintained contact with Solanus by phone. Meanwhile, Solanus steadfastly supported his friend.

Around the same time, some complaints came to the chancery of the Archdiocese of Detroit concerning Solanus's promotion of the four volumes, which some thought was burdening people already under financial strain. When the Capuchins were told about these complaints, the local guardian, Marion Roessler, felt sure that Solanus was not using his influence sufficiently to curb Garland's alleged excesses. The provincial, Father Theodosius Foley, became very firm with Father Solanus. He forbade him to have any connection with this man. Father Solanus told the provincial very simply that the man was being misunderstood. Then he begged Father Provincial to give him a different position, even working in the kitchen. Father Theodosius told him he didn't want to take him out of the office, but just to sever all connections with the fellow.

For the next several years it seems that Father Foley's order held. When the Chapter of 1945 was completed, it was decided that Solanus should be moved from Detroit. Officially the decision for his transfer was made to protect his failing health; unofficially, at least in part, it also arose because of the controversy around *The Mystical City of God.* Some also believe, without foundation, that part of the reason for his transfer was in response to his failure to be present in Detroit during the holding of a Provincial Chapter.

Solanus heard about this decision upon his return from an extended family visit in Washington State in the middle of June 1945. He had been given permission to visit his relatives there, more specifically to attend his Jesuit nephew's First Mass and to welcome his brother Edward from a four-year internment in a Japanese concentration camp during the war.

On the previous March 23, U.S. troops had stormed the camp before the Japanese had time to massacre their two thousand prisoners. Among the detainees were 125 religious women, 2 bishops, and 150 priests, including Monsignor Edward Casey. (Despite the oppression his brother and the others suffered at the hands of the Japanese, Solanus never was known to utter a racial slur against them; the only reference he used of the Japanese was "Japs," a word used at that time even by prestigious journals such as *The National Geographic*).

However, when other relatives in California cajoled him to visit them, he went, even though California as such was not listed specifically in the letter of "obedience" given for his trip to Spokane and Seattle. In his mind, since he had received the "obedience" to visit his relatives, it was okay to visit to California as well. Besides, once he got there, a local bishop wanted to spend some time with him.

Unfortunately, he did not anticipate the consequences of traveling in postwar time. The trains were very crowded. Once there he discovered that he would not be able to return to Detroit by the deadline indicated on his "obedience" — by the date of the Provincial Chapter. He wrote to his superior in Detroit, Father Marion Roessler, about his dilemma. He explained that the Capuchin superior in Los Angeles, Father Stephen Murtagh, tried to get him reservations on the train on his clergy pass. However:

the very best he could do — in regard to transportation, was to get reservations for next Thursday (July 12) instead of yesterday (July 9) for Seattle, so that I may use my "pass" to St. Paul. To get on the train as I proposed, without reservation, he stressed, would be foolhardiness. So here I am still — hoping to make the best of missing the privileges of the Chapter.

Solanus's rationale made perfect sense to Father Marion, who was sensitive to the thought processes of Solanus. Furthermore he was not going to interfere if a bishop wanted to talk with him. He found Solanus's behavior fully in accord with an obedience that Solanus exhibited then and always to the point of heroicity: "As his superior several times in Detroit, I always found him obedient; he would do anything you told him. In my opinion he had all the virtues required for the making of a saint."

Solanus prided himself on the cross-country nature of his trip from the West. He wrote to his sister, Margaret:

We'd come in from Los Angeles the night before (July 12) and offered Holy Mass in the Cathedral — and had a nice conference with the archbishop. At 1:30 p.m. Owen left me on the train for Seattle. That was Saturday. Sunday and Monday I had Holy Mass at the Convent (in Seattle). Father Joachim served. I stopped over 24 hours in Spokane. We were on the train all day Wednesday from 7:20 a.m. until Thursday at 10:30 when we arrived in St. Paul. I said Holy Mass Friday in St. Paul, got to Chicago on Saturday, Detroit on Sunday, New York on Monday and Tuesday in Brooklyn. I missed two Masses from Los Angeles. Thanks be to God for all things. Praised be Jesus!

On July 21, 1945, when Solanus returned, he was informed by Father Bernard Burke, the newly appointed superior, that he had been transferred to St. Michael's in Brooklyn, New York. Bernard later recalled that Solanus received this surprising news as if he had been told that it was time for the next meal. It was just the next thing the Lord was calling him to do. Without registering disappointment, surprise, complaint, or question about the continuance of his front-door ministry, Solanus immediately began to pack his bags. He arrived in Brooklyn the following Monday, July 23, 1945.

Chapter 7

Semiretirement for an Untiring Solanus: 1945–56

The Year of "Quiet" in Brooklyn: 1945–46

Although the people in Detroit were shocked and disappointed when they heard that Solanus had been transferred to Brooklyn, Solanus himself did not share their feelings. He viewed the transfer not only as part of "the will of God" but as a respite from the busy schedule of Detroit. In a moment of confidence, he noted to Brother Ignatius Milne that he was tired out and wanted to get away. Now that he was a semiretired porter in Brooklyn, he seemed relieved.

In so graciously accepting his transfer, Solanus already was evidencing that kind of "practical penance" that comes from obedience, as demanded in the Rule. To a group of people who came from Detroit and asked him why he had been changed, Solanus simply responded: "I guess they thought I was too besieged by the people in Detroit."

Once settled in Brooklyn, Solanus was able to get some much-needed rest. He also was able to make his annual retreat, that he might "try again to be converted for another year." He went the fifty miles to the province's Beautiful Immaculate Conception Monastery on the Hudson. The theme of the retreat was "To imitate St. Francis, who so perfectly followed Jesus, our divine model." Either the retreat provided many insights for Solanus or he was inspired to write more than usual: his retreat notes filled nine pages and included reflections on the vows, the beatitudes, and the "last things." Elaborating on the conference on penance, which had as its theme "Unless you do penance you shall all perish," Solanus made some astute observations:

> God knows as no one else knows that we all and each need penance. God knows we need humiliations whereby we can foster humility. Hence in His love, He never fails to provide occasions for each one to

practice penance, which means in other words to check self-conceit and, with God's help, to get somewhere in humility. Hence for a religious, the most practical penance is that naturally and logically connected to the Rule.

Returning from his retreat, Solanus found "quite a stack of letters awaiting opening." One of the many came from a Mrs. Kenny. He responded shortly afterward:

> I just came to yours of the 23rd and sure do sympathize with you and your family. However, we've had so many decidedly worse reports than that about your Pat which turned out most reasonable after several months of suspense and anxiety, that I shall still hope for a good word about son Patrick.
>
> At all events, I have just enrolled him in the Seraphic Masses as requested and we shall not be surprised at any favorable report to come. We'll pray and hope, trusting in God for the best. After all, if we look at things in light of faith, the worst (as the world considers things) is only our victory, according to our dear Lord's words: "Greater love than this no one has that a man lay down his life for his friends." I think that this ought to buoy us up as it is needed in millions of sad bereavements these days. God bless you again and give my love to all the family and friends.

Mrs. D. Edward Wolfe of Brighton telephoned Solanus saying her infant daughter, Kathleen Anne, was dying from "early" celiac disease. Feeling that the doctors were not helping her baby get better, she told Solanus she wanted to bring the baby to Brooklyn for his blessing. Solanus would hear none of it. Not only was the baby deathly sick; the expense was too much to consider. Then, contrary to all rules he may have been taught about not being able to "transmit" blessings through media more than fifty feet from the recipients, Solanus said, "Kneel down with the baby and I will give you my blessing over the telephone." When he had finished praying, he suggested that Mrs. Wolfe use the money that she would have spent coming to Brooklyn to "do something for a poor family." Kathleen Ann recovered.

As more Detroiters discovered Solanus's address in Brooklyn, letters to him increased. Some came from Ray Garland and others in his group, relating their activities and their promotion of the insights of Mary of Agreda in *The Mystical City of God*. Commenting on an "interesting meeting" the group seems to have had a few weeks before, Solanus noted the controversy surrounding Ray and the group. It seems that Solanus had been reported (wrongfully) as having been telephoning Ray and the "Agredan Society" long distance. "Whatever the source," Solanus wrote, "it seems to have given important offense, if not scandal." With his usual faith-filled approach to life, Solanus felt it was time for God to act in this situation, since Ray's efforts and his own had generated too much controversy. Consequently he asked to be left free of involvement:

> Therefore, I wish that for the present and until you be better known and your efforts recognized, you leave me out of the picture. After all if Venerable Mary of Agreda is a saint, about which I find it personally unreasonable to doubt, then, in my way of thinking, it's high time she get active in working a miracle of some kind, in clearing away the prejudice or jealousy or at least misunderstanding that has hampered her work [*The Mystical City*] — which is not hers but God's work—and has pressed on your shoulders for three years and on mine for at least seven.

Although the letter makes it clear that Solanus believed fully in Ray's innocence and commitment, his superiors had told him to be disassociated from the man and Solanus obeyed. No further communication between the two has been discovered. However, other correspondence indicates that his written communication with others was definitely increasing. He wrote to his brother Edward that his coming to St. Michael's had been a "decided relief" compared to the drain and strain of twenty years at St. Bonaventure's in Detroit: "I do have perhaps hours as long but it's a change. Here it's correspondence that takes most of the time. There, I simply had to leave most of that to others. And while I meet with pathetic cases to solve or try to alleviate, the strain and tension is by no means so pressing."

With more free time available in the first part of his stay at St. Michael's Solanus used the Christmas of 1945, the first after the end of the Second World War, to extol the birth of Christ in verse-form. One of the poems he sent (written perhaps as early as 1934) went to his niece Helena Wilhite:

ALWAYS CHRISTMAS EVE

With love and Christmas greetings to all
Comes the Infant once more to free us from sorrow.
Whose smile and whose power and whose gentleness call
To each heart and each soul for a manger tomorrow.
Whose love and whose goodness—whose wonders proclaim

Him, the Son of the Virgin, as promised of yore.
Oh, may He estrange us from sin and its shame!
And reign in our hearts, as His crib evermore!
...Ah, the rest of us, on Calvary
Mary conceived under the Cross
Thirty-three years later. Glory to God!
Peace to men of GOOD WILL.

In some of his correspondence with Detroiters, Solanus reflected on incidents of God's healing power that he had witnessed among people visiting him at St. Bonaventure's. He related what happened as though he were a mere observer, a reporter. From his perspective, any healing came through divine means, especially the SMA, not his own. His letters spoke of doctors being surprised, God's will being done, and "hoping" for happy resolutions to people's difficulties. In an extended letter written to Miss Mildred Maueal, he wove spiritual reflections related to the shortness of life and to the need for confidence in God. The material on confidence seemed chosen especially to address the woman's sagging spirits:

Confidence in God — the very soul of prayer — hardly comes to any poor sinner like we all are, without trials and humiliations, and your failure, though simple and possibly single, has no doubt been quite a little cross, at least for a "little soul" to carry. There is a little verse I am sure will prof[it] you to keep in mind and ought help you foster confidence in God: *"God condescends to use our powers if we don't spoil His plans by ours."* God's plans are always for the best: always wonderful. But most especially for the patient and the humble who trust in Him are His plans unfathomably holy and sublime.

Solanus closed his letter to Miss Maueal with one of the most beautiful reflective prayers that have thus far been discovered in the collection of his writings:

Let us, therefore, not weaken. Let us hope when darkness seems to surround us. Let us thank Him at all times and under whatever circumstances. Thank Him for our creation and our existence. Thank Him for everything — for His plans in the past that by our sins and our want of appreciation and patience have so often frustrated and that He so often found necessary to change. Let us thank Him for all His plans for the future — for trials and humiliations as well as great joy and consolations; for sickness and whatever death He may deign to plan; and with the inspired Psalmist let us call all the creatures of the universe to help us praise and adore Him Who is the Divine Beginning and the everlasting Good — the Alpha and the Omega.

Increasing Numbers of People Invoke Solanus's Help

Within a short time, word about the wonderful things happening through the intercession of the new Capuchin at St. Michael's traveled around the parish and beyond. Astoria Mahoney, a Girl Scout leader in the parish, was twenty-seven years old and married for eight years. However, she and her husband were childless. Upon his return from World War II they consulted various doctors who told them the "heartbreaking news" that it would be very unlikely that they would have their own children. Her husband then suggested that they adopt a child. She was very hesitant because it would be "a first" for both their families. She wondered if their "children would be accepted and loved as the other grandchildren, nieces and nephews." She recalled:

> It was not generally known, but I had heard that Father Solanus was in our parish, that he was a very saintly man, well loved and sought after for counsel and advice by the people in Detroit, where he recently served.
>
> One afternoon after a Girl Scout meeting, I rang the monastery bell and asked if I could speak to Father Casey. Brother asked me no questions and ushered me to a small conference room when very soon Father Casey came in with a friendly smile. I told him about my marriage, how much I wanted a family, and my fears about adoption. His answer to me not only answered my questions, but will remain with me forever. He said, "If it wasn't for people like you, who would take care of the unfortunate ones?" When I left him, I was happy and convinced that this is what I was meant to do and shortly applied to the N.Y. Foundling Hospital to adopt a child.
>
> On June 12, 1946, we brought our first son home. He was exactly two months old.

When people like Astoria Mahoney were unable to visit Solanus at St. Michael's, some friend would take Solanus to visit them. Sometimes the process of getting him through New York's complex traffic created humorous incidents for his drivers. One such incident has been recounted by Art

Lohrman. It seems that his wife, who knew Solanus, sometimes asked Art to take him to the houses of various people in the metropolitan area. One time their destination took them over the Triboro Bridge to the Bronx. Coming back, Mr. Lohrman wanted to have a little extra time for conversation with his traveling companion. So he acted as though he couldn't find the bridge. "Oh," Solanus said, "Let's say a rosary to the Mother of God that you find it." By the time the rosary was prayed, they had "found" the bridge. "Now in thanksgiving to the Mother of God," Solanus said, "let's say another one." Finally, after three rosaries and no conversation with Solanus, Art decided that he would never say anything "whether I was lost or not."

As word of people's experiences with Solanus Casey spread, the numbers of those seeking time with him increased. Because he kept long hours either seeing people or answering correspondence, Solanus did not always get the hours of sleep that his body needed. So he inaugurated a method for a quick "catnap," which he had devised earlier at St. Bonaventure's. He would push his chair back from the desk and crawl under it. Then he would snuggle up like a little child and take a quick snooze. He'd stay there until he was relaxed, or until the phone or doorbell rang. Then he'd get up, brush himself off, smooth down his hair, and look refreshed.

As had happened at St. Bonaventure's front office, the front office at St. Michael's gradually witnessed a line of people waiting to talk with him. One of these was Ruth Keck, whose son became Father Barnabas Keck, OFMCap. Years later he was the director of the Solanus Guild at St. John's in Manhattan. He recalled:

> When my mother still lived in St. Patrick's (Brooklyn), she had been in a hospital. The doctor wanted her to go home and then come back for surgery. She asked him, "If I ask you straight questions, will you give me an honest answer?"
>
> He said, "Okay."
>
> "Do I have cancer?" she asked. At that he turned and walked out of the room. So my mother turned to the woman next to her and said, "What's that supposed to mean?"
>
> She left the hospital and told my aunt Agnes what happened. "Ruth," she said, "let's go over to St. Michael's and see Father Solanus." So she went to the friary and waited in line. When my mother's turn came, Father Solanus said, "And what's your problem, dear."
>
> "I think I have cancer," she said.

All he said was, "Don't you know God can cure cancer just like a toothache?" So she knelt down and he put his hand on her and blessed her, praying over her.

She went home and never went back to the doctor and was eighty years old when the story was told in 1983.

Deepening Bonds with the Friars, Friends, and God

Although he left much behind when he left Detroit, even to the point of having many pictures destroyed, Solanus brought his violin with him to St. Michael's. Soon after he arrived he decided to entertain the friars at their regular Sunday evening recreation. So he brought his violin to the recreation room. When the friars saw him with the violin, recalled Father Walter O'Brien — who was present — they thought: "Well, he is an old man trying to entertain us." So they endured his squeaking fiddle. This reaction on their part was interpreted as so positive by Solanus that he thought he had done very well. The next Sunday night he showed up with his violin again. However, this time the friars were not so generous. As he began to play, one of the men went to the radio and turned up the volume. "Without saying a word," noted Father Walter, "Solanus left the room and went down before the Blessed Sacrament and continued his playing. Each Sunday night after that he would go with his violin and 'play before the Lord' for a half hour or so, playing various hymns."

The place where Solanus played was the friars' chapel. It overlooked the main church. One day Father Walter discovered that the altar boys had been severely reprimanded by the sisters for their antics after the Sunday evening Holy Hour. When he asked the servers why they had misbehaved they exclaimed, "'Oh, Father, there were some squeaks coming from your chapel and we couldn't help but laugh.' There was Solanus, it seems, oblivious to everything, playing before the Blessed Sacrament. All I said to the altar boys was, 'The next time it happens just try to control yourself!'" Walter concluded: "And it did happen every Sunday night."

Besides recreating with the St. Michael's friars and with Jesus in the Blessed Sacrament, Solanus found time to renew contact with other friars and parishioners he had known in former assignments. Concerned as well about his physical fitness, he went occasionally to the monastery in Garrison, New York, to swim in the pool there. He also made it a point to go to the Labor Day Festival in Yonkers. He loved to see the excitement of the children, to watch the games being played, and to eat the food being served. He especially enjoyed hot dogs with onions.

Such occasions made Solanus's presence in the New York area much more known, hardly something envisioned by the superiors when they sent him to Brooklyn. Although Solanus had been transferred from Detroit to Brooklyn in part to relieve him of the burden of seeing so many people, the superiors' best intentions were subverted by the people's needs, which did not recognize boundaries or state lines. So, looking around the province for a place that would be far enough removed from the major cities served by the Capuchins (New York, Detroit, and Milwaukee), as well as have enough community presence to nourish Solanus in what they thought would be the twilight years of his life, the superiors decided to send him to the province's House of Novitiate at Huntington, Indiana. He would leave Brooklyn April 24, 1946, nine months and a day after his arrival.

The "Twilight Years" in Huntington, Indiana: 1946–56

Soon after Solanus's arrival at St. Felix Friary in Huntington, word came from Detroit that a person with whom he had corresponded while at St. Michael's was very upset. It seemed that the friars had made a rubber stamp of Solanus's signature, thinking this would make it easier for Solanus to handle SMA enrollments and sign checks. They knew his arthritis made it very difficult for him to write and type his letters and even to sign his name. However, for at least this person, receiving Solanus's signature by means of a rubber stamp rather than his own hand was an affront. She complained quite strongly to Brother Leo Wollenweber, the porter who replaced Solanus in Detroit.

Solanus wrote a letter in response to the woman and copied it in a cover letter to Leo. The letter is representative of the nonviolent way Solanus tried to deal with anger, impatience, and tensions in others. It also reveals, to a small degree, the way the seventy-six-year-old Capuchin was being plagued (or blessed) by various ailments, especially with his legs:

Dear Brother Leo:
    God bless you and all at St. Bonaventure's.
    I am sending the original of this carbon to Miss Lyke. I hope it may smooth the thing off in a manner, though I am not just clear

to what she really complains about. Perhaps she expected a personal acknowledgement of some kind rather than just a rubber stamp.

I've been getting so many checks — both here at St. Felix and at St. Michael's — that I would have to possess an extraordinary memory to recollect particulars like this little mix-up might require. One thing I do remember, that during the nine or ten months I was at St. Michael's it was very seldom, if ever, that I was without letters to acknowledge, even though I sometimes worked on them until after midnight.

God be praised, however, I did not mind it and my health kept fine. Sometimes my two faithful old sentinels would threaten to go on strike and to quiet them down I felt I'd have to give it up.

Well, she will possibly write again. After all if she got her checks back, she ought to know that things were okay.

We'll hope for the best anyhow and pray for the dear Lord's gentle guidance.

Praying in the meantime for one another's conversion, till someday we can sin no more and the angels will be able to bear us off to eternity. There, forever, really and truly CONVERTED, we'll be able to sing on with the angels awaiting that blessed day: "O all you works of the Lord, bless the Lord, praise and exalt him above all forever."

Fr. Solanus Casey, OFMCap.
Praised be Jesus Christ.

One of the first items the house chronicle at St. Felix noted after Solanus's arrival was his blessing of the orchard, lest frost hurt the newly forming apples. When he heard that the friars were planning to light a smudge to save the tiny apples, "Father Solanus volunteered to bless the orchard instead with the oration 'Ad Omnia' and one to Blessed Ignatius, a Capuchin brother. Now it appears that only the grapes froze. When all around us the neighboring apples were destroyed — ours were unharmed."

The fact that the friary chronicler did not make any elaboration on the incident serves to indicate that such events had come to be perceived as quite normal from Solanus, even by the brethren. The friars recognized Solanus's gifts and, unlike parallel examples of other people recognized by "outsiders" for their holiness only to be rejected by "their own," they accepted the phenomenon of Solanus in their midst. As a whole they did what they could to place no obstacle to God's work through the instrumentality of their brother.

Solanus's Interaction with the Capuchins at St. Felix

With Solanus's transfer to Huntington he was officially "retired." He was given the directorship of the SMA as his only assignment. Thus, with more time on his hands and before the people could know where he was, Solanus had the leisure to admire his surroundings, with gratitude. As he noted in a letter to one of his sisters, a simple walk behind the friary led him from a sense of appreciation for the environment to a deeper reflection of human connectedness to God and God's Mother:

> I was strolling in the orchard and vineyard this a.m. [They are] beautifully loaded. Deo Gratias. And kneeling in the little Capuchin cemetery all behind this ideal monastery, I was thrilled by the chimes of SS. Peter and Paul in their tower smiling at me less (than) two miles away. Thoughts multiplied of the wonderful past. Wonderful indeed to muse over! Thanks be to God. Still how comparatively melancholy when, anchored in holy faith, we turn to the spring of Eternal blessedness — assured our perseverance. Indeed, what is the past, aside from the privilege that ought to be our supreme aim, to have fostered and to foster appreciation of our being children of our Heavenly Father and of our Blessed Mother Mary?

The thirty acres at St. Felix afforded Solanus the opportunity to thrill at the wonders of God's creation in the apple trees, the grape vines, the gardens for flowers and vegetables, and, above all, the beehives. Often on his strolls he would sit near the beehives and wondrously observe the coming and going of the bees. Now and then they would alight on his hand. As he would watch them move on his hand and around his fingers, Solanus would be fascinated by their intricate construction and way of functioning. He would often pray some word of praise such as: "My dear God, how could you have created such a marvelous thing!"

Almost from the beginning, because he was so relaxed with the bees, Solanus was asked to become involved in their care. A year or two after arriving at Huntington, Solanus ordered a queen bee for the apiary; on July 27 of the following year Solanus and another friar extracted forty pounds of honey from one of the hives.

Each class of new novices would have their own stories about the credulous soul who would come upon Solanus talking to a bee as he held it in his room or in the friary corridor. Solanus would ask the novice to take the bee outside. Invariably, as the story always ended, the novice would be stung. Father Elmer Stoffel (no great supporter of Solanus while he lived) recalled to the Tribunal "my own case of healing" when asked to describe "a case of healing" and its details:

> When we were at Huntington I had charge of the bees and Father Solanus was helping me. I was smoking the bees to calm them down. Father Solanus would stand there and calm them with his harmonica. But one day I had not taken the proper precautions to tighten my clothes and three of the bees got up my leg and stung me. I had an immediate reaction to them and fell to the ground extremely ill. I thought I was going to die. Father Solanus blessed me and said, "God will make you well." Immediately the pain and the illness left me and I was perfectly well and never bothered by it again. Some of the other priests said to Father Solanus after this, "How come you cured Elmer? You never cure the rest of us when we come to you with our aches and pains." Father Solanus merely smiled and said, "But Elmer was dying."

It was commonly known among the Capuchins that Solanus would not respond favorably when they asked him to pray for healing of their own "aches and pains." In his mind, Capuchins were called to suffer and to do so patiently. The only known exception (besides Elmer) to this rule of thumb which guided Solanus in his relations with the friars was a brother-novice, Daniel Brady, in Detroit. He was experiencing very severe teeth problems, and Solanus blessed him; the problems went away.

Among the friars, Solanus asked for no favors and received none. He intermingled with the professed and the novices as any friar at that time could (given the rules which limited relationships between the two groups). When he was able, he would play volleyball or tennis with the novices; he did so enthusiastically and competitively. If he fell, he would pick himself up and continue as though he had not fallen. Indoors he loved to play billiards, especially when his legs were not too painful to keep him from standing. Often he would be the fourth man in the game; thus, when a visitor wanted to play, Solanus would be excluded. When the visitor left, he would be invited to return to the game to make the foursome. Blase Gitzen's recollections of Solanus's having little expertise at the game have been countered by another regular visitor, Father James Conroy. Father Conroy, later a monsignor and a columnist for *Our Sunday Visitor*, the national Catholic newspaper based in Huntington, recalled that Solanus "was sly and beat me most of the time; you couldn't talk to him at all while you were playing; he had no mercy." Yet, he added, he had "a keen sense of humor."

At Huntington, as elsewhere, Solanus kept the practice of putting all his food together in one bowl. While Father Blase interpreted this as a "penance" he performed, he also acknowledged that Solanus's practice made others practice penance as well! Father Benedict Joseph Groeschel recalled: "If he had one eccentricity it was the fact that he put all of his food in the same dish at the same time; it could be mashed potatoes and ice cream but it still went in the same dish." The friars allowed each other worse "eccentricities" than they found in Solanus. Besides, they were mature enough to balance any questionable table patterns with the rest of his life, which continually edified them. The only other pattern of Solanus that irritated some of the friars was his tendency to extend the telling of his stories with details they considered unnecessary. Father Colman Boylan remembers that, when this happened, "the older friars would chide Father Solanus by saying, 'Please Solanus, give us the main point of the story and forget about all the sidelines.' Unperturbed, Father Solanus would do as he was told, again manifesting all kindness and no rancor at the gibes of others."

Although it might be expected that a senior friar could be exempt from the regular horarium of the house, not only did Solanus observe it, he also surpassed it — at least by rising earlier than the 4:55 a.m. signal, a clapping of two pieces of wood which announced the dawn of a new day. Solanus would often be observed in chapel at prayer by friars getting up before 4:00. While this was not a daily occurrence, usually Solanus would already be in chapel when the rest of the community arrived for morning prayers at 5:15. Solanus would either participate in the community Mass at 6:15 or, like most priests of that period, offer Mass privately at a side altar. After Mass he would join the community for breakfast (always in silence). At 8:00 he attended the Mass celebrated for the novices. Often he remained long afterward, absorbed in prayer. But by the time the mail arrived at 9:30 he was ready to get to work answering letters until noon prayers and the noon meal.

After dinner he went to the "Priests' Recreation Room" (in those days brothers, novices, and priests had their own recreation rooms). Sometimes he would tell tales about his family and childhood (often repeating them to the frustration of some friars), or listen to stories from the others. Or he might play billiards. At 1:30 he would take a "siesta" until 2:00 or 2:30. If he had finished his mail, he would often walk outside, many times praying the Little Office of the Blessed Virgin. He would then do work assigned him by the superior (such as taking care of the bees or killing the weeds on the lawn) and then say the Office with the community at 5:00. At 6:00 he would have supper, followed by a short recreation and night prayers at 7:15. His evenings were usually spent in his room, reading and praying. If he slept on his bed, he apparently slept on its springs because he had no mattress under the bedspread.

Often in the middle of the night he would get up and go to the chapel for more extended prayer time. Father Giles Soyka, whose room was next to that of Solanus in the friary, often heard him get up around 3:00 to "go to the chapel to pray." Friars might come upon him sprawled on the floor, face down, as if in total adoration or, in contemporary charismatic terminology, "resting in the Lord." Benedict Joseph Groeschel recounted:

> On a particular evening when it was very warm in the monastery, I arose because I was unable to sleep — about 3 o'clock in the morning. I walked around the cloister and came to the chapel, which was in darkness. I paused to say a brief prayer at the side door of the chapel adjacent to the altar. Without much movement I was able to reach over and put on two large electric spotlights which filled the sanctuary with illumination. Father Solanus was kneeling on the top step of the altar. His eyes were partially open and his gaze was riveted on the tabernacle. His arms were extended in a form of prayer. He seemed to be totally unaware that I was present, or even that the spotlights had gone on although they were very bright. Father Solanus was a very self-effacing man, and would have moved immediately, I believe, if he knew that I was present. It was not typical to see him in such a posture. I observed him for several minutes, and he did not move at all. I was filled with a sense of both awe and embarrassment, feeling, I remember, that I was observing something that I was really not supposed to see. Eventually I put the light out and left him there in the chapel.

The friars knew that prayer was not just something that Solanus performed now and then; it was a way of life. Frequently after receiving phone calls, he would go to the choir, where he would kneel down and become very prayerful. Father Blase remembered that "at times he was so absorbed in prayer that it seemed he was in some sort of mystical state. At such times one could not get his attention by motioning or calling to him; he had to be shaken."

While prayer might have been the element of Solanus's life that inspired the impressionable young novices most, they may have overlooked the normal, everyday kinds of charity that Solanus performed—from willingness to play his violin for friary talent shows to taking care of his old classmate, Damasus Wickland, who was blind. Solanus would go to the infirmary, where Damasus spent most of his time. He would reminisce with him and pray the Little Office of the Blessed Virgin with him.

The novices may also have been unaware of the way Solanus never would allow even a friar to make any possibly derogatory statement about something holy. While he loved to joke and had a quick wit, if jokes were directed to or about matters of piety, he did not hesitate to correct those who joked, even if the one he corrected happened to be his superior. One person who experienced his fraternal correction was his own superior, Father Thomas Aquinas Heidenreich. He recalled:

> One time I mistakenly, or more jokingly, referred to Mother Agreda as Mother O'Grady. Father Solanus immediately corrected me, very nicely but very firmly, and told me that he did not think it was proper that I should make fun of a woman whose writings had been accepted by the church and is considered at least to be Venerable.[40]

While Solanus cared deeply for his brothers, it is quite evident that they cared for him. They tried to protect him from the excessive demands of the people who called, who wrote, and who came to share with him their burdens and concerns. This care of the friars for their brother Solanus probably is most evident in the fact that, during his time at Huntington, Solanus was given a fellow Capuchin to act as his secretary for the many letters which came to him each day.

Solanus's Need for Secretaries

Besides keeping in good correspondence with his family, Solanus was forced, by the sheer number of letters written to him and the requests for enrollments in the Seraphic Mass Association, to correspond actively with many other people. Invariably his letters to others were initiated by their correspondence to him, often asking for his prayers and insights on difficult issues.

Unless the letters were written to his family, with whom he reminisced more, they tended to be short and to the point. His sister-in-law Martha recalled that "he could get more on a postcard than I could get on a large sheet of paper." Sometimes Solanus would make a point from the past that would surprise the recipient. For instance, when Sr. Mary Cecilia Eagen, SC, whom Solanus knew when she was a child, wrote him during her novitiate, his return letter to her called her by her baptismal name, Dorothy. To friends like Sr. Cecilia and to others whom he knew better he might send a card, but always in it there would be a prayer. As one recipient recalled, "it always seemed to fit in with the situation at the time; that is, if I had been depressed, not feeling well, the prayer would seem to just fit into the situation and could bolster me up." When the letters were from benefactors, he often answered by writing on the same piece of paper between the lines of the original letter. More often than not his responses thanked God for whatever was happening and assured recipients that they were in God's loving hands. Many times they closed with a request that the recipient pray for his conversion.

In his latter days at Detroit, Solanus had been given Brother Leo Wollenweber as a secretary to help him handle his increasing correspondence, which usually related to SMA requests. At St. Felix, the superiors gave him a succession of very competent friars upon whom he relied to answer the ordinary requests of his correspondents and who would know when Solanus should be involved more personally. These secretaries were Capuchins Ambrose DeGroot (1946–49), Blase Gitzen (1949–51), Simeon Keogh (1950–52), Justinian Liebel (1952–53), and Booker Ashe (1953 until Solanus was transferred to Detroit).

The sheer volume of letters coming to him led the superiors to give him these secretaries. Booker recalled that he would open his mail and read it and then discuss it with Solanus, who would tell him what to say: "Most of it would be in a spiritual vein, telling the people to believe in God and trust in God and everything would be all right." He would answer more difficult cases himself. Father Blase remembered:

Naturally, in looking through these letters I came across four or five in each mailing that were particularly pitiful cases. In my heart, I prayed that Father Solanus would answer these himself, and almost invariably, those were the letters he chose to answer personally. The rest I would acknowledge with a short note. In the course of the day, I would receive the answers he had crashed out on an old battered typewriter. They were typed, mostly, on three by five cards. The spelling was bad, pure fifth-grade stuff, but the contents simply amazed me. With a few words he was able to come to the heart of the problem. His understanding of people, his sympathetic response, his grasp of theology just astounded me. He may not have passed his examinations, but his wisdom was far beyond mine.

Many times people would send Solanus money, which he would just place loosely around his room. Thus, another reason why the superiors wanted friars to be his secretary was to collect the monies that came. Because Solanus didn't keep track of the money and often didn't even know where he had put it, the secretaries were ordered to open his mail. To this Solanus never objected.

The testimonies of Solanus's secretaries are especially significant because these friars related to Solanus more closely than any others. From Ambrose DeGroot's perspective, the "characteristic notes of his spirituality were his deep confidence in God, his confidence in Divine Providence, and prayer." Another characteristic that Ambrose appreciated in Solanus was his humility:

> I am convinced that he was not aware that others held him in such high esteem. If he did, then all I can say is that he was a very good actor. But no one can put on an act for such a number of years without giving himself away. I just know he was not aware of the esteem in which others held him. Nor did he care.
>
> He was not the kind of man who put himself on trial before anyone, nor did he reveal he was on trial. He was on trial before his God. And he loved his God and he knew that God loved him. That was all that mattered. His whole conduct showed that this must have been the case. I cannot help but marvel how God can hide such mass esteem for a person without that person being aware of it. But God does. And I'm convinced he did it in the case of Father Solanus. He was genuinely humble — without any pretense.

Despite having a secretary to handle the ordinary flow of his correspondence, Solanus still handled much of his own mail. In the early days at Huntington the apostolate of the pen took more time than did office calls. Just as previously he had had to keep people waiting in the office, now he had to keep them waiting for responses to their letters. To one correspondent who commented that he was late in answering, he wrote: "It is not audiences with callers now but answering letters that is my problem. So please have charity to overlook my tardiness."

Reflecting on his work with Solanus, Ambrose noted that the letters

Solanus wrote to the people were not initiated by him, but always were in response to their letters to him. If people couldn't come to see him or reach him by telephone, they wrote him letters. Writing him letters seems to have been their third alternative after personal visits or phone calls to St. Felix: "I know that it wasn't long after he arrived there that people knew he was there and began to seek him out," Ambrose has noted. "He was constantly seeing people, and if they didn't come to see him they telephoned him. He was constantly being called to the telephone."

Blase Gitzen took the place of Ambrose DeGroot as Solanus's secretary. In his work with and observance of Solanus, Father Blase noted that, although Solanus's many contacts with people took him away from community recreation at various times, he always was present for religious exercises. Sometimes, Blase recalled, "he was so involved with the people that he would miss recreation and even meals. It was not because of something that he intended to do, but rather because of the call upon his time. His absence from these various activities was understood by his superiors."

Solanus received from thirty to forty letters a day, most of them containing money. According to Blase, it was his duty to open all Solanus's mail, determine what the money was for (Masses, SMA, alms), and record the information.

When people wrote to Solanus with their problems and their monies for Masses, SMA, or gifts, Solanus got so involved in their problems and how to address them that he paid little or no attention to the monies when he opened his mail. Solanus absentmindedly would stuff the money into his habit pockets or place it in the cubby holes of his desk or use it as book marks or misplace it, because he did not perceive it to be of importance, given the real concerns of the people. One day, with the permission of the guardian (and without the knowledge of Solanus), Blase did a thorough cleaning of Solanus's room and located $153 that had come to rest in many different places. He noted that "he never said anything, but I got the impression that he wasn't very pleased that I cleaned up his room," probably, Blase surmised, because "I lost his place in many a book!"

In Solanus's letters to people who wrote for favors, he often recalled incidents from his past experiences that might serve to give them hope. Early in 1950 he wrote from St. Felix about an incident that had happened while he was at St. Bonaventure's. It involved a married couple who were neither Catholic nor white. As he was fond of describing situations from his past in as graphic detail as possible, this letter reveals his attempt to characterize the style of conversation that ensued between him and the people, who were definitely from the South: "It must be ten or more years ago that a certain modest lady, having waited close to an hour, until all else had gone, introduced herself. 'I's not Catholic, but I would like to get a blessin' too. I's always had headaches.' Her accent rather than her color indicated something of her particular origin."

About three hours later "a well-featured but very dark visitor of the same name and identical accent asked for a rosary. I told him of his name-sake who had been in about 11:00. 'That's my wife.' He went on to explain that she had come home without any headache." Thanking God, Solanus continued:

> They had been praying for a family for thirteen years and were natu-rally discouraged, or were becoming so. They believed in Christianity but had never been baptized.... It is next to "unbelievable," what dif-ficulties they met with and, by God's grace overcame, before being received into the church — and even for months afterward. All Hell just seemed determined to keep them from their purpose.

More than three years later the "convert darkies" returned. This time, however, "there were three of them instead of two. The good God blessed them with a decidedly promising youngster, the picture of his appreciative Daddy."

While the story remained in Solanus's memory and could be recalled to his correspondent ten years later, Solanus noted that he used it only as a "practical lesson — one case in thousands." As for Blase, he too had "so many" stories about "cures that had been effected through the intercession of Father Solanus" that he "eventually threw them away." However, before the Tribunal, he did recall one case concerning a family from Michigan:

> I think the name of the family was Brewer, but I am not sure. At any rate, these people had come down to visit Father Solanus at Hunting-ton. The woman had a diabetic sore on her arm that wasn't healing. As they wrote in their letter later, they felt that Father Solanus had almost ignored this problem while they were talking to him. How-ever, as they were leaving — they were already in the car — he did lean in and say to the woman, "When you reach the Michigan bor-der, why don't you take that bandage off of your arm." The woman wrote in her letter that they raced to the Michigan border in silence, and when they crossed the borderline, they unwrapped the bandage

and thought the wrong arm had been bandaged because there was nothing of the sore that remained.

When Simeon Keogh took Blase's place as Solanus's secretary, the stories continued. Simeon noted that, as with his approach to the young black couple, Solanus "never showed preference among people" of any race or religion. During the time Justinian Liebel acted as Solanus's secretary (1952–53), the province was divided into two provinces: the "East," St. Mary's Province, composed of the northern states, from New York to Maine, and the "West," St. Joseph's Province, from Detroit to Montana. The novitiate was returned to St. Bonaventure's, and the house of philosophy was located at St. Felix in Huntington. Solanus chose to be part of the St. Joseph's Province.

Justinian was followed by the one who served the longest as secretary to Solanus, Brother Agathangelus (later Booker) Ashe. When Booker went to Huntington as a postulant in 1951, he made such a positive impression on Solanus that the latter wrote to Brother Leo: "Thank God we have a very promising bouquet of brother-candidates, including a very carefree, happy darky." To anyone who possibly might hypothesize from his use of the term "darky" that Solanus might have had prejudice against African Americans, the very context of thanksgiving indicates that that was merely the way white people spoke of them; the tone of the letter indicates Solanus was most welcoming to Booker as well as to all the other brother-candidates. According to Booker himself, Solanus Casey treated all people equally:

> I am the first black member of the Capuchin Order in the United States and I think he was ahead of his time in the way he treated me. At least I felt nothing of the racial character in the way he treated me or the way he accepted me. He saw all persons as human beings, the image of God; their physical characteristics were mere accidents that he would pay no attention to — whether it would be race, color, or creed.

From Booker's perspective, it was Solanus's encouragement which enabled him to persevere. Solanus's prophetic indications to him while he was secretary came to fulfillment in later years: "He told me that I would make solemn profession, that I would see my twenty-fifth jubilee, and that I would help to bring about a lot of changes in the province. Now I think that many of those things have really come to pass. He even told me that I would do things that no brother had ever done."

After various other assignments around the province, Booker helped found and direct the House of Peace, a large direct-ministry and service program for inner-city poor people in Milwaukee, where he also served on many civil rights boards. He became the first brother in the history of the modern Capuchin Franciscan Order to become a provincial councilor, serving two terms. He was president of the clergy group of the National Office of Black Catholics and represented the North American Capuchin Order's Plenary Council on Prayer at Taizé, France.

Upon hindsight, Booker feels that Solanus's way of communicating with people seeking help was somehow extended to them through himself. Often he experienced a kind of power within him that enabled him to say just the right thing in the right way at the right time. He has well described the way he "translated" Solanus's thoughts:

> Every day, I opened his mail, read it and informed him as to what people were writing about and he usually had a word or so to say to people and somehow I was able to get them out. I think it was sort of a miracle in itself, because I certainly was never experienced in that. The letters just came off. And, they were, I must admit, rather beautiful. I'm not an experienced typist but I used to sometimes get out one hundred or two hundred letters a day. And around the various holidays like Christmas, Thanksgiving, Feast of St. Francis, his name day, and other days like that, mail would just double or triple.
>
> If I asked him a direct question that someone wrote, he usually would tell me what to answer. Otherwise he usually would tell me what to write back, or he would tell me just a word or two to write. He would sometimes say, "Well, you tell Mrs. So-and-So that she doesn't have to worry about that. She doesn't have to see the doctor again, or, when she sees him again, he will discover there was nothing wrong. But she really doesn't have to because it may be a waste of money since she would have to pay a price to see him."
>
> Sometimes people would write back in reply to those kinds of prophecies. At one time, I kept a separate file of such replies. What happened to them after I left, I don't know. But I would say that during the time I worked for Father Solanus, there must have been five or six hundred such letters from people who were helped through his words of encouragement, through his prayers, and so on.

It made me very humble, too, because people would write back and thank him for the beautiful letters and words of encouragement. It was what they really needed to resolve the problems they wrote about. Even though I typed it, I looked upon it, certainly, as Father Solanus's words.

Usually we put his rubber stamp on the letters because at that time it would have taken him several minutes just to sign one letter. He was a very popular person in that sense, that so many people wrote to him for his prayers and his help.

Many of the letters Booker wrote were in some way connected to requests that enclosed money for the SMA. As promoter for the SMA over many years, Solanus had built up quite a clientele. After fifty years of supporting the Capuchin missions through the SMA, Solanus received a commendation for his "magnificent work for the Seraphic Mass Association," accompanied by other fine reflections about Solanus himself from the head of the Capuchin Order in Rome.

The working rule at Huntington was that, if people planned to come, they should come by car and not in busloads. The rule was made to save Solanus from the strain of seeing so many people at one time. One day, Benedict Joseph Groeschel recalled, two busloads of people — "close to one hundred" — arrived at St. Felix from Detroit:

> The guardian would not permit Father Solanus to go out and meet the people. Father Solanus spent the whole day in the chapel. He even omitted going to lunch. The people remained outside by the buses, and about every 5 minutes there would be a blast from the horn of these buses. About 4:45 p.m. the guardian finally relented and allowed Father Solanus to go out and meet the people, but he had only ten minutes to do so. I observed this: Father Solanus went out, the whole group from both buses poured out and fell to their knees. Father Solanus quickly went to each one of them, blessed them, and I noted that at five o'clock he was in his place in the chapel.

Solanus's Understanding of Suffering and Healing

Letters written by Solanus, from early in his time at Huntington, offer a unique insight into his own reflections on the way God's healing power was extending itself to others through his ministry. He wrote about suffering in a series of letters, all within a few months of each other. These give a clear expression of his own understanding of what was happening to others as a result of his ministry of healing.

Solanus's letters reveal his own approach to the problem of suffering. First of all, with almost all other human beings, he confessed: "I don't understand why children have to suffer." Even though he was not familiar with the contemporary theology of suffering that sees children's suffering as part of the human condition connected to original sin, Solanus viewed God from the revelation of Jesus who healed "sickness and disease of every kind" (see Matt. 4:24; 8:16–17; 9:35). He believed this Jesus wanted to extend the power of his compassionate healing to his followers (see Matt. 9:36; 28:18–20). He wrote that we are called to have our lives "blend" with God's. This blending enabled God to continue healing in us as God did in Jesus. "In his divine economy," he also wrote in this early period at Huntington, "God has honored His creatures — most especially rational ones — by giving them each according to his ability, a part of his own work to do — by participation in His own divine activity."

On one day, December 14, 1946, Solanus wrote letters to two different people. These are among his best on the subject of healing extant to date. In one he reflected on prayer for healings that were "successful." Such healings came, in part, he believed, because of people's generosity to God shown through their own activity, such as support for the missions. In the other letter he reflected on prayer for healings that were "not as bright." These had to be understood in light of God's "mercifully loving designs" which demanded not just resignation, but even thanks "beforehand" from God's people. For Solanus, both cases demanded faithful confidence and generous thanks.

In Solanus's mind, the healings took place because the people requesting them promised to do three things: (1) believe, (2) pray with faith, and (3) make a promise. The promise to do something would manifest the people's efforts to respond to the divine concern that all come to a deeper knowledge of God and God's ways. It did not matter whether the people needing the healing were Catholics, Protestants, or Jews. As God worked in the world of Jesus of Nazareth to heal "all" who were afflicted, so now in the world of Solanus of Prescott, God's same Spirit became manifest in the healing of all who were broken.

Solanus believed that God willed to heal; thus his approach to healing manifested a faith or a stance toward God that assumed there would be such healing. But what about those times when prayers for healing, good works toward those in need (such as contributions to the soup kitchen in Detroit, or enrollments in the SMA), or reading to know more about God and God's plan for the world (as indicated in *The Mystical City of God*) did not bring about the desired healings? How would these disappointments be reflected upon?

Once, in a letter, Solanus tried to explain to another person in Detroit why not all prayers are answered in the way people might hope. Manifesting the same confident faith in God and for the persons to whom he was writing, Solanus noted:

> I was pleased to receive your kind favor of the 9th even though it was not as bright, as of course, we all would like to see it. However, God knows best, and, while we'll still hope for a favorable surprise, we can hardly do better than not only being resigned to whatever God permits, but even beforehand to thank Him for His mercifully loving designs.

Sometimes when Solanus might not put one's suffering in the perspective of God's overall designs, he would be jolted by the person's confidence in this perspective and his own faith would be reinforced. Ambrose DeGroot recalled how Solanus told a story about the time he was talking to a group of people sitting in a car in front of St. Bonaventure's in Detroit. One of the occupants of the car was a woman who had been crippled and unable to walk for thirty years. Solanus wanted to sympathize with her and said, "My, but thirty years is an awful long time to be suffering this way." To this she quickly replied, "Yes, Father, but eternity is worth it."

The more he reflected on this story and the more he recalled that Solanus would say at various times, "Religious are people who have the leisure time to suffer," the more Ambrose came to believe that such reflections on suffering by Solanus revealed a very significant theology:

> He saw it [suffering] as having redemptive value in the life of the Mystical Body — that certain people are chosen by God to suffer as an apostolate. It recalls St. Paul's statement: "I rejoice now in the sufferings I bear for your sake; and what is lacking of the sufferings of Christ I fill up in my flesh for his body which is the church" (Col. 1:24). It's the church's doctrine of vicarious or redemptive suffering. I really think he understood this well and was the reason why he made such statements; and it was the reason why he never obtained cures for his own brethren.

Above all, Solanus believed, whether one received a desired healing or not, one should always give thanks to that God who, as creator of heaven and earth, can do all things. Giving thanks ahead of time — for healing or for continued suffering — should characterize true believers. Giving thanks beforehand reflects a deep trust in God's power always at work in us. "This is the way we can foster confidence in God," he wrote to the Detroiter explaining why not all prayers are answered in the way people might hope:

> This confidence is the very soul of prayer, and consequently heightens our hopes for supernatural intervention. Not only this, but in fostering this confidence we greatly eliminate the danger of sadness, want of resignation and impatience. While these are not necessarily sinful in themselves, nevertheless, they sadly frustrate God's merciful designs. Hence the little verse: "God condescends to use our powers if we don't spoil His plans by ours."

From Huntington Solanus wrote also to a couple whose little girl had eye trouble. In the letter he shared quite clearly his reflections on the "giving thanks before and after" attitude we are to take when approaching God for healing. First of all, he wrote, "Shake off the excessive worry and instead exercise a little confidence in God's merciful providence by first promising something — even a little sacrifice of some kind in thanksgiving if things go favorable." However, thanks, too, must be given, not just after the favorable result, but before: "To show your confidence in His goodness, start and thank Him whenever you think of it. Give Him thanks for whatever He may see best to do for the little one and for her loving friend."

The unique element in Solanus's approach to God's healing revolved around confident thanks shown in good deeds. These constituted the heart of the "proposition" which he suggested people make when they asked for healing. In a letter of February 8, 1947, Solanus recalled the "proposition" approach. A Methodist woman had come asking for help for her husband, who had a brain tumor removed but then developed an infection which demanded another operation. Yet a third operation was required and the woman told Solanus that the doctors offered very little hope for his recovery.

> "Now Mrs. Wheeler," I pleaded, "do not take it so hard. We will pray for your husband and enroll him in the Association and try to in-

duce our dear Lord to take over the case Himself." So I recorded his name, etc.

Then I said, "Now Mrs. Wheeler, I have a little proposition for you to make yourself to the good God in your own honest way."

"I'll do anything to please the good God," she interposed, "if He will only spare my poor husband!"

"Well this is the proposition or promise I want you to make, if you choose this rather than something else, whereby to please God. It is more a suggestion, therefore, that you promise or earnestly resolve in your own mind to look into the claims of that Mother Church divinely planned and proclaimed infallible, and the claims of any other denomination or system of religion. Or I might say that you look into the connection between them."

Mr. Wheeler came home the next day, the day before yesterday. He came here with his wife and neighbor today. A patch of about three inches square was taped around his right temple. While I was noting the surprise (in the healing), he remarked to the party who had given him his place (in line): "It is great to feel normal again, although I feel a little weak. The doctors in Ann Arbor, Peet and Wood, call it miraculous...that a patient should talk intelligently inside of twenty-four hours after such an operation."

"Thanks be to God!"

I had not heard from them for over a year and a half, when Mrs. Wheeler came to lament that her husband was not very well of late. I asked her if she had kept her promise as I had suggested and if she had read the book I lent her, *The Mystical City of God*. She humbly admitted that she had not. She had come without him, as she said, because she wanted to tell me about him first.

I told her without hesitation, "The whole trouble is in your failure to keep your promise, or your proposition, whatever it was."

She promised to return next night with her husband and in the meantime to do something to show her good will. It was a very stormy evening, the next night, so she phoned her inability to come as promised but that they would come the following evening. Following is the note that I made under the original:

October 18, 1944: Thank God they are both here today. [Even] He has started to read the wonderful life of the Blessed Virgin, *The Mystical City of God*, and is quite enthused about it.

Among other things in praise of the wonderful work, *The Mystical City of God*...he remarked: "I find so much in it that I have often wondered about."

Solanus's Activities beyond St. Felix

Although Solanus tended to stay at the Friary of St. Felix and on its grounds, he did have occasion to leave it for various reasons. Near the friary was the motherhouse of the Missionary Sisters of Our Lady of Victory ("The Victory Noll Sisters"). In the early 1950s, he was invited regularly to speak to the sisters on some devotional topic. The sisters would come to the large hall to listen to his reflections, the postulants seated in the front.

Invariably Solanus would talk on the love of God and, at some point, would become so involved in what he was saying that he would become very emotional, his eyes filling up. At this he would pull from his Capuchin habit the large bright blue and white handkerchief that he carried. Automatically the postulants would burst into giggles until they realized the possible consequences of being perceived as laughing at such profound ideas or at such a holy person. However the pattern of talk-pause-tears-hanky-giggles repeated itself over and over without Solanus ever being aware of what was happening.[41]

When Solanus would journey beyond St. Felix, he would always ask that the rosary be prayed. Often, Booker Ashe recalled, it would be more than one rosary, maybe three or four. When Solanus would be late for meals, the friars would tell him jokingly: "For your penance for being late, we will not say the rosary next time we drive in the car." If they followed through on their "penance" and did not say it, Solanus accepted the jest and prayed the rosary by himself as they traveled.

Each year Solanus went some place beyond St. Felix to make his annual retreat. He also joined a Third Order pilgrimage from Huntington to Carey, Ohio. There he visited the shrine of the Blessed Virgin which was conducted by the Conventual Franciscans. The house chronicle noted periodic visits to Detroit for various occasions. Sometimes when he knew in advance that he would be going there, he would call Evelyn Cefai at St. Paul's Maltese Parish in Detroit. Because he loved her spaghetti and her Maltese cheese cakes, he would, "as simple as a child," ask if he might have some of her spaghetti. Outside of this, Ms. Cefai recalled, he never indicated his desire for anything special.

Another place Solanus visited at various times was Milwaukee. Since

Solanus's schooling there the Capuchins had expanded their ministries beyond St. Francis Parish to St. Elizabeth's Parish and St. Benedict the Moor, a mission established for African Americans by the province's Stephen Eckert. Solanus had been stationed with Stephen at his first assignment in Yonkers. After that Stephen had followed his desire to work among the "colored race" and had been instrumental in the creation and development of St. Benedict the Moor Mission with its school and hospital and other social services open to those who otherwise probably would not be able to succeed in the white system.

In late April 1949, Solanus and three other friars drove to Milwaukee for the unveiling of a statue of Stephen Eckert which had been created to mark the twenty-fifth anniversary of his death. As they drove through Chicago, Solanus suggested they stop to see his friends, Mr. and Mrs. Joseph O'Donnell. The O'Donnells were wealthy benefactors who lived in a high-rise building along Chicago's Lake Shore Drive. They had told Solanus, it seemed, that he would always be welcome at anytime into their home or for a meal. One of the three Capuchins with Solanus was Ambrose DeGroot, who recalled:

> I personally felt embarrassed, calling on these people unannounced, and expecting an invitation to supper. I was rather amazed to see these people brighten up when they saw Father Solanus. They felt sincerely honored and just could not do enough for us. They called a caterer and had a beautiful dinner sent to the apartment. It was borrowed glory as far as I and the rest of us were concerned. It was Father Solanus all the way — the wealthy couple just hung on his words.

As far as Solanus was concerned, the O'Donnells were as good as their word; this just evidenced that he and his fellow friars would always be welcome in their home. As to "the fuss made over him," Ambrose concluded: "Father Solanus took it all in stride and just did not notice."

Ham was served at the celebration for the statue's unveiling in Milwaukee. However, the ham was spoiled and a large number of people became ill with food poisoning. Solanus's reaction was more severe; he had to be rushed to St. Michael's Hospital, in serious condition. He stayed there two days.

In June 1953, Solanus was again in Milwaukee. This time he was there to testify in the cause for the beatification of Stephen Eckert. Solanus did so most willingly, for he firmly believed in the holiness of his confrere.

In some reflections entitled "Rev. Father Stephen, as I Remember Him," Solanus recalled him as being "the popular Father" at Yonkers, and "from the first he seemed to me to be a really earnest, zealous priest; always, not only willing but solicitous to help whom and where he might, without exception, high or low, rich or poor, learned or ignorant, Catholic or 'atheist.'"

One of the times that Solanus traveled to Milwaukee, he called his niece and her husband, Mildred and Dean Conley, in Chicago asking to stay overnight. That night Mr. Conley was able to observe Solanus at prayer in a way few if any other people were privileged to do. His narration of what happened has been told by Leona Garrity, the first biographer of Solanus:

> About 10:30 or 11:00 o'clock, Mr. Conley retired, as was his usual habit. He assumed that Father Solanus did the same. However, about 2:30 a.m., Mr. Conley awoke and saw a light was still burning in the living room. Thinking he had left the light burning, he got up. As he quietly came into the room, he saw Father Solanus on his knees. He was kneeling before a small table with a prayer book braced against the lamp. His arms were outstretched above his head. In seeing him thus engaged in prayer, Mr. Conley quietly withdrew so as not to disturb him. Father Solanus gave no indication of having noticed him. At about fifteen minutes to 6:00 in the morning, Mr. Conley arose. Coming out of his room, he saw the living room light still burning, and he found Father Solanus in the same position, praying with his arms outstretched. He still had his suit on and there was no evidence that he had gone to bed or slept at all that night. As Mr. Conley came into the room, Father Solanus noticed him and said casually, "Oh, are you up?" And Mr. Conley said: "Father, we have about an hour to get down to the station." Father Solanus said to him, "I will be finished in a few minutes."

When people like Dean Conley witnessed such holy experiences in relation to Solanus, they naturally told about what happened. Consequently stories about Solanus circulated, and far more people than those in Yonkers at the turn of the century heard of "the holy priest" who now was at St. Felix in Huntington. For instance, when Booker Ashe visited his mother in Chicago after becoming secretary to Solanus, he told her of his new appointment. "Oh, I have heard of him," she immediately responded; "he is that holy priest."

Solanus's Jubilees and the Affection of the People and Benefactors

On the occasions when Solanus celebrated various anniversaries of his vows and of his ordination, the extent of his reputation and the esteem with which he was held by relatives and friends, benefactors and Capuchins, was apparent.

A year after he arrived at St. Felix, Solanus celebrated the golden jubilee of his religious vows. However, it was decided that the ceremony for the people should be held at St. Bonaventure's in Detroit. At this time the people of Detroit had not been told where Solanus was living. Consequently, when the *Detroit News* ran a story about his jubilee in its January 25, 1947, edition, thousands came to celebrate with him the next day.

Solanus had been asked to write a message on the back of a holy card which could be given the people as a memento of the occasion. Realizing that people would be looking for a message which summarized the story of his life's commitment, Solanus wrote and rewrote his thoughts until they finally expressed what his life might be about:

PAX ET BONUM

IN MEMORY OF MY

GOLDEN JUBILEE IN RELIGION

St. Bonaventure's Monastery

Detroit, Michigan

Thanks be to God for uncountable

mercies — for every blessing!

Thanks be to my neighbor for his

charitable patience.

Fifty years in the Order — almost unnoticed — have slipped away from me into eternity. Thither I hope to follow before half another fifty — trusting in the merciful goodness of God!

Fr. Solanus, OFMCap.

DEO GRATIAS

If the superiors had any second thoughts about Solanus staying at Detroit, the large number of people converging upon him at the jubilee made them realize they had made a good decision to send him to Huntington. Staying at St. Felix would be best for his welfare. When he returned to Huntington a week later, Solanus brought many gifts: money, a chalice, vestments, and altar linens. Among his letters of thanks was one to Father Simon Hesse, spiritual director of the Third Order of St. Francis Fraternity at St. Bonaventure's. He and the fraternity had hosted the jubilee celebration. Besides reflecting the elaborate style of such letters at that time, this letter also indicated the fact that the ceremony was attended by people of many different faith expressions.

With so many people "hanging on his every word," or "eager to make a response" for favors granted them, or "asking what they could do to help Solanus," Solanus developed an idea that would tap into their desire to help him in his concerns. Because the postwar period had created a new communist approach to nonbelief, and since he could not fathom anyone not believing in God (since only fools could say in their hearts that there is no God), Solanus decided that, once and for all, he would try to spearhead an effort open to all "atheists" to prove that God *did not exist.* Such an undertaking was in keeping with his enterprising personality: when he saw an opportunity, his determination directed him to take the steps needed to meet his goals. Thus he proposed that atheists could try to prove that God did not exist. He would inaugurate an essay contest with a million dollars available to whoever could prove the nonexistence of God.

Solanus shared the dream about his "essay proposition," as he called it, with his fellow Capuchins and his benefactors. One of these was Mrs. Montgomery Ward Thorne, a member of the well-known retail-store family. "Without an effort," he wrote to his provincial, she "could donate the whole Prize ($1,000,000) and possibly will do as much." Others who indicated an interest in the "proposition" were the O'Donnells and the School Sisters of Notre Dame in Milwaukee. However, in spite of his zealous effort, the project failed to materialize.

Another celebration that brought out large crowds of Solanus's devoted followers was his fiftieth jubilee of ordination at the end of July 1954. Again, the *Detroit Times* featured a story about the coming celebration. It described Solanus in glowing terms:

> At 83 [he] stands amazingly erect, although his tall frame is gaunt in its brown homespun habit from many decades of fasting and self-denial.
>
> But his most striking characteristics are his eyes and his voice. The eyes...are the eyes of a man 50 years younger. At times they are shrewd and penetrating, but when he speaks of his faith they shine like the eyes of a child.
>
> His voice is low and warm and somehow it can make his simplest remark sound like a benediction.[42]

This time the celebration took place in Huntington. Because the large numbers of anticipated guests were not expected to fit into St. Felix's chapel, the liturgical ceremonies were held at St. Mary's in Huntington. The reception and dinner followed at Sts. Peter and Paul, a few blocks away. The dinner began at 12:00 and did not conclude until 3:00, "due mainly to the number and length of the after-dinner speeches," the house chronicle noted. "It was a terrible day and not too conducive to sitting in one place for a long time."[43] For his part, Solanus concluded the day with a talk which stressed his usual theme: the need to show gratitude and thanks to God.

The following day, Solanus and Brother Pius Cotter were talking. In that conversation Solanus let slip an underlying motive for his seeming bravado in making sure that people would "thank God ahead of time" for favors requested. When Pius asked Solanus why he always urged people to "thank God in advance for the grace you are requesting," Solanus said that in doing so we sort of put God on the spot so that he could not deny us the favor or grace that we need. If Jesus promised a response to those who would ask, people could always "put God on the spot" and assume God would be faithful.

Some months after the jubilee celebration, under the leadership of Mr. and Mrs. Daniel Ryan of Detroit a "purse" was raised and presented to Solanus totaling $6,000. As Solanus read the list of hundreds of donors — who had given donations from twenty-five cents to a hundred dollars, tears of thanks glistened in his eyes. Nothing like this, he managed to say, had ever happened to him before. Repeating his oft-used phrase in thanking God and the people who had been so generous, he said, "The first sign of intelligence is gratitude to God." The money was used to redecorate the chapel at St. Felix.

Because of his presence at St. Felix the friary was able to procure needed items at reduced cost, or even free, simply through people's affection for Solanus. Father Francis Heidenreich, who was the superior in the last years of Solanus's stay at Huntington, recalled how the community received a car through the good graces of an automobile dealer in Detroit by the name of Jerry McCarthy, and how other benefactors gave laundry equipment to the friary:

One time we needed an automobile at Huntington and through Father Solanus we obtained this car from Mr. McCarthy. Father Gordon Garske drove Father Solanus and I to Detroit to pick up the automobile and I was amazed at the reverence with which Father Solanus was received by the people at the automobile dealer's office. Everyone there had just the utmost respect for this nondescript simple priest. He was never very concerned about the clothes that he wore and yet he was the one to whom they showed deference. Evidently, they were all deeply impressed by him. On another occasion, I needed laundry equipment for the house. I happened to mention it to Father Solanus and before long I had a new washer and dryer. Friends that he had who were financially well-off used their money to further spiritual or religious programs. It was this type of a relationship that he had with these people.

Another influential friend and devotee of Solanus was Frank J. Brady, the president of a company in suburban Detroit which bore his name. He became aware of Solanus by reputation in 1955 or 1956 when his wife was seriously ill and slated for an operation that was very close to the brain and had little possibility of success. At the suggestion of an acquaintance, he called Father Solanus and told him that his wife was in the hospital and would be having the operation which would necessitate being separated from their four children. Solanus listened for a minute or so and said, "Oh, no, she won't have the operation. She'll be all right. She'll be out in a few days. She'll be back with those children." Having finished the part of the conversation pertaining to the preoccupation of Brady, Solanus then followed with a question of his own — a very practical one from a former baseball player: "Now, tell me how the Tigers [baseball team] are doing." Mrs. Brady came home without having the operation, and gradually improved. "As far as I am concerned," her husband declared, "it was miraculous."

Solanus's Growing Physical Ailments

Toward the end of 1955 Solanus's age and infirmities had begun to take their toll even for a man who was one of the original joggers and whose other exercises included raking and gardening. For years Solanus was known to have had skin problems of some kind. Some doctors called his skin disease "weeping eczema"; others called it psoriasis. Its symptoms were especially apparent on his legs. His first Huntington secretary, Ambrose DeGroot, remembered that "he had a bad leg; it was turning black and covered with sores." With age his leg condition became more acute.

Although he had been hospitalized at other times, the chronicle at St. Felix noted that his trips to the doctor and his hospitalizations were becoming quite regular.

Toward the end of 1947 and the beginning of 1948 the chronicle noted that Solanus was so ill that he had to be confined to his room. On Christmas Day he wrote his sister and brother-in-law, Margaret and Frank LeDoux, that his "weeping eczema" had "thwarted" his effort to write them before. At the end of the letter, in a postscript dated January 18, he wrote: "Am still mostly on the mattress, though saying holy Mass every day. I lost four daily Masses including two on Christmas. I am hoping things brighten soon." The chronicle noted on January 24, 1948: "Father Solanus came to dinner today in the refectory — the first time in many days. He is feeling better but is still far from well."[44]

The first extended hospitalization came in the spring of 1949, after he returned from the unveiling of the Stephen Eckert statue in Milwaukee. On the return trip, some of the friars noticed Solanus rubbing his legs together as if they were itching. Once back at the friary, he walked very deliberately up the stairs to his room. His pace was very different from that of a man known to have taken the stairs at a run. Father Blase noticed that something was wrong with Solanus's legs and his feet. Blase recalled that, after a bit of persuasion, Solanus let him look at them. They were "as raw as a piece of meat":

> We literally had to bathe his socks off of his feet. He was then put in the hospital, in Fort Wayne, Indiana.... There was fear for awhile that they might have to amputate his legs because of this illness. I later talked to him about that, and it didn't disturb him. It didn't upset his equanimity. I supposed he felt that if they had had to amputate his legs then that was the will of God.

Solanus stayed at St. Joseph's Hospital, in his words, "two long weeks — 16 days." Because the doctors feared they would have to amputate, nurses were told to monitor his circulation every three minutes. Meanwhile the friars decided that word of his hospitalization was not to be communicated to the public. However, the next day, when he went to Solanus's room, Blase discovered that the friars best intentions had been for naught:

> To my utter surprise, despite a big "DO NOT DISTURB" sign on the door, I found fifteen people in the room.... Some had come from as far away as Detroit. How they found him, I'll never know. But here he

was, propped up in bed, with a white canopy over his legs, amiably chatting with his visitors. And sure enough, every three minutes, a disapproving nurse came in to check the pulse in his legs.

In just over a year, in June 1950, Solanus was hospitalized again in Fort Wayne. His legs had become covered with the sores and were giving him great pain. Two weeks later the legs were healed enough for him to return home. Throughout 1951 he spent much time in Fort Wayne getting relief. In 1952 he was in Grace Hospital in Detroit where he made a great impression on those who tried to help him. The fact that he did not want anyone to make his bed, but would make it himself, contributed to making him so popular that, when he left the hospital, "doctors, nurses, patients and visitors all formed two lines from his room to the entrance door all seeking his blessing." In 1953 he referred to himself as a "poor, clodding, stupid brother—just at the present a stumbling, three-fourths invalid." In May 1954, blisters broke out all over his body when a doctor gave him the wrong medicine to combat infection.

By early January 1956, the pain was becoming so great that it was quite difficult to hide it. Since no further relief could be found in Huntington or Fort Wayne, it was decided that he should be driven to Detroit by the brother-infirmarian, Brother Gabriel Badalamenti. They left on January 12 amid wishes that things would go well with the doctors and that, as had happened in the past, Solanus would return quickly to Huntington.

This time, events would not let their wishes be fulfilled.

Chapter 8

The Return to Detroit (1956–57)

Solanus regularly referred to the period 1956–1957 as unsettled, yet favorably blessed, times. Although there were various manifestations of threatening forebodings, much of the unsettlement arose from the increasing arms race between East and West and the rapid rise of materialism in both blocs, under different guises. However, balancing these manifestations of "worldly-inclined humanity," Solanus had a sense that this period was also particularly blessed. Part of this blessing involved an increasing number of people entering seminaries and religious congregations.

In the United States, seminaries and religious orders were overflowing with new recruits. The St. Joseph Province had 119 candidates for the priesthood, quite possibly the largest number of any Capuchin province in the world. The college at St. Felix was "bursting at the seams"; a new college would have to be built, and plans had to be made for anticipated expansion at St. Anthony's theologate at Marathon, Wisconsin. On March 17, 1957, the novitiate at St. Bonaventure's in Detroit was relocated in Baraga, Michigan; the same day, Solanus noted that the world received the "sad news of President Magsaysay's tragedy" in the Philippines; namely, his assassination.

With the division of the province in 1952, St. Bonaventure's again became the novitiate. Thus, by coming to this place, Solanus had returned to where his life in the Order had begun in 1896. The superiors wanted to ensure that here Solanus would have peace and quiet. Father Bernard Burke, the guardian, informed all the Capuchins at St. Bonaventure's that they were not to make known Solanus's presence in the city.

Tests taken when he returned indicated that Solanus had some skin cancers on his legs. After a successful operation, the doctors indicated that, in spite of his other skin ailments, Solanus was in relatively good condition for an eighty-year-old man. He stayed in the hospital for three weeks.

When Solanus returned to St. Bonaventure's, Father Bernard limited his acceptance of phone calls and visits to the monastery office. Furthermore, he was not to use the phone or go to the front office without special permission. Bernard's rationale for these restrictions on Solanus was to "save his strength," and, as far as he knew, Solanus complied with this decision. However, as the days of isolation moved into weeks and months, this restriction became most difficult for Solanus. Brother Ignatius Milne recalled:

> After several months of not being allowed to see people because of ailing health, he remarked to me, "Why don't they let me see the people?" He stated this very spontaneously and without a hint of bitterness but rather wonderment that the superiors considered his health more important than the needs of the people.

To make sure that Solanus would abide by Bernard's restrictions, Brother Gabriel Badalamenti, who had accompanied Solanus from Huntington, was put in charge of his health care. Gabriel not only faithfully executed the guardian's wishes; he imposed his own on Solanus as well. From Gabriel's perspective, keeping Solanus away from the people improved his health, despite Solanus's protests to the contrary. Gabriel explained:

> I was taking care of him at the time when he was ill, and I was preventing him from seeing people.... He told me I was being difficult, and here I was always harping on obedience and then telling him not to do the things he wanted to do. He was really a little bit upset with me because I was restricting his practices, but I took care of him and I got him better. When somebody else began to take care of him and let him go back to his activities, then his health began to fail again.

This account by Gabriel represents the only known time that Solanus became upset with one of his Capuchin brothers — to whom otherwise he referred as "dear brother Gabriel." It is not difficult to realize that his irritation was not really directed at Gabriel, but at the situation itself.

Father Lawrence Merten, Bernard's vicar at St. Bonaventure's, recalled that, when exceptions were made and Solanus was allowed to visit individuals, the people's stays were to be limited to thirty minutes. Naturally the people were inclined to overstay their allotted time and Solanus would be oblivious to the overtime they were enjoying. Consequently, Lawrence would go to the room and "conclude the visit." He remembered that it was "hard for Solanus to say goodbye, as his natural inclination would be to spend a longer time." Yet he "very readily acceded. There were never any arguments. His attitude toward authority was always marvelous."

With more time available, Solanus went increasingly to chapel. His devotion was a constant subject in the conversation of the novices. They liked trying to determine if his prayer and devotion would pass their scrutiny for authenticity. One of the novices in the first year of his return to Detroit was Capuchin Dan (then Nevin) Crosby. He recalled:

> He would be so completely absorbed in the Lord that the novices would frequently decide to test out the depth of his absorption. On their way to their place in chapel a novice would deliberately detour to walk directly in front of Father Solanus. Other novices would have previously been alerted to the test being conducted. Kneeling in their place they would watch to see if Solanus's eyes would open or at least flutter because of the distraction. To their amazement no change was ever registered. Solanus always passed the test.

Solanus liked to take some of his additional prayer time to participate in other Masses after he celebrated his own. Sometimes he would have the "privilege" of serving others' Masses (especially Father Rudolph's); other times he would go to the choir loft to observe the liturgy being celebrated at the main altar of St. Bonaventure's small chapel. One of the priests for whom he served was Father Michael Dalton, a priest of the London, Ontario, diocese, who was visiting St. Bonaventure's.

Father Dalton did not know who his Mass server was but was "quite impressed when I saw him kneel and kiss the floor when he passed in front of the tabernacle." After Mass Solanus took him to the refectory for breakfast. When he learned that Solanus was a priest, Father Dalton asked him to "hear my confession." Solanus simply responded, "I'm only a simplex-priest — no faculties to absolve." He went on to explain that, while he could not absolve sins, he found his work with troubled humanity at the office was quite similar to confession. Years later, in recalling this visit, Father Dalton called Solanus his "oldest altar boy."

Capuchin Dan Crosby recalled one Sunday morning in 1956 when he and his fellow novices gathered in the choir loft for the 9:00 High Mass. Solanus sat directly in front of him. In the sermon, the celebrant told a story about a farmer and his donkey, using the term "ass." This uncustomary word brought spontaneous laughter from the novices. Dan's laugh "was more of a loud snort." Solanus turned around and said to him: "The trouble with us is that we don't appreciate what he is trying to tell us. If we did appreciate it, we wouldn't think it was so funny." At this, Dan recalled, "I only laughed the louder, but I have come to appreciate his meaning of appreciation."

Dan also recalled the last Christmas Solanus celebrated in Detroit. On his way to community recreation on Christmas evening, Dan decided to stop in the friary chapel for a visit to the Blessed Sacrament. While kneeling there he heard "a familiar squeaky noise" coming from the larger church. Knowing it had to be Solanus, Dan decided to investigate further. He opened the door from the friary chapel to the main church to find Solanus alone in the choir-loft playing Christmas carols on his violin and singing them to the Christ Child.

While the novices, as well as almost every other Capuchin at St. Bonaventure's, found such manifestations of devotion from Solanus to be evidence of his holiness, they were criticized regularly by his tablemate Elmer Stoffel. At that time Elmer served as novice master. Because of this position, he always sat next to Solanus in seniority at the table. When he would see Solanus picking at his food or not eating very much, he would challenge him, "Are you trying to be a saint?" At other times, referring to the many people trying to visit him, he would say to Solanus, "You're trying to work miracles and taking the honor for them while the Seraphic Mass Association is doing the work." Lawrence Merten recalled:

> These accusatory remarks got a little strong at times, but Father Solanus just looked down and continued eating. He would never in any way be grieved or get mad. He took it. Sometimes he laughed, and other times you could see it hurt a little. Other friars kidded him a lot about many things, even mispronouncing a word. Some would say that he was bluffing the people, but they couldn't get him angry.
>
> I thought that Father Elmer might have meant seriously what he said. In order to clarify whether he was kidding or not, I made it a point to question Father Elmer in recent years. Father Elmer indicated to me that he did think Father Solanus was trying to "steal the show" when both were stationed at St. Bonaventure's. However, he is now convinced of the sanctity of Father Solanus and said that he retracts that.

Elmer Stoffel's "Testimony" before the Tribunal of judges convened to interrogate witnesses who knew Solanus regarding his life and virtue contains none of these allegations, thus reinforcing Lawrence Merten's reflections about Elmer's retraction.

Elmer did not limit his confrontations with Solanus to the reported healings that were taking place. He would not allow the novices to talk with Solanus because he believed some of Solanus's advice countered his own. This would give the novices a double message. He also challenged him on his promotion of *The Mystical City of God*, but after further discussion with Solanus, he, too, read the work. He also confronted him on the way he dealt with non-Catholics: "I used to accuse him of not showing sufficient justice toward nonbelievers. I thought he should be more strict with them. But he would just smile and say, 'Well, they can get to heaven, too.' "

If Solanus's nemesis was Elmer Stoffel, he was almost idolized by another friar at St. Bonaventure's. This was the provincial, Father Gerald Walker. As provincial, Gerald had been instrumental in transferring him from Huntington to Detroit, permanently reassigning him there (as of May 10, 1956). In Gerald's mind, Solanus's faith continually challenged his own, as happened one day in the last year of his life at St. Bonaventure's:

> Faced with what seemed to me would be a tragedy, I asked him to pray that God would spare me from it. He promised that he would. A week passed by. The situation seemed more threatening. I went to see him again to ask if he was praying, as he had promised. He assured me that he was. I went back to my room.
>
> Soon there was a knock on the door, and there was Father Solanus, the tears pouring down his cheeks. Evidently hurting very much, he said, "Gerald, I am so disappointed in you."
>
> Pained to hear that from him, I asked, "Why?"
>
> He said, "Because I thought you had more faith than that!" Then, referring to Jesus' words in the Gospel, he said, "Remember that Jesus said, if you ask you shall receive."
>
> It was a lesson in faith I needed.
>
> By the way, I then received what I asked for.

The first passage from the Gospels that Solanus had written in his notebook in 1897, during his novitiate, had become so embedded in his belief-system that he could not fathom his provincial superior being weak in faith. Did not Jesus mean what he said? It was precisely this faith that enabled Solanus, throughout his life as well as in his last year, to be the conduit for the requests the people continually brought to him.

Solanus's faith enabled him to share with others prophetic insights as to their future. Father Rupert Dorn recalled that in the spring of 1957 he and a group of novices were in a group which included Solanus. Some in the group said to him, "Pray for us, Father." Immediately he turned around and pointed directly at Rupert and said, "Better you should pray for him." This statement frightened Rupert at the time because he did not know what it meant. However, when he was elected provincial ten years later he realized that "this was probably what he meant," because Rupert would be the provincial in the most difficult period faced by the modern province, the years 1967–1973.

Infrequent Communication with the People

At first, very few people knew Solanus was in Detroit. Those who did know were asked to keep the information confidential. Consequently not many people came to see him at St. Bonaventure's. One of those who did was a friend of Rupert Dorn, William (Bill) Sinatra. He was a high school student who suffered from a severe case of arthritis. The effects of the disease already were beginning to show in his hands and fingers. Rupert took the teenager in to see Father Solanus. Solanus prayed over Bill and blessed him. Rupert noted that "nothing spectacular" happened at the time, but later when he met the young man he asked him about his health. He responded very simply, "I was cured." Sinatra later became a priest of the Archdiocese of Detroit.

To those people he was able to see, Solanus continued his effort to have them be more dedicated to their faith. Father Giles Soyka recalled being asked to hear confessions of people who had talked to Solanus and been challenged by him to reorder their lives or to deepen their relationship to God through the sacraments. Sometimes, however, Solanus used the opportunity of visits as an occasion to reminisce about his childhood and his family. In the case of Earl and Adeline Striewski and their son Tommy, the visit spanned two hours. Solanus spoke of his brothers and sisters as "bright," adding: "But I was not very bright; all the others were more brilliant than I." Mentioning the difficulties he had in school, he said, "But God was good to me." During this expanded conversation in which he talked also about the people who had come to him with their trials and troubles and how they had been helped, he said several times, "Oh, God is so good." Meanwhile tears of thanks and joy rolled down his cheeks.

Another way Solanus kept in touch with people was through the intermediary of the other friars. People discovered they could ask these friars to take their problems to Solanus on their behalf. On one particular Friday, Brother Ignatius was asked by a family with a hydrocephalic child to petition Solanus for prayers because the doctor had told the parents that their boy wouldn't live beyond twelve years of age. Ignatius relayed their concern to Solanus. He told Ignatius to tell the family they should all go to Mass and Communion the following Sunday in honor of the poor souls in purgatory. On Monday the family called Ignatius back with some good news. They had taken their boy to a specialist who wondered why they were bringing him because there was nothing wrong.

When not talking with the people personally or on the phone, or through intermediary friars like Ignatius, Solanus continued to write notes thanking people for their enrollments of themselves, their families, and their friends in the Seraphic Mass Association. Frequently his notes included some of his reflections, often on faith and the need to be concerned about the poor. To Mrs. Betty Kopplin of Milwaukee he wrote: "Where there is real faith and *confidence* in God there is no such thing as a hopeless case." To a "Mr. Hoffa," Solanus repeated his definition of religion: "The science of heaven come down to earth: the science of our happy dependence on God and one another; the science whereby Almighty God makes men like to Himself, viz. — men cooperating with the grace of God." Another undesignated note reflected: "Real busy men are not, as a rule, too religious. The Lord who died for us, however, will always find something good if the busiest at least now and then have a heart for His poor."

When the people were able to visit Solanus personally or write him or call him on the phone, he increasingly encouraged them in their faith and in deepening their relationship with God. A phone call from Milwaukee told Gerald Walker that a child was ill with meningitis, and asked him to pray for the child:

> I said I would, but I also referred her to Father Solanus. She did call him, and later called me back thinking that Father Solanus was out of his mind. I asked her why, and she said that Father Solanus had told her that she and her husband should go to Mass the following morning in thanksgiving because in ten days her child would no longer have meningitis. This child today is now a woman 30 years of age.

Although Solanus was able to see very close friends, who kept his presence a secret, he communicated with others by mail. With the Korean War just ended and with the continual news about atheistic communism and the nuclear threat, Solanus was keenly aware of the need for global peace.

While in Detroit he had come upon a "Prayer for Peace" which "filled up" his heart when he read it. Consequently he shared it with others.

For almost a year, until December 2, 1956, Solanus's presence in Detroit had been kept relatively quiet. The silence was broken when the *Detroit Sunday News* ran an article on the Capuchins' centennial of establishment in the United States. While noting the various ministries of the Capuchins, the St. Bonaventure's chronicle recorded that "Father Solanus was spread all over the front cover of the Rotogravure section."[45] Furthermore, while the article purportedly was about all the Capuchins, the only Capuchin to be featured was Solanus. When he was asked how a Capuchin felt about the Franciscan life of prayer, study, and work, the article stated, "Father Solanus Casey, who is 86 and in his 60th year in the Order, said, 'It's like starting heaven here on earth.' "[46]

Immediately, the monastery was deluged. People not only came to the front office. Friars answering the phone, the chronicle noted, suffered "a headache from answering the avalanche of telephone calls from the people who wanted to know whether Father Solanus was available for consultation and blessings."[47] The answer was a kind but firm refusal, in the interest of preserving Solanus's health. The people were disappointed, but could understand.

On the morning of January 14, 1957, Solanus celebrated the sixtieth anniversary of his investiture in the habit of St. Francis. During the liturgy, as was the custom, he renewed his vows. As he did so, he began to choke up. The realization of all the good that God had done for, in, and through him was too much to bear. By the time he came to the part where he would rededicate his life to "live in obedience, without property, and in chastity," the thought of God's gracious love overwhelmed him. He could not continue. Father Giles finished the renewal for him. Although the ceremony was very private, in Solanus's eyes, "it could [not] have been more beautiful, under the simple circumstances." In a letter written to his brother Edward on March 14, Solanus described the events that, sixty years before, had brought him to St. Bonaventure's:

> I had come to the holy novitiate Christmas eve. It was six months ahead of the seven other students who joined me the following July. They are all gone to Heaven now, we hope, with the senior of them all, Father Damasus, in his 90th year. Had he waited five months longer, he and I would have had our golden jubilee together. He was patient and joyful to the last. May he be privileged to await

in the peace of the saints, the inconceivable glory of the general resurrection.

Please pardon the digression. Today, Deo Gratias, it is sixty years and sixty days since I was invested.

The Agony and Death of Solanus Casey

Not long after writing this letter Solanus had to be hospitalized. In early May, skin eruptions appeared again on his body. As the condition worsened, the doctors diagnosed the lesions as severe erysipelas. When the condition became even more serious, on May 15, it was decided an ambulance should take him to St. John's Hospital. Once there his condition again worsened; it appeared he was close to death. He was anointed, and an oxygen tent was placed over him to help him breathe.

With the oxygen, he seemed to rally. Out of danger, one of the first things he did was to begin singing a hymn of thanks to the Blessed Virgin. Almost immediately Brother Gabriel told him to stop; he needed to conserve his strength. Without any argument he obeyed. As his strength improved he was able to joke and banter with the staff and visitors. In response to a nursing sister who said, "Father, throughout the years I have so often heard people speak of you," he responded: "Yes, people often speak of Jessie James, too." When she said more seriously, "But these people, Father, spoke of wonderful things that occurred through your prayers for them," he conceded that she was right. However, he added, "Many wonderful things have happened — but the people had faith." Another time she came into his room and said, "How about a blessing, Father," to which he replied, "All right; I'll take one!"[48]

As he improved, he liked to be taken in his wheelchair to the hospital chapel. On one occasion as he entered the chapel, he dipped his fingers into the holy water font and, before blessing himself, flipped the water to all about him saying, "Glory be to the Father and to the Son and to the Holy Spirit." In the chapel, various people would read to him from *The Mystical City of God* or pray the rosary with him. When he was strong enough he would celebrate the liturgy. If he went to the chapel, the word would get out that he was there, or on his way there. People would come into the corridors asking for his blessing, or they would ask for it after Mass. With everyone he would be gentle and generous, even though he did not like the personal attention he was receiving.

Because of his continued improvement, Solanus was able to leave
St. John's Hospital and return to St. Bonaventure's, but not for long. He
returned June 14 for more treatment. Again he improved enough to return to the monastery. However, on July 2 he was forced to go back to the
hospital. He remained there until his death.

This time, only the closest friends, Capuchins, priests, and relatives were
allowed to visit him in room 307. He was checked in under the name of
Father Casey instead of Father Solanus to keep people from discovering
his room. Nevertheless some found devious means to get to him with their
problems. Brother Daniel Brady recalled that one very determined woman
was adamant about getting to see Solanus:

> She had always wanted to have children and had never been able to
> have them. She snuck up the back stairs to the floor that Father Sola-
> nus was on. Fortunately the nun was not present, and she was able
> to get to the room that Father Solanus was in. They were just about
> to ask her to leave when she cried out to Father Solanus, "I've always
> wanted your blessing. I want to have a child, please help me." He
> told her simply, "Go home, you will have a boy and a girl." I am told
> that the following year she had a boy, and then she had her second
> child — a girl.

Solanus's skin became so sensitive that the hospital attendants could not
put a sheet on him. Despite his terrible pain, he neither complained nor
asked for anything to alleviate the pain. It was apparent to everyone, including Solanus, that his days were numbered. He received the Sacrament
of Anointing from the hospital chaplain, Father Hoey. One of the sisters assigned to nurse him, Sister M. Margretta Hughes, recounted various
encounters with him as his last days approached:

> A sister companion and I often read to him — always from *The Mys-
> tical City of God*. Always, too, he would precede the reading by asking
> us to recite with him a prayer to the Holy Spirit. As we read, he
> would close his eyes, and seem to doze. But let the word be misread,
> and he would open his eyes, and we'd note a twinkle in his eyes as
> he corrected us. Or some passage would strike him, and he would
> exclaim — "Glory to God."
>
> He told us that he had "prayed" the four volumes of *The Mystical
> City of God* through three times, kneeling.

His sickness brought excruciating suffering. He developed a skin reaction that enveloped his entire body. This alone caused Solanus intense pain. Tubes, needles, examinations — these added to his discomfort.

Yet there was never a complaint from him, and he was lucid at intervals even on the morning of his death.

In his presence it was impossible not to feel his Christ-likeness, his genuine simplicity and humility, his great love for mankind, his selflessness. Even in his pain, he wanted to continue working to bring more people closer to God. "I can't die," we overheard him say, "until everyone loves Him."

Yet he realized that death was not far off.

As Sister Arthur Ann entered his room one evening, he asked — "What time is it, Sister?"

The sister, who had learned that he relished a little bantering, replied, "Now, Father, why should you care? You're not going any place."

"Oh, yes I am. I am going to heaven."

"Well, if you're such a little prophet, when are you going to heaven?"

"I'll tell you when — when it is God's will. I don't want to go until I have learned to appreciate heaven."

He frequently spoke of God's mercy with such childlike tenderness that tears came into his eyes. "God is so good," he would say, and then repeat slowly and quietly, "Glory be to God, Glory be to God."

The sisters realized that he was suffering intense pain, and sought to alleviate it. "Where do you hurt, Father?" one compassionately asked.

"Oh, I hurt all over — thanks be to God," he responded.

Because of poor nutrition and continuous intravenous feedings, his hands had become red and raw. "Your poor hands," said Sister Arthur Ann, as she prepared to remove a needle. "I hate having to remove the adhesive tape."

"Well, Sister, don't feel badly about it," he comforted her, "Look at our Lord's hands."

Sister Carmella, one of those who read to him, noted that one would go in and out of the room, and he wouldn't know it. His mind was elsewhere. He seemed to be thinking continuously of the love of

God. "The love of God," he would say, "is everything." As he said this, his face would shine with an inner light.[49]

Around July 26, Solanus's brother, Monsignor Edward Casey, arrived in Detroit just as Solanus's condition worsened. In reaction to a drug that had been given him, Solanus's skin condition erupted all over his body. Edward found him not wanting to eat or drink. His only request was that Edward would read from *The Mystical City of God*. As his health deteriorated, the friars notified the Casey family. On July 29 Martha Casey flew to Detroit to be with him in his last days. Her nursing skills and knowledge of health-care administration proved helpful in keeping people from seeing Solanus. She testified:

> When I went to his room, he knew me and said, "Martha, Martha, such a long trip just to see me, and on the Feast of St. Martha too." I could see that he wasn't long for this world, in fact, just a matter of hours. He suffered and was in great pain and discomfort but never a word uttered of complaint. His body was covered with a burning rash, his legs were black to the knees. He was past caring for food, a little broth or a sip of water. When I asked if there was anything I could do, it was always the same, "No Martha, just pray for my conversion." "Say the rosary with me." So we said it over and over again. Then he would ask me to read to him from the *Mystical City of God*. Father thanked me for coming, asked about my family and all the relatives in Seattle. He seemed to know just about the time he would die.

On July 30, Elvera Clair was in the room with Monsignor Edward and Martha. Solanus said, "Tomorrow it will be all over. I want to go to heaven, but with all Christendom." That night he repeated this desire to be one with humanity and, with all humanity, to be one with God. When Gerald Walker was visiting him that last evening of his life, he was writhing in pain. Gerald leaned over and asked where it hurt. He said, "My whole body hurts." At the same time his face was "literally radiant," and he said, "Thanks be to God. I'm offering my suffering that we might all be one. If only I could live to see the conversion of the world."

When Brother Ignatius Milne went into the room to visit him, Solanus was scratching himself. "Gee, Father, you must be hurting quite a bit," he said. Without hesitation, Solanus responded: "Would to God it were a thousand times worse."[50] His pain, united to the pain of Christ Crucified, was meant to bring conversion to the world.

Being especially mindful of his brother, Monsignor Edward celebrated an early Mass on the morning of Wednesday, July 31. Then he went to Solanus's room about 8:00. The last days had found Solanus drifting in and out of consciousness, but he now seemed his old self, better than at any time Edward had observed in the last few days. Even though Edward tried to keep his brother from talking, Solanus seemed totally preoccupied with the need for the world's conversion and his desire to do all he could to bring the world to unity in God's love. Relieved that Solanus seemed so much better and so alert, Edward returned to his room in the hospital to write the relatives that things were looking better.

Shortly before eleven o'clock a nurse came to bathe Solanus. She took the rosary and a relic of the True Cross, which he often carried with him, from his hand and slipped the hospital gown from around his frail body. As she gently bathed him she heard Solanus whispering, but his voice was too weak for her to understand his words. Suddenly he opened his eyes and stretched out his arms as though greeting an old friend. He said very clearly: "I give my soul to Jesus Christ." With that declaration of his dedication, he died.

He who once had told his Jesuit nephew that he was eager to go to heaven but was not "in a hurry to go" now went to meet his God.

Martha, too, had been out of the room when Solanus died. After joining in the prayers for the dead, she gathered together his personal belongings and took them with her to St. Bonaventure's. His habit was old and patched in many places. The superior explained that whenever they would issue a new habit to Solanus, "he would soon give it to some younger priest."

One of Solanus's closest lay associates was Clare Ryan. Two days previously she had called the monastery to ask about Solanus. She asked the name of the person who answered the phone; he replied: "Father Francis." When she inquired whether he was a priest or a brother, he said that he was a priest. She then asked him if he was from Huntington or Wisconsin. He replied, "Well, you could say that" and then went on to tell her that Father Solanus wanted to see her. She testified:

> I told him I didn't think that anyone but the priests or brothers from the monastery were allowed to go to the hospital. He said it would be all right. I could go in. The next day I had planned to go to the

hospital immediately after dinner, but my husband was delayed in
getting [home] from work and so we were not able to go. After dinner, I called the monastery again and I spoke to this Father Francis.
I said that I would go the next day and if necessary I would take a
taxicab to the Hospital. He said that there would be no need for me
to go because Father Solanus would be "going home at three minutes
to eleven." I said, "Well then, I will be able to see him at the monastery." The priest said, "Yes, you will be able to see him but you won't
be able to talk to him."

Father Solanus died the next day. It wasn't until almost three years
later that I was at the monastery in conjunction with the establishing
of the Father Solanus Guild and I spoke with Father Gerald who was
the superior at the time. I asked him if there was a Father Francis still
there. He told me that they had never had a Father Francis stationed
at St. Bonaventure's Monastery. I do not know how to explain this
incident, but I believe that somehow it was Father Solanus telling me
almost the exact time of his death.

The "exact time of his death" had come fifty-three years, to the very
hour, after the celebration of his First Solemn Mass with his family,
brothers, and friends, in Appleton, Wisconsin. Now his own sacrifice of
thanksgiving was complete. He had given his body and soul for the life of
the world and its unity.

The People Respond to the Death of Solanus Casey: An Outpouring of Grateful Love

Immediately upon the news of his death the friary was inundated with
phone calls. At the request of the Detroit Police Department, which was
concerned about preserving order among the large numbers of people expected, it was decided that the crowds would be better handled if the wake
for Solanus were at a regular mortuary rather than in the friary chapel
where Capuchins' wakes usually were held. The Van Lerberghe Funeral
Home, not far from the monastery, was the mortuary chosen as a matter
of course.

On various occasions, during the time of his first ministry in Detroit,
Solanus would stop to see the Van Lerberghes "more or less just to say
hello" when their original funeral home was just two blocks from St. Bona-

venture's. Around 1937, Arthur Van Lerberghe needed money to build a new funeral home but could not obtain financing anywhere. He went to Solanus and asked if he would pray for his intention, and he said he would. "The following morning," Arthur testified, "I received a call from a man who was willing to cosign the note for the loan of $100,000, which he did, and I did build my funeral home." In thanksgiving, Van Lerberghe had begun the practice of burying the Capuchins gratis. Now he would prepare for burial the body of his friend and benefactor.

When the body was brought to the mortuary Arthur found it "very well preserved." He testified:

> I found only on the back of his hand and the palm a little bit of sca-
> liness. Their location reminded me of the stigmata. I did not notice
> any sores on his legs or any other part of his body. When it came to
> the embalming of the body, the embalmers finished doing their work
> in less than an hour when ordinarily it would take about an hour's
> time. When I asked them why they were finished so soon, they said
> they did not need very much fluid to preserve the body, which was
> unusual in itself. There was little need for any cosmetics to adorn
> the body.

Capuchins of the Province of St. Joseph are buried in a cloth-covered casket made of wood. However Van Lerberghe insisted that, at his own expense, he would provide an inexpensive metal casket. The superiors relented; they also reluctantly acquiesced when he ordered a cement vault to hold the casket in the cemetery.

The funeral home placed the pertinent information in the newspapers, which notified the people that visitation hours would be from 1:00 p.m. until 10:00 p.m., Thursday. However, as early as 5:00 a.m. people were ringing the doorbell; a line extending for a full block was already waiting to pay their respects to the man they had come to revere and love. Among the first was Mrs. Marguerite Baker. She returned later in the day and discovered "thousands of people outside of the funeral home waiting to get in. There were all types of people present both at the wake and at the funeral — lay people, religious, priests."

One of the thousands who came was Bernadette Nowak. After the birth of her first child, Mrs. Nowak had lost three babies by miscarriage and had been desperate to have a second child. Because her blood was RH negative, the doctors questioned whether she could have a live baby. When she began to suspect she might be pregnant in December 1956, seven months before

Solanus's death, she immediately wrote a letter to the Capuchin who had helped her at another time fifteen years before:

> I addressed it to the monastery with a note attached saying that if Father was too ill, not to bother him with my problems. In the letter I asked him to pray that I could have a living, normal baby. I also explained my previous medical history. Shortly after, I received a reply saying Father Solanus had been very happy to have the letter and would indeed pray for such a good intention. He urged me to name my child *now* after two of God's saints and enroll the intention in the Seraphic Mass Association along with enrolling the Poor Souls. I did so. I also promised God to call my child, if a boy, Anthony Joseph. I cannot remember the girl's name I chose, but I think it was Mary Anne. My pregnancy progressed uneventfully and the baby grew.
>
> Father Solanus died a month before the baby was due. I went to the Van Lerberghe Funeral Home to view his body. The baby had lain so quietly within me the past few days, and when I approached the casket, the baby seemed to leap inside. I could see my dress moving and I was embarrassed. I felt sad because I wanted to tell the good news to Father Solanus and now I could not do so....
>
> During the labor I, indeed, felt a comforting presence although I was in the "preparation room" all alone the entire time except for an occasional visit by a doctor or nurse. It was a swift, easy, uncomplicated delivery. Joseph was born with the cord around his neck, twice, and it had a knot in it. Despite all these things, the baby was fine and I never felt better. I was up and around and at home in three days.

The line at the funeral home continued all day long until 2:00 a.m., when Father Rupert Dorn and a brother had to stand at the door and tell the crowds that the funeral home had to close. They assured the people that they could pay their respects the next day at the monastery.

Once Solanus's body was brought to St. Bonaventure's, large crowds continued to come, morning, afternoon, and evening — an estimated twenty thousand people "of all walks of life": "ordinary people, rich people, women, children, priests; every class of people. There was nothing done directly or indirectly by any member of the Community to encourage such a gathering. This was an entirely spontaneous outpouring of love and respect by the people who came to see him." Even the City Council recognized the man who was more loved than any other in Detroit; it memorialized him with a testimonial resolution. It read in part:

Whereas, the City of Detroit with profound sorrow expresses regret in the passing of Rev. Father Francis Solanus Casey, advisor to thousands of troubled persons;...who won his many followers mainly as a spiritual guide;...Therefore, be it resolved that the members of the Common Council of the City of Detroit take this opportunity to express their deep regret in the passing of so loved a person.[51]

Detroit newspapers carried many articles in praise of Father Solanus and his good work that touched so many people. One headline read: "Fr. Solanus, Advisor to Thousands, Dies." Another declared: "Famed Priest Helped Feed Souls and Stomachs in the Depression." The *Michigan Catholic*, the archdiocesan paper, said in part:

Sixty years a Capuchin friar, fifty-three years a priest, a potent, persuasive counselor and comforter to thousands beset by physical, mental and spiritual tribulations, Father Solanus Casey, died Wednesday morning in St. John's Hospital here....Father Solanus was active for twenty-one years at St. Bonaventure's Monastery. In that time he became widely known as the friend and helper of persons in need, whether spiritual, mental or material. He gave sound advice and spiritual consolation to some. He helped the sick and procured aid or work for others. His desk in the monastery office was surrounded all day, week in, week out, by persons in need or in trouble. None went away unaided.[52]

Whether at the funeral home or at the friary chapel, people approached the various Capuchins to tell their stories about Solanus. Gerald Walker recalled how people would say things like:

"Meet my son. Fifteen years ago he was dying of polio; Father Solanus blessed him, and today he is in the best of health." Someone else would introduce an elderly lady, saying: "Father, meet my mother. She was dying of cancer and Father blessed her, and she is here tonight." Others would tell us that they themselves were here because he (allegedly) had cured them of some serious illness when they were doomed to die....One lady began to cry and pointed to him saying, "He was the best friend I had in the world. Some years ago I was in utter despair and just wanted to die. I spoke to him and began to live again."[53]

That night the chapel was closed to visitors at 10:30. On Saturday, after the regular 8:00 a.m. Mass, Father Bernard Burke asked the crowds to leave the chapel that it might be prepared for the funeral liturgy. He was amazed that they left without anger or frustration.

The Funeral Liturgy and Burial

When the chapel was reopened, all available places were filled immediately. Loudspeakers were set in place outside to share the service with the people who now lined the sidewalks on both sides of Mt. Elliott Avenue. The busy street had been closed to accommodate the crowds. The people were kept in order by a squad of police who had been sent to make sure no disruptions would take place from eager enthusiasts. To their surprise the thousands who had assembled remained unbelievably composed. "I was present for the funeral," Capuchin Bernard Burke recalled. "The calm and the order that pervaded the crowd, to my mind, was a miracle itself. Even the police officers were surprised at the calmness of such a large crowd."

Monsignor Edward Casey celebrated the funeral liturgy. Auxiliary Bishop Henry E. Donnelly of Detroit, Solanus's friend, presided and paid a final tribute on behalf of the clergy and the people of the Archdiocese of Detroit. Father Gerald Walker, the devotee of Solanus as a young man who had become his provincial, eulogized him. In his remarks, Gerald spoke not so much as the provincial superior of Solanus, but as the spiritual son of a man he considered the holiest Capuchin in the history of the province: "Father Solanus was a man I loved dearly," he began. As he continued, he often had to stop, choking back his tears. But the tears did not stop — a response to his close friend's passing from this life as well as to the realization that so many had been brought closer to God because of his faith. In concluding, Gerald declared: "His was a life of service and love for people like me and you. When he was not himself sick, he nevertheless suffered with and for you that were sick. (When) he was not physically hungry, he hungered with people like you. He had a Divine love for people. He loved people for what he could do for them — and for God, through them."[54]

After the liturgy, Solanus's Capuchin brothers brought his body to the small friary cemetery south of St. Bonaventure's. There he was laid to rest with the other brothers for whom he had so often prayed. Not long after his burial a grave marker was placed over his grave. It was the same style as that placed at the burial sites of all the Capuchins in St. Bonaventure's cemetery. It stated:

Rev.
Francis Solanus Casey
O.F.M.Cap.
Born Nov. 25, 1870
Ordained July 24, 1904
Died July 31, 1957
Age 86 Religious 60
R.I.P.

While the stone of the grave may have been the same as those of all the other friars, something quite different immediately began to take place at his grave site: from the day of his burial, a regular pilgrimage of people began to come through the gate of the cemetery to visit the burial place of the man they considered a saint.

Original tombstone placed on
Fr. Solanus's grave in the
Friars Cemetery in Detroit,
before his body was moved to a
crypt in the church in 1987.

Fr. Solanus at St. Felix Friary in Huntington, Indiana. Taken about 1948.

Fr. Ed   Leo   Fr. Solnnus   Jim   ELLEN   Pat   Owen   Gus
Traynor

Maurice

John T   Margaret   Ellen   Genevieve   Bernard   Grace   Tom   August 14, 1892

The Casey Family in Superior, Wisconsin,
on August 14, 1892. Bernard Casey Jr.
is third from the left on the porch.

Close-up of Bernard Casey Jr.
at age 22. At this time
Bernard Jr. was studying during
the school year at St. Francis
Seminary in Milwaukee.

Bernard Casey Jr. was a conductor on one of the first electric street cars in Stillwater, Minnesota, around 1889. (Courtesy of Minnesota Historical Society)

After his novitiate in Detroit, Solanus joined this class of Capuchin Clerics to continue his studies for the priesthood at the Capuchin Seminary at St. Francis Monastery in Milwaukee. Solanus is in the middle of the second row.

Solanus at the farm of Mr. and Mrs. Ed Bishop near Detroit in 1935.

Solanus at the Porter's Desk, St. Felix Friary, Huntington, Indiana, in 1952. Behind him is a picture of Capuchin missionaries with a map of the world. Solanus encouraged people to support the foreign missions prayerfully and financially.

St. Bonaventure Monastery in Detroit, Michigan. Here Solanus made his novitiate in 1897-98. Later he served here as porter from 1924 to 1945. He returned in 1956 and remained here until his death in 1957.

Close-up of Solanus in 1912 at age 42 while at Sacred Heart in Yonkers.

Capuchin Community at Sacred Heart Friary, Yonkers, New York, in 1912.
Solanus is in the center, back row. The young men were prospective candidates for the Capuchins.

Though not a virtuoso, Solanus loved to play the violin,
usually Irish tunes or his favorite hymns.

Three Casey priest-brothers in 1912 at Edward's ordination:
l. to r., Maurice, Edward, Solanus.

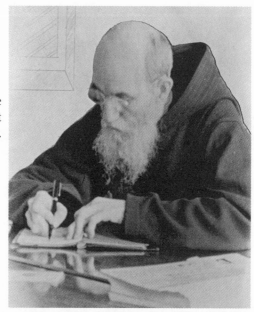

At his desk in the Monastery Office at Detroit, 1939.

Solanus at the Soup Kitchen distributing bread with Fr. Mathias Nack and a lay volunteer, c. 1942.

In January 1947, Solanus returned to Detroit from Huntington to celebrate his Golden Religious Jubilee. Standing are his sister, Grace Brady, and brother, Owen Casey. Seated are Fr. Damas, Capuchin from Canada, Fr. Solanus, and his brother Msgr. Edward Casey.

Fr. Simon Hesse, Third Order Director in Detroit, presents Solanus with a chalice, the gift of the Third Order Fraternity (Secular Franciscans) in honor of his Golden Religious Jubilee.

Portrait taken
on a visit to
Superior,
Wisconsin,
around 1937.

Portrait taken
at Detroit in 1956.

Portrait taken in the
Monastery Garden at
Detroit, 1956.

Solanus at St. Felix Friary,
Huntington, in 1954.
(Courtesy of Detroit News)

Solanus blessing one of the novices, Albert Sandor, in 1956.
(Courtesy of Detroit News)

Praying at the Blessed Virgin Shrine. St. Bonaventure Monastery
Garden, 1956. (Courtesy of Detroit News)

Solanus's friends at his funeral on August 3, 1957, processing
into the Friars Cemetery for the burial.

Part Two

THE PRACTICE OF THE VIRTUES BY SOLANUS CASEY

Chapter 9

The Theological Virtues

In Solanus Casey's eyes the "triune virtues" of faith, hope, and charity were "essentially one" because they revealed the "trace of the Holy Trinity in our immortal souls." Since the three were united, they stood together in positive contrast to society's atheism, despair, and hate. Through God's indwelling presence, those baptized into the Trinity were to grow in faith, hope, and charity with God and each other. As someone who knew him from his Yonkers days (1904–18) noted: "Everything was one's hope, one's faith, one's love for God." Aware that living these virtues demanded continual conversion, Solanus once wrote, "Breathe a little [prayer] for the conversion of this poor sinner Solanus who makes so little progress in faith, hope, and charity." Love, faith, and trust were the three points that he preached to the people at all times, someone once said of Solanus Casey. But not only did he preach these theological virtues; in his own life there was the greatest consistency in his extraordinary practice of faith, hope, and charity.

Solanus, the son of Irish Catholic immigrants, was schooled in the theological virtues from his childhood. His "greatest consistency," according to one priest, an author of books on spirituality, was "in his extraordinary practice of faith, hope, [and] charity," which "flowed from his entire personality." Not only did Solanus manifest the theological virtues throughout his life; he regularly promoted their practice to others. To a woman experiencing anxiety and a sense of failure, he once wrote encouragingly: "Why do we have discouragement as long as we have a spark of faith left? What a different view we get by exercising and by fostering the triune virtue — FAITH, HOPE, CHARITY!"

For Solanus, "religion" meant being rational; it constituted the "great science of faith, hope, and charity" as well as the "science of our happy dependence on God and our neighbor." This religion contrasted sharply with humanity's apathy and atheism. As early as 1917, in response to indifference in society, Solanus recommended the cultivation of the virtues.

157

Especially with the rise of communism after the Second World War, Solanus came to believe that "this generation" was "fearfully apostatizing from faith in God, which of course means from hope in the divine and from supernatural charity." Solanus believed that the faith "of perhaps the great majority of men these days" had become weakened as well as "hope and charity, its necessary accompaniments." In consequence, he concluded, "religion, the great science of faith, hope, and charity," is refused recognition.

While faith and hope "were pretty much dependent on" love, faith was "theoretically first — as is the Eternal Father in the Holy Trinity." Consequently, as this section of the book considers the virtues, we begin with faith, for without faith, hope and charity wane.

Faith

According to a Capuchin who was a fellow student with Solanus and who knew him well, Solanus's whole life was one that was grounded on faith in God. A staff member of the Archdiocese of Detroit noted, "Father Solanus nourished the faith of a whole generation."

Solanus Casey's uniquely personal form of faith cannot be separated from the fact that through his parents, Bernard James Casey and Ellen Elizabeth Murphy Casey, he belonged to the families of two ardent Catholics, who were very confirmed in their faith. Solanus considered his father's father as a martyr for the faith.

Barney Jr.'s (Solanus's) "faithful parents" emigrated from Ireland, known throughout the world for its own unique Catholic faith in God. He was one of sixteen children who would "follow their [parents'] footsteps in keeping the faith." He had an uncle who was a priest, a cousin who became cardinal archbishop of New York (Cardinal John Farley), and two brothers who became priests, one of them eventually becoming a monsignor.

Without a doubt, the Casey's family faith nourished his vocation. Once Bernard Jr. entered the Capuchins and became "Solanus" Casey, he joined another community of faith. In his writings as a Capuchin, Solanus considered faith to be "divine," "God-given," a "gift," in fact, the "greatest gift on earth." "Have faith in him who loves us so much," Solanus once urged some friends. A lay person who knew him well testified:

Father Solanus was a man of supernatural faith. He showed it by his words and his deeds. He always spoke about faith. He would say that we always had to have faith. We had to believe that God could do all things, and if he could develop and cultivate faith in persons like myself and others, he certainly first had to be a man of faith himself.

For Solanus, the only adequate response to the gift of faith was gratitude. "Thanks be to God for the True Faith," he often noted. "Oh, the Faith," he would say, almost in rapture. Capuchin Ambrose DeGroot recalls that Solanus "was a man of living faith, and he lived in an aura of the supernatural. As an example of his living faith, if any noteworthy event or calamity occurred Solanus would ask, 'I wonder what reason God would have for allowing this to happen?'"

Sometimes Solanus reflected thankfully on the "wealth" of one person's faith or another's "wonderful faith." "How little it is possible for mortals this side of heaven to appreciate our holy Faith or to be fully grateful for its blessings, its outstanding excellence," he wrote. Another time he wrote: "If we could only learn to appreciate the holy faith and the innumerable blessings flowing from it and the blessings otherwise surrounding us; we could never have time to worry about anything, except that we're so little appreciative."

For Solanus, faith had a twofold expression: it reflected his approach to life and relationships with God and others, and it meant his Catholic religion, or the "True Faith."

Faith as a Personal Relationship with God and Neighbor

Solanus expressed his notion of grace and a human's share in the divine life as a "blending" of God's life and ours. "We are continually immersed in God's merciful graces like the air that permeates us," he wrote. Living in God's presence demanded that people of faith manifest God's presence and action in the world. He wrote: "In His divine economy...God has been pleased to honor His creatures — most especially His rational [ones] — by giving them, each according to his ability, a part of His own work to do. Rather I ought to say, by participation and cooperation in His own divine activity."

Since all life and creation is thus graced, the only response people of faith can make is to respond to God's gracious initiative. One woman recalled him saying, "God wants to be close to all of us if we will only turn to Him." Often he reminded people that "God condescends to use our powers if we don't spoil His plans by ours." To a woman who thanked Solanus for a favor received, he said, "Don't thank me. Thank God. Just have faith in him; if you have enough faith you can move mountains." Gerald Walker, Solanus's provincial at the time of his death, notes that "the only time he ever criticized me was for what he considered my lack of faith."

Like all relationships, faith had to be expressed. Faith with God and in God's redemption had to be practiced in face of all events, including poverty and struggles. Such faith had to be nourished by prayer. One witness testified that the only rationale for "such deep convictions about his faith" was that, for Solanus, "prayer was the foundation for them." Thus Solanus urged others always to pray for more faith. On Good Friday, 1955, Solanus penned a quick note to a friend on the back of a postcard:

> Would that you and I, dear Tom,
> Had a spark or two more of holy Faith!
> Do we appreciate the little faith we have?
> Do we ever beg God for more?

This personal and relational dimension of faith, Casimera Scott noted, made Solanus "a man of great faith" whose own faith helped hers. She testified:

> I don't know how I can put it into words, but you just had the feeling when you were with him that he believed very strongly in God and he passed on that same feeling to you. He always spoke of God when you were with him, and when he would bless you he would say, "May God be good to you and God will be with you." He made you feel the presence of God in your life. He is the only one in my life who made me feel that way. And by that, I mean that I felt that God was with Father Solanus and he was transmitting that same presence of God to me.

Another witness testified, "When I was with Father Solanus, I felt that God was around us."

For Solanus, faith represented our response to the word of God (Luke 8:11), which invites us to bring forth works of faith. Such faith enables us to approach problems in the world. Like charity, faith "prompts us to rejoice with those who rejoice" and "requires us also to weep with those who weep." In face of "the unbelieving world," which interprets difficulties in terms of "failure," Solanus asked, "Why [should we have] discouragement as long as we have a spark of faith left?"

In one of his early sermons (1917), Solanus referred to the "cockle of indifferentism and lukewarmness in God's service of those who profess to be Catholics and are but withered branches." Reflecting on the unbelieving world and its problems in the middle of the twentieth century, Solanus felt a compelling desire to "rescue" people whose faith was weak. "Alas for our want of faith these days," he wrote in 1949, "and consequently, for our lack of appreciation between physical and spiritual values and between the momentary and the eternal. Well, therefore, do the words of Jeremiah the prophet apply to any people or power or individual that has little or no [faith]: 'With desolation is all the world made desolate, because...none thinketh in his heart.'"

Those who would consider in their heart would come to faith, for as he said, "to know is to appreciate." But not all people had such appreciation. Solanus noted two kinds of atheists: the theoretical kind and those who manifested "practical atheism." The latter professed faith but did not practice it, because society and its values undermined their faith in God. In both cases the self supplanted God. "Have you ever heard my definition of an atheist?" Solanus once asked a young man: "An atheist is a person who knows there is a God but denies it because he wants to live life his own way. He continually tells himself 'there is no God,' and finally convinces himself there isn't. He eventually gets to the point in his life where he has completely convinced himself there is no God. This is a form of insanity."

Especially with the rise of communism and its atheistic philosophy after the Second World War, Solanus's reflections and communications are replete with concern about atheism and people's lack of faith. "The direct and immediate object of atheism in the designs of Satan,"[55] he wrote, "is to weaken belief in the supernatural and to rob souls of their life-giving faith in Almighty God." Given his own faith, he could not fathom anyone proclaiming to be an atheist. Atheism was "blasphemous," "a diabolical cancer," "the climax of stupidity," the "climax of insanity," "the climax of intellectual and spiritual insanity," the "omega of intellectual and moral depravity." "The poison of modern atheism," he said, "doped consciences."

Solanus believed that atheism brought humans "to the level of the brute beast"; this made any atheist "wanting in intelligence."[56] To a policeman who declared himself an atheist, Solanus wrote in 1946:

I have often thought of you, Walter McClellan, since that night when you took the pledge and, thank God, you kept it. Many a time, however, I have wondered if "big W. Mack" ever tried to realize in any way what he has been missing in refusing to believe in RELIGION and in God, and in failing to foster faith in Jesus Christ. I am sure Walter would be a quite different, altogether happier man if he only had the faith. Ah! that faith which down the centuries has been the consolation and the stay of uncounted millions. Of course, the very fact that I respect you as I do ought to be proof sufficient that I am confident you cannot be a real atheist, except possibly such a one as have been heard to thank God for their atheism! For as a matter of fact, Walter, in my opinion there can hardly be anything worse for the individual or for society than atheism.

In Solanus's view people's individual atheism was inseparable from societal attitudes of atheism, especially materialism and a kind of "worldly inclined humanity." It also could be found in the mentality that lay behind the discovery and possible use of nuclear weapons. In 1948 he wrote apocalyptically: "And just these days of atomic invention, it would seem that God might be permitting men without faith to be preparing the fearfully poisoned lightning fires with which He will arm His angels of wrath on an adulterous, defiant, atheistic generation."[57] In 1956 Solanus noted an "avalanche" of atheism, and connected it with its condemnation by Popes Pius XI and Pius XII.

For Solanus, atheism was not limited to the Soviet Union; it could be found equally in the materialism of his own country as well as countries like England, Germany, and France. The result was "weakened" faith (as well as hope and charity). He considered the postwar period "unsettled," "threatening," and "foreboding." Yet, though the times might be difficult, his faith gave him hope: through the mercy of God, the times were "greatly privileged." "For men of faith," they were the "most promising of days." He believed atheism would surely bring "believers together."

As noted earlier around the middle of the century Solanus began discussing the creation of a "million dollar" proposition to confront the spread of atheism. He proposed that one million dollars be collected from individuals "Christian and Jewish, possibly pagans, too — who would be happy to donate the whole million at once." The money would be awarded to anyone able to write a convincing fifteen-hundred-word essay on why God does *not* exist. If a person could prove that God does not exist, he or she should be rewarded; otherwise, such a person is proved foolish, for only the fool says in his heart that there is no God (Ps 13:1).[58] Capuchin Pius Cotter testified to an event that took place in the office that showed how he dealt with people who proclaimed themselves "atheist":

> This man looked at Father Solanus and said, "Father Solanus, I am an atheist." And Solanus immediately retorted, "You are a damned fool." I want to tell you, the man was taken aback. I was taken aback. Everybody who was sitting in the office was taken aback. But the man then sat down and had a long discussion with Father Solanus, and when he left the office his attitude was certainly a great deal different than it was when he came in.

The only remedy for the disease of atheism, Solanus believed, was religion. And the foundation of religion and piety rested in the individual's personal relationship with God. Solanus related to God as a Father,[59] Jesus Christ as his personal friend and brother, and their Spirit as the guiding principle of his life. A close friend noted that Solanus conveyed the message that "God wants to be close to all of us if we will only turn to him," and that "when he talked of God the Father, the Holy Spirit, and of Jesus, and of the Blessed Mother and St. Joseph, it seemed as if he were talking of his family." Indeed, his oft-repeated definition of religion as the science of "our happy relationship with and dependence upon God and neighbor"[60] seems to summarize his personalized approach to faith.

Solanus's personal, friendly relationship of trusting commitment to the Lord was nourished by his life of prayer. His one-time secretary, Capuchin Blase Gitzen, noted: "I would like to say that in his prayer life he exhibited a personal relationship between himself and God. It was a relationship characterized by great warmth and a feeling of closeness." Another priest noted how he "would stress that in our prayers we should be on friendly terms with God." For Solanus, confidence in God constituted the very "soul of prayer."

This confidence in God was already manifest when Solanus was fifteen or sixteen years old when the family's wheat crop failed. He said: "We will all pray that the other crops will flourish and that we have a good year without the wheat." The other crops yielded heavily; along with money Bernard earned at temporary work, the family had a financial surplus that year.

Once in the Order, Solanus was faithful to regular observance but went far beyond the very extensive prayer-forms that constituted the liturgical and devotional forms of prayer then practiced in the Order. One of the first entries in his novitiate notebook highlighted "meditation on the passion of Jesus Christ," "mental prayer — meditation and contemplation," and intercessory "prayer" as "Means for Acquiring the Love of God." Throughout his life he always kept his breviary close at hand. Many have noted that he often was found for extended periods on his knees or prone on the floor in chapel or even in the homes of relatives.

This pattern of spending late hours or the early morning hours in prayer seems to have begun very early in his Capuchin life. Later in life, when he lived with the novices, they "tested" him (without success) to try to see if he could be distracted. At the end of his life it seemed enough for him just to sit in his room or chapel and contemplatively gaze at God. As one witness testified:

> He prayed all the time. Prayer, I would think, was his practice of piety. He prayed in the chapel before the Blessed Sacrament, so he had a devotion to the Blessed Sacrament. He also had a great devotion to the Blessed Mother. I recall one time my wife and I were visiting him in Huntington. We were sitting around the table, and suddenly he said, "Let us go say a prayer." On the way to the chapel, which was just across the hall, he said, "Wouldn't it be awful to have the enemy, the communists, take over our country?" We went into the chapel and said a prayer. As we left, he said, "Now everything will be all right." I had a feeling that he must have had a vision at the time because his invitation to go say a prayer was so sudden and out of context with what we were talking about.

Solanus's Profession of Faith in Catholicism

Another aspect of the personal and relational dimension of Solanus's faith involved his participation in the community of faith of Catholicism itself. At the same time, his openness to everyone of any color or creed was considered far in advance of his times. He may have learned his tolerance from his parents, whose home was always open to people of other faiths. "I know from childhood how to appreciate German Lutherans," Solanus wrote to some Catholic friends who were considering hiring a Lutheran to be their farm manager:

> The whole trouble with honest Protestants — and thank God there are a lot of such — is that they simply do not know the real rela-

tionship between their own denomination and the Mother Church. Otherwise equal, I would take a conscientious Lutheran ten times in preference to just a nominal Catholic.

Solanus's attention to people of other faiths was manifest from his first days at Yonkers, where he showed keen interest in dialogues with them.[61] He affirmed all sincere members of other "faiths," as long as they acted on the beliefs of their expressions of Judaism or Christianity. Rabbis and ministers of at least sixteen different Protestant congregations visited him for discussions and counsel.

Cardinal John Dearden of Detroit noted, "Father Solanus was practicing ecumenism long before Vatican II came up with that idea." Yet, in Solanus's mind there was only one Christianity and, thus, only one faith. Despite the various "systems," there was but one "religion." In this vein, he wrote to Raymond T. Taylor:

I think it is slightly an error for one who is Christian (as I presume you are) or who believes in Jesus our Redeemer, to intimate that he does not belong to the same faith as another who, though believing in Jesus Christ and professing Christianity, happens to differ with him in some details, possibly not even essential. Because I claim that there is really but one Christianity, as scientifically there can be but one religion, though there be a thousand different systems of that "greatest science of all times and of all generations: THE SCIENCE OF OUR HAPPY RELATIONSHIP WITH GOD AND OUR NEIGHBOR."

If people were satisfied in their own religion, he would simply encourage them to live up to their own religious convictions. While honoring the faith of those who were not Catholic, at the same time Solanus invited them to consider the "claims" of Catholicism; he believed his was the true faith and Catholicism was the true religion.

During his first assignment at Yonkers, Solanus copied a statement from the recently converted son of the archbishop of Canterbury: "The Catholic Church promises a great deal, but to my experience she gives ten times more, and if you put on the balance the most successful life outside the church, and the most unsuccessful and disastrous life within her fold [I would] a thousand times rather choose the latter."

When Catholics came to ask for help, Solanus would ask about their own practice of the faith: when they last went to the sacraments, how often they went to Mass, and whether they made their Easter duty. If they were lax, he would tell them they had to improve. Leona Garrity recalls:

> When people came to him he encouraged them to practice their faith. If they were practicing Catholics and perhaps received the sacraments once a month, he would encourage them to receive the sacraments weekly. If they received the sacraments weekly, he would encourage them to try to receive the sacraments during the week.

For those who were faithful to all these practices, he would always find a way for them to "do more" to deepen their faith. Faith, for Solanus, always invited deeper conversion. According to Capuchin Bernard Burke: "His eagerness for the propagation of the faith and conversion of sinners was one of the foremost topics in his mind and in his actions."

One of his confreres noted: "He had a great love and respect for the church. I know that anything that came from Rome or from the bishops, he would say, 'this is it,' sort of in the spirit of St. Augustine, 'Roma locuta est, causa finita est' (Rome has spoken; the matter is over)." This applied in a special way to statements of the popes, whose words he noted from his early days in formation. "He believed everything that the church taught," noted Brother Dan Brady. "He had no reservations about any of the doctrines. Any proclamation by the Holy Father was accepted by him without question, no matter how difficult it might seem. His attitude was, 'Peter has spoken,' and that was it."

While he was at Our Lady of Sorrows on Manhattan's Lower East Side, Solanus's notebook reveals a sermon based on the Petrine text of Matthew 16:16–19. He noted, "It is easy to know that Jesus has been and is still with His church. It is easy to know that His church has triumphed and triumphed over error of every shape and color and form [and] that She has stood the test of 1900 years." It was "easy to know" this about the church for someone like Solanus, for he found in the Catholic Church the fullness of God's presence and revelation, the life of the sacraments and sacramentals, and the structure (around the pope as vicar of Christ) and communion of saints that sustained his faith. At the same time, as happened with his involvement in the Irish cause, he found no problem challenging bishops if their political positions differed from his commitment to Irish liberation.

Because of faith, Solanus believed, people could profit from "the Holy Bible, the Holy Gospel, etc., because the church has declared them to be inspired writings." Brother Ignatius Milne remembers that "Solanus had a great love for the scriptures" and used them often in his talks and letters. "Something he said in regard to this was: 'If we call ourselves Christians then we have to believe in His word and practice it.'" Solanus's whole life, especially his life of prayer, was nourished by the scriptures. Capuchin Pius Cotter gives a specific example, "I know that he was fond of that particular passage from St. Mark about, 'Do not hinder the little children coming to me.'" Solanus transcribed other favorite scripture passages in his third notebook. He often advised people who wrote with requests "to read such and such a verse and see what God says about this."

Besides its grounding in the scriptures, Solanus treasured the Catholic Church for its sacraments and sacramentals. "When we were baptized, we became candidates for heaven," he once wrote, "and every time we receive the sacraments of Mother Church, we take another step forward. How wonderful and legion are our privileged opportunities." "He had a great reverence for all the sacraments," Father Blase Gitzen notes. "I felt it when he came to confession to me — that he was awed, as it were, by the presence of God and the fact that God was touching him through that sacrament."

For Solanus, the church's sacramental life for the baptized revolved around the Eucharist, "the soul of the church"; he linked people's faith with their Mass attendance. According to Doris Panyard, "He said time and time again, 'The answer to all problems is Mass and Holy Communion.'" It made no difference where he might be assigned, for "after all Christ is present there in the Blessed Sacrament." He wrote: "Frequent Communion brings peace into a family and into the soul. It also fosters faith in God and heavenly relationships with all God's dear ones in heaven." To nourish such faith Solanus encouraged daily Communion.

Solanus's devotion to the Eucharist was noted from his first days in the Order as well as his first assignment as sacristan. It continued throughout his life, as did his use of quotations from the encyclical on the Eucharist by Pope Leo XIII. In 1918 he recorded in one of his notebooks the Johannine foundation for the Eucharist.

In Yonkers word spread among the altar boys to avoid Solanus's Mass because it took too long. Later, Brother Ignatius Milne commented on Solanus's prayerful celebration of the Mass: "It almost seemed like he was praying the Mass, although he did not go into ecstasy or anything of that nature. He was really totally aware and attentive to what he was doing. He was a real source of edification to everybody. He was truly absorbed in the whole spirit of the Mass."

Possibly because, as a child, Solanus was not able to participate in the liturgy each Sunday, he found it very difficult to understand why people did not attend Mass regularly or, when they did, why they might not receive Holy Communion. It seemed so clear to him that families that communed together stayed together and had their prayers answered. According to William Tremblay, who drove Solanus to St. Joachim's Church in Detroit for the 10:30 Mass:

> When it came to Communion time, he turned around and held the Host waiting. But there was nobody that came to the holy table for Communion. There weren't many people in the church. Maybe one hundred people, but it used to happen that nobody went to Communion. He was so surprised and seemed to be hurt about it. He said to the people as he held up the Host, "Please come, the Lord wants to go to you, please." And everybody was so surprised that they all just looked at him. Then he turned around and put the Hosts back in the tabernacle. It was just another incident to show you his love for the Holy Eucharist and how he wanted the people to be helped. He knew that God could help them though Holy Communion. He was just surprised and hurt that nobody went to Communion, and he just had to tell them.[62]

On the other hand, when people did go to Communion, Solanus made note of it, as we find in his notes following the feasts of Corpus Christi, the Immaculate Conception and Christmas, or the Portiuncula.

Solanus's devotion to the Blessed Sacrament was widely known. Brother Ignatius Milne found it to be a concrete manifestation of his "heroic faith": "He had a tremendous reverence for the Blessed Sacrament.... It was the custom among the Capuchins to kneel down and kiss the floor, and this Father Solanus would do, but he would always pause momentarily in seeming rapt adoration." Even when he was in his eighties, he would kiss the floor — until his superiors told him not to, in order to preserve his health.

Whether in Yonkers or Brooklyn or Detroit, lay people and friars recalled times when Solanus stood near the tabernacle of the Blessed Sacrament playing his violin before the Lord. If he were carrying the Blessed Sacrament while he was being driven to visit hospital patients, he would not speak; upon his return "he would talk very freely." If anything could make Solanus angry, it was a friar's "sloppy genuflection" in reverencing the Blessed Sacrament, or when altar boys misbehaved during

Mass, or when laughing and frivolity took place during these and other prayer times.

So great was his desire to share in the Eucharist that he urged people who could not partake to make a "spiritual communion." James Maher recalled Solanus urging him to make a "spiritual communion" when he could not "go to Mass or receive Communion." Maher asked:

"Father, how do you make a spiritual communion?"

He said to me: "This is what I say, 'Lord please come to me in spiritual communion. Send your Body and Blood gushing through my veins; your love to my heart, my soul and my mind. Lift me up to your bosom, and infuse me with your Divine Love.'"

From the beginning of his ministry, Solanus made use of the sacramentals of the church, especially holy water. One time he advised a young man: "Use holy water frequently. It keeps the devil away." He believed in the power of a blessing, whether it came from a priest like himself, a brother like Brother André, a nun who nursed him, or in the simple greeting he invariably used in his letters: "God bless you and yours."

Solanus's deep commitment to the Sacred Heart went beyond the piety then manifest among the laity and Capuchins. Solanus lived in a province whose cofounder, Francis Haas, had helped to inspire the friars to a deep devotion to the Sacred Heart of Jesus.[63] In the first pages of the notebook that covers the period of his novitiate and simple vows, Solanus devoted a section to noting the twelve "Promises of Our Lord Jesus Christ Made to Blessed Margaret Mary in Behalf of Those Devoted to His Sacred Heart." Solanus's first assignment was to the parish in Yonkers dedicated to the Sacred Heart. There, one of his first tasks was to be chaplain to the League of the Sacred Heart, to whom he gave a spiritual talk at its monthly meetings.

First Fridays and their devotions to the Sacred Heart provided Solanus with the occasion to talk to others about the love of God manifest in the Heart of Jesus. In 1917 he drafted a short reflection to celebrate the Feast of the Most Sacred Heart:

"Behold the Heart that has loved men so much!" If, in regard to men, the saying is true that "familiarity begets contempt," it can never truly be said in regard to Almighty God. On the contrary, the more we learn to know of His divine Majesty, the more we are drawn to reverence Him, to love Him, to adore Him. The more thoroughly we understand any of His works, the more we must admire the wisdom of the Creator till, with St. Paul (Rom. XI), we exclaim in utter astonishment, "O the depth of the riches of the wisdom and of the knowledge of God! How incomprehensible are His judgments and how unsearchable His ways!"

At Huntington Solanus gave badges of the Sacred Heart to the people who came to visit him. Often he signed his letters "Sincerely yours in the Sacred Heart." He endured suffering for the "intentions of the Sacred Heart."

Accompanying his devotion to Christ's Sacred Heart was his devotion to the cross of Christ. Both devotions were nourished by the work of Josefa Menendez: *The Way of Divine Love: Or the Message of the Sacred Heart to the World.* The Way of the Cross, Solanus said, was "the best school wherein to learn appreciation for and love of Jesus Crucified, [the] divine lover of souls." When asked how he prayed, Solanus once answered: "I unite myself with Jesus being nailed to the Cross."

Father Benedict Joseph Groeschel — who believes Solanus made the stations of the cross daily — recalls an incident that took place when he brought a small crucifix to Solanus to be blessed. Solanus stopped writing a letter, took the cross in his hand, and then "very tenderly kissed it before he blessed it and then gave it back to me. I remember very distinctly that he paused for several seconds and looked at the crucifix with great reverence and love."

Solanus found in the passion of Christ a source of hope for people who were in pain. Elvera Clair found in Solanus's love of the cross a manifestation of his faith: "I remember, too, that he said: 'People despair by the loss of faith. They must be made aware of the great mercy of God. Just look at a Crucifix. Our dear Lord died for each one individually. Meditate on the depth of His love.'"

Solanus often spoke of venerating the True Cross and had great devotion to its relic. He often blessed people with this relic, which also served as the key sacramental at each Wednesday's service in the chapel. "When he blessed the people with the relic of the cross, he was extremely devout. You just felt the aura of holiness surrounding him. You knew that you were blessed and that he was truly praying for you."

Besides deep faith in God, Solanus showed a great devotion to the communion of saints, which centered in Mary. It also included those who had preceded him. Consequently he had a great devotion to the Poor Souls. Solanus told people, "If we, by our prayers and sacrifices, freed a soul from

Purgatory, we would then have another intercessor for us in heaven." The woman relating this continued, "I feel that this was like missionary work for him, to work for the souls in Purgatory." When a member of the family died or, for that matter, when any true believer died, Solanus's faith was nourished by the belief that the person would join the saints in heaven, a reward for a life of fidelity. He or she would rest in the peace of the saints. To his niece Helena, whose husband had died recently, Solanus wrote:

> Now you are not only an orphan but a widow also. What does that mean? For you and for anyone who have real faith and Christian hope it ought to mean: "Another string broken that tends to bind our hearts to earth." It ought to mean that you have now another faithful dear one as we confidently hope, a loving husband to pray for you beyond the grave together with your saintly Mother and Father and so many who have loved you and gone ahead. What a wonderful doctrine and [how] consoling to think of our dear ones awaiting with not only lighted candles but greeting us at our arrival with music and hymns of heavenly sweetness.
>
> I've been thinking often of the really touching family reunion last summer in Seattle. But what about the great reunion awaiting the arrival of the just in heaven!

Solanus's devotion to the Blessed Virgin throughout his life was nourished in his family from the beginning. It was especially sustained in Solanus's conviction that God's mother had saved him from drowning by pulling him from the water by the scapular he wore. At the center of the communion of saints, in Solanus's faith, stood Mary, whom Christ gave us orphans as mother under the cross. He attributed his vocation to the Capuchin Order to her, since he received his notice to "go to Detroit" on the feast of her Immaculate Conception.

One nun who knew him well noted that Solanus evidenced a sense of joy when talking about God, "but when he spoke of the Blessed Mother he seemed to become even more vibrant and alive. He would speak of her with the same familiarity that he would speak of his mother or his sister."

Solanus could not separate Mary from her Son: "When Jesus is in our hearts, Mary will be not far away." To love Mary is to love God's Son. "Next to Jesus Himself," Mary was the "most meek and humble of heart." Coming to know Mary would lead to deeper knowledge of God. For this reason Solanus urged many to study Mary's life and imitate her, especially in her practice of the Christian virtues.

Solanus's desire to study Mary's life and imitate her resulted in the promotion of Mother Mary of Agreda's "autobiography" of the Blessed Virgin contained in her *Mystical City of God*. While the rationale and expression of this have been discussed earlier, he believed it to be of "supernatural origin" and regularly noted that it had been approved by a host of popes and bishops. He recommended invoking the Holy Spirit before a daily reading from *The Mystical City*.

Solanus read *The Mystical City* no fewer than four times on his knees. One time, when Father Anthony Kerry came to his room at St. Bonaventure's in 1957, Solanus "seemingly was in meditation and almost in a state of ecstasy." According to Father Kerry, he was reading from the Revelations of Mother Agreda. When he saw me, he was glad to see me and said, 'Now, listen to this.' He read me a passage from the Revelations. He said, 'Oh, Father, this is truly inspiring.'"

His devotion to this book lasted until the end. In the days before his death he loved to have people read from one of the four volumes as he lay in his hospital bed.

Because of her union with God, Mary stood as powerful intercessor. Although he prayed the Litany of Loretto each evening with the other friars, Solanus's writings contain a virtual litany of titles that he used to exalt Mary: God's Living Tabernacle, God's Own Mother, Virgin Mother of God, God's Own Immaculate Virgin Mother Mary, Blessed Virgin Mother of Wisdom, Blessed Mother of Redeemed Humanity, Mother of Redemption, God's Most Outstanding Masterpiece, Supreme Masterpiece of All Masterpieces of the Universe, God's Mother Suffering, Most Merciful of Tenderest Mothers, Mother of Fair Love and of Fear and of Knowledge and of Holy Hope, Jesus' Sorrowful Mother, Our Dear Blessed Mother, Mother and Mistress of the Apostles, Mother of Missionaries, Our Mother, Our Confidence, Queen of the Most Holy Trinity, Singularly Chosen and Privileged Blessed Queen, Eternally Chosen Queen of the Universe, Blessed Queen of the Entire Creation, Queen of the Heavens, Queen of Mercy, Queen of Peace, Queen of Apostles, Queen of Martyrs, Queen of All Saints, Queen of the Holy Rosary, Queen of Lourdes, Mistress of Heavenly Wisdom, Mistress of Earth, Morning Star of Christianity, Clear Star at Morning in Beauty Enshrined, Co-Redemptrix with Jesus Her Divine Son, Refuge of Sinners, Our Refuge, Heaven's Greatest Gem, Humanity's Solitary Boast,[64] Virgin of All Blessed Virgins, Our Divine Model in All Things.

"Blessed Be God in the Maternity of Our Blessed Virgin Mother Mary," he once wrote. His notes also contain frequent references about devotion to Mary, which almost every witness noted as a clear manifestation of Solanus's faith. At his first assignment he served as chaplain for the Young Ladies Sodality of Our Lady. He rejoiced in 1950 when Pope Pius XII solemnly declared the Assumption of Mary as dogma of the Catholic faith. He loved to pray the Angelus, and he tried to make sure that he prayed the Little Office of the Blessed Virgin daily; he chided himself when he omitted it. He made novenas to Mary. He prayed to Mary under her titles of Our Lady of Perpetual Help and Our Lady of Lourdes.

Like the other friars, Solanus always stopped for a short prayer when he passed the outdoor grotto honoring Our Lady of Lourdes at St. Felix in Huntington. He also made a pilgrimage to a Marian shrine in Carey, Ohio. Solanus was concerned when he noticed at a retreat house that a shrine to Mary had been neglected; to do his part in honoring Mary he placed some fresh flowers there.

But Solanus's favorite way of expressing his love for Mary was to recite the rosary and to encourage others to do so. As a boy and young man at home, Solanus said the rosary each night, "kneeling straight up as he had learned from his mother." Sister M. Solania Manturuk, a Felician Sister named after Solanus, recalls that he always had a rosary in his hand, even when he was in the office talking to the people. His routine on a trip included recitation of the rosary with his companions:

> I know that the rosary was one of his favorite devotions. The day that I was to drive him to Huntington we were delayed for about five hours because I had to get the brakes fixed on my car. Someone from the monastery drove him out to the place where my car was being repaired. The car was ready to go when he arrived, and I thought he would be anxious to leave, but he asked me if there was a church nearby. I told him that Presentation Church was close at hand. So he said, "Let's go over and say some prayers." We went to the church and he said, "Let's say the rosary." Which we did. In other words, he was more anxious to get his prayers said than he was to get started on the trip. We said five decades of the rosary at the church; then on the way to Huntington, we said the other ten decades of the rosary.[65]

Whenever he was asked to lead the rosary for a deceased person he "always recited the Glorious Mysteries, indicating the hope that we should have in the life hereafter." The rosary served as a mainstay in his dying days as well.

Besides his devotion to Mary, Queen of Angels and Saints, Solanus often made the ejaculation: "Blessed be God in his angels and in his saints," which was used in the prayers at the close of benediction of the Blessed Sacrament. He spoke familiarly of the angels and especially of the guardian angels. "We are not angels, but poor sinners," he noted. As for the saints themselves, they had triumphed over the world, the flesh and the devil. Thus they served as a source of intercession with God and an example to be imitated. For this reason, he believed it was helpful to read the lives of the saints with reverence and to celebrate their feasts. "One of the great advantages of a study of the lives of the saints," he wrote, "is the supernatural courage that such studying tends so positively to foster. And at the same [time, it fosters] appreciation for one's vocation."

From his first notebook and throughout his letters, Solanus had a habit of copying various quotations from the saints. It can be assumed he had a deep dedication to the founder of his Order, St. Francis of Assisi. And while he had devotion to such a wide range of saints as Ignatius Loyola and Gerard Magella, he seems to have had special devotion to St. Joseph,[66] Anthony of Padua,[67] the Capuchin saints, and particularly St. Therese of Lisieux, the "Little Flower."

It was mentioned in the introduction that Solanus was a devotee of Therese's *Autobiography* since at least 1915. Father Anthony Kerry recalled that Solanus told him that he had read it nine times. Father Kerry believed that Solanus "saw in her life much of his own. The Little Flower never did extraordinary things. She had the simple tasks to do about the convent, and that was also his life in the Order. He had the simple and the menial tasks to perform. He believed in doing these little things as well as he could."

Although Solanus encouraged young women to have a devotion to St. Therese, like all the saints she took second place to Mary. As Brother Dan Brady recollects:

At Detroit there was a woman who once a week would bring a bouquet of beautiful gold or yellow roses to be placed before the statue of St. Therese. After she would leave, Father Solanus would take half of those and put them in front of the Blessed Mother's altar. One time I jokingly told Father Solanus he shouldn't do that, that was stealing. He just laughed and shrugged it off and said, "I'm sure St. Therese will understand. She knows that the Blessed Mother comes first."

Finally, Solanus supported the notion of contemporaries being proclaimed saints by the Vatican. He lived with Stephen Eckert in Yonkers and developed a great admiration for him.[68] When the cause for his beatification opened in 1948, Solanus jotted down recollections of him. As for the possibility of being a saint himself, he refused to comment.

Hope

Among the theological virtues, hope follows faith, or as Solanus believed, it is "inspired by faith." While theoretically different in their dependence on each other, faith and hope "coexisted" for him. In his ministry to others, according to Capuchin Pius Cotter, "one of the first things he did for the people was to encourage them to have a great trust in God, and somehow out of this encouragement to trust in God came the notion too that they would first of all have to have faith in God." Solanus not only connected faith and hope with encouragement, but especially with confidence. In fact, it might be said his notion of hope was manifest as confident faith as well as faithful confidence. For Solanus, "Where there is real faith and *confidence* in God there is no such thing as a hopeless case." He declared that "our sad weakness today is our lack of faith and, consequently, [our] want of confidence in God."

While he was serving in his first assignment, at Sacred Heart in Yonkers, Solanus wrote a letter to his sister Margaret. One section of the letter contains almost every element of hope that the virtue includes — from its reference to the limitations of natural goods in light of eternal life and God's provident guidance, to thanksgiving for all the events that help shape our lives and especially for and from the perspective of hope and belief in a heavenly reward for God's faithful ones. Solanus wrote:

> What is nature in light of the supernatural? Ah, a substratum! And what are natural blessings compared with the hope of immortality? I believe that I'd go crazy, yearning for something higher if I had nothing to enjoy or to hope for but the natural, even had I all the natural gifts and blessings enjoyed by man. But thanks be to God for the True Faith! Thanks be to God for the simple, honest, faithful parents that God gave us! Thanks be to God for vocation and for strength to follow the call, at least imperfectly! Thanks be to God for the blessed hope that he gives us here in our exile of once being eternally united

with His chosen ones in the peace of our true home, in the love of His Sacred Heart! What are the struggles and victories of men, if only natural? What are they all compared with the victorious struggles of a Christian soul leaving its exile to brighten Heaven!

Solanus's roots in Irish Catholicism and his pioneering spirit helped create his hope. However his faith in God was what made it so strong; for him God was "the divine source and foundation of individual hope" and even "international confidence." God was to be first in people's lives. One of his superiors adds: "I think one could say that he was constantly breathing in God, that he was constantly surrounded by God in his life and therefore from this came his great trust in God. I truly believe that he promoted this virtue of hope in others by encouraging them to believe in God and to trust in God and to place themselves in the hands of God." "God is always available and never too busy," he would say. "He is always waiting for you individually."

In his dealings with the many people who came to him in the hope their prayers would be answered, "he would inevitably always add: 'Well, let's leave something up to the good God to do.'" Brother Dan Brady recalls:

> Hope was an outstanding virtue in his life. When he talked to the novices, he would remind us of the hope we should have for eternal life. He would quote the Scriptures, "The eye has not seen, nor the ear heard, the things that have been prepared for us." It was one virtue that he sought to instill in the people, constantly reminding them to have trust in God.

People could have confident trust in God because of God's provident will. This notion guided Solanus's approach to people as he encouraged them in their needs. It was God who healed, not he. Consequently he had an "unconditional trust in God" that flowed from his conviction "that good would come out of any situation that came up." This unconditional trust in God might be considered a chief characteristic of his spirituality and the unique message for our times. "Blessed be God in all His designs," was one of his favorite expressions. One of his superiors referred to Father Solanus as a man of hope: "His thoughts were constantly directed heavenward. He brought and inspired hope in all those he met in life. He was a man who had implicit faith in the trust of God." The superior added that Solanus summarized hope by saying: " 'Let God's will be done,' and I am sure he was confident that in some way God's will would be done."

Because of Solanus's conviction about God and eternal life, he evaluated all events in light of God's plan and eternal life itself. "He stressed the regard that one should have for eternal life," a lay friend noted. "He said that we are only here for a time, that everything should be directed to the eternal life and that we were here only to do God's will. He would say, 'Don't worry about tomorrow; worry will never change it. Let us not be presumptuous; God decided tomorrow years ago.' "

He continually urged people to hope, to trust. It was the "one thing" he instilled in others; that which "he constantly preached." Even though many came for material assistance or for "cures," hope was "his principal form of assistance," which he shared with others "to carry on in spite of all of their difficulties and troubles." "With Father Solanus," his confrere Elmer Stoffel recalled, "everything was placed in God's hands. He not only encouraged the people to have that same trust; I would say he almost demanded it of them." Because of his hope, others had hope in what he said to them about their concerns. Sister Mary Cecilia Eagen, whose father was a close friend and co-worker of Solanus, said that he sought to promote "this trust in God. I know. I asked my father what he thought when Father Solanus told him that he would be better. He looked at me and said, 'Daughter, I never doubted it.' "

"God's will would be done in whatever way it was intended, and the people for whom he prayed would be able to bear with their crosses" if their request was not granted. This was especially true for people who had to prepare for dying. William Tremblay, who drove Solanus to visit people in need, noted the case of a woman in Windsor, Ontario, who was suffering from tuberculosis. She was in her late thirties and had two children. She had been on the verge of dying for many months, but she struggled to live because of her children. Tremblay relates the situation:

> When he entered the house, the first thing she said was, "Oh, you look just like Jesus Christ Himself." His dark beard and his tall, lean frame in the brown habit, combined with his gentle blue eyes and peaceful composure had often brought such a response. Solanus had learned to take such comments in stride.
>
> "Well, I'm taking His place," Solanus replied. "I was sent here by Him. I came here because the Lord has a crown waiting for you. Why don't you resign yourself to go to heaven and forget about your children? The Lord has a lot of good mothers, especially the Blessed Virgin, and she will take care of your children."

"Oh, I feel so different now," the woman responded, sensing a calm which so many others seemed to receive in Solanus's presence and words. "Well, if you do," Solanus said, "let's all pray for you and you pray with us."

Everyone knelt down and Solanus led a decade of the rosary. There was not a dry eye in the room. When he finished, Solanus said, "I promise you the Lord will help you today."

By 11 o'clock that same night the woman was dead, relieved from her pain.[69]

Solanus continually promoted people's confidence in God; as he wrote, "Confidence in God is victory assured." As "a great grace in itself," it constituted the very "soul of prayer." Hardly anything could be more pleasing to God or more profitable to our souls. The very fact that Solanus promoted prayer emphasized his confident trust that these prayers would be heard. Whether with the countless people who came to him in need or to ask God to supply bread for the Soup Kitchen, confident prayer guided Solanus's life.

He particularly sought to "foster confidence" in God's providence, in God's wisdom and goodness (and in the powerful intercession of Mary),[70] in God's mercy, in God's generosity, and especially by "thanking God ahead of time" for whatever is best for us. Even mistakes could be the source of fostering confidence, as happened to St. Peter. Such fostering of confidence would result in "real peace" in one's soul.

Confidence, wrote Solanus, "is courage divinely reinforced." It is the "soul of courage." When confidence and courage go hand in hand, victory is assured. He wrote: "Let us foster it [confidence] in every way and pray for it, always for an increase of faith and confidence and of reverence for God's holy servants and service. How little it is possible for poor mortals to appreciate, this side of heaven! Blessed be God in all His designs!"

One way Solanus promoted courage in others was by encouraging them: "Keep courage," he would recommend. Father Ambrose DeGroot, one of his former secretaries, notes: "He had great confidence in God. He encouraged the people who came to him to pray and to have confidence in the Providence of God. To people who were discouraged, he encouraged perseverance and trust in God. In this way he instilled hope in them. Of course, the greatest way he could enkindle courage was to encourage those discouraged 'to trust.' It was rather circular."

We have already seen how Solanus fostered confidence by promoting thanksgiving. However, if one would ask Solanus to summarize his "privileged" life, as he tried to do at the golden jubilee of his religious profession, it would be thanks "to God for uncountable mercies — for every blessing!" as well as "Thanks be to my neighbor for his charitable patience." The times he said "Thanks be to God" and "Deo Gratias!" each day or the number of times he began or closed his letters with these ejaculations would be difficult to ascertain; however, it would be safe to say that thanksgiving characterized the vast majority.

The day after the celebration of his fiftieth year as a priest, Solanus revealed an underlying rationale for his seeming bravado in making sure that people would "thank God ahead of time" for favors requested. When asked why he always urged the people to utter their thanksgiving before receiving a response, Solanus responded: "It's like putting God on the spot." Jesus had said, "Ask and you will receive" (Matt. 7:7); Solanus was not at all reluctant to take Jesus at his word.[71]

Another notion that Solanus equated with thankful hope was gratitude. Hope is gratefulness for everything God has done, is doing, and will do in our lives. "Oh, God is so good," he often said. Gratitude was Solanus's unique way of manifesting the "happy" part of his relationship with God and neighbor. Because "gratitude is the first sign of a thinking, rational creature," ingratitude, whether toward God or neighbor, had to be "poor humanity's sorrow or unhappiness." He warned, "Be sure if the enemy of our souls is pleased at anything in us, it is ingratitude of whatever kind. Why? Ingratitude leads to so many breaks with God and neighbor."

Besides linking thanksgiving and gratitude, Solanus identified both with the concept of "appreciation." For him, "to know is to appreciate." In Solanus's mind the only response to knowing God's existence was to appreciate, love, and serve God; thus he wrote a reflection called *Think Over* on these words:

> To know is to appreciate, to love, and to adore . . . things divine and to glory in the service of the known. What an outlook this ought to afford us! What an outstanding horizon. If "hope is the soul of happiness here" and if the revealed purpose of our creation — "to know God" — is kept in mind, what a horizon for poor sinners [there will be] if we but stop to think and remember that to know God covers everything.
>
> > God made me to know Him. Oh, what a bless'd aim!
> > To love Him and serve Him sure rests in the same.

It's "Heaven begun" for the *grateful* on earth;
To treasure aright! Highest heaven its worth.

For Solanus, "humanity's great weakness" could be found in "want of appreciation." Solanus's idea of appreciation, like his approach to faith itself, involved the personal dimension of his relations with God and neighbor. "To know and appreciate is to advance in the one science necessary — sanctity," he wrote. He also brought appreciation to bear regarding the gift of "the faith" itself. Capuchin Dan Crosby, who lived with Solanus as a novice, stated: "The word I heard more than any other on Solanus's lips was 'appreciate.' To me it sums up his whole spirituality."[72]

Finally, Solanus saw happiness and joy themselves as consequences of living in confident hope. "Thank God for hope, the soul of our happiness here," Solanus once wrote. "The fool sayeth in his heart, 'There is no God.' He refuses to be happy in refusing to hope." Yet Solanus made it clear that he considered happiness to be spurious without hope:

> You tell me you see others so happy. Oh, yes we see such people. Thank God they exist, though many of those who seem happy — who try to appear so — hardly know just what happiness is. Many do not realize or stop to use their faculty of reasoning that the very soul of happiness for mortals — those who are to die someday — is *hope*. Children are happy as a rule because in the mind of any normal child there is always [a] bright star of hope: "Some day I'll be grown up." "I'll be a woman." "I'll be a man." Herein we must imitate the children.

Hope not only was the soul of happiness; it presaged "a supernatural taste of heavenly joys." Joy, in Solanus, was "evidence of his love and trust in God." The only obstacles to happiness and joy are worry and anxiety. The latter reflects want of confidence in God. "By all means, shake off that anxiety of yours," he wrote to correspondent Winifred Goodwillie of Chicago. "Last year it was about something that now you smile about. Today it's about something that will not be serious if you raise your heart to God every time it comes to your mind and thank Him for whatever is to come."

In another passage, he quoted St. Therese as the source of his connection between worry and confidence:

> But why worry? "To worry about anything," St. Therese, the Little Flower, claims, "is to indicate a want of confidence in God." She very likely speaks of excessive worrying, and yet, why should we worry

about anything. Tumors? Cancers? Death? Why not rather turn to God, whose solicitude for our individual welfare — temporally as well as spiritually — puts all created solicitude out of the picture. Why not foster confidence in His divine providence by humbly and in all childlike humility venturing to remind Him — remind Him in the Person of our divine Brother Jesus — that we are His children — that we are, and at least want to be reckoned as among His "little ones"; and therefore, thank Him frequently, not only for the blessings of the past and present, but thank Him ahead of time for whatever He foresees is pleasing to Him that we suffer. This is not only in general but in each particular case, leaving everything absolutely in His divine disposal, including with all its circumstances, when, where and how He may be pleased to dispose the event of our death.

Besides making a connection between worry and confidence, this passage also shows how Solanus recognized the surpassing greatness of God's solicitude or providence to "created solicitude." Above all, it highlights that nuance of hope that might be considered characteristic of Solanus's spirituality: the continual offering of thanks for what has been, is, and will be happening in our lives, even to the point of becoming abandoned to the way God "may be pleased to dispose the event of our death." For his own part, he was in no rush to die. His nephew Jesuit John McCluskey testified to a conversation he had with his uncle: "He had great trust in God and the will of God. I know that during our conversation I asked him if he was eager to get to heaven. He smiled and raised his eyes to heaven and he said, 'Yes, but I'm not in any hurry to go.'"

While containing many of the elements that Solanus used to articulate the virtue of hope, another letter he wrote to a regular correspondent, Miss Mildred Maueal of Detroit, offers in its seven paragraphs elements of almost everything that has been said thus far about Solanus's practice of the virtues. Although it is quite lengthy, it provides a fitting conclusion to this section on the virtue of hope:

My Dear Madam: M.M.M.: God bless you and yours.

I hope this finds your outlook brightening. I just read your letter of the 11th — pathetic indeed. And [I] surely do sympathize with you. Perhaps I ought rather to congratulate you on the unusual experience [from which] you are of course inclined to learn and which the unbelieving world must look upon as a sad indication of failure.

But Oh! Why discouragement as long as we have a spark of faith left? What [a] different view we get by exercising and by fostering the "triune virtue — FAITH, HOPE, CHARITY!" In the first place "life" here in this world is so short — comparatively so momentary — that in regard to its success or failure one is inclined to think: "After all, what is the difference?" "Life" so short, that worldlings are so inclined to worship [it] as the only LIFE — as everything [of] worth.

How is it possible that man can be so shallow-minded and still be considered "rational"?

Your failure, yes, is an indication of weakness of some kind, somewhere. But if "the weak thing[s] of this world hath God chosen to confound the strong...," as St. Paul so wonderfully assures us (and the history of religion abounds in examples and all creation says Amen), then why ever be discouraged, unless it be that our faith more or less weakens?

Why dear sister, you ought to rather thank God for having given you such an opportunity to humble yourself and such a wonderful chance to foster humility — and by thanking Him ahead of time for whatever crosses He may deign to caress you with, [having] CONFIDENCE in His wisdom. Confidence in God — the very soul of prayer — hardly comes to any poor sinner like we all are without trials and humiliations. And your failure, though simple and possibly single, has no doubt been quite a little cross, at least for a "little soul" to carry. There is a little verse I am sure will profit you to keep in mind and ought [to] help you foster confidence in God: *"God condescends to use our powers if we don't spoil His plans by ours."* God's plans are always for the best, always wonderful.

But most especially for the patient and the humble who trust in Him are His plans unfathomably holy and sublime.

Let us, therefore, not weaken. Let us hope when darkness seem[s] to surround us. Let us thank Him at all time[s] and under whatever circumstances. Thank Him for our creation and our existence. Thank Him for everything — for His plans in the past that our sins and our want of appreciation and patience have so often frustrated and that He so often found necessary to change. Let us thank Him for all His plans for the future — for trials and humiliations as well as for great joys and consolations; for sickness and whatever death He may deign to plan. And with the inspired Psalmist, let us call all the creatures of the universe to help us praise and adore Him Who is the Divine Beginning and the everlasting Good — the Alpha and the Omega.[73]

Charity

Father Solanus showed clearly the virtue of charity. I would say that his intense love of God was the very core of his life. Everything that he said or did was in some way related to the love of God. Faith and hope were pretty much dependent on this virtue in his mind. I think his intense love for God was shown by the fact that he almost seemed to be enraptured when he spoke of God and the love we should have for God.

From the testimony of one witness who knew Solanus Casey well, "His particular message to all of us would be to love God and to love your neighbor." According to Matthew's Gospel, in response to the question regarding the "greatest commandment," Jesus responded: " 'You shall love the Lord your God with all your heart, and with all your soul and with all your mind.' This is the greatest and first commandment. And a second is like it: 'You shall love your neighbor as yourself.' On these two commandments hang all the law and the prophets" (Matt. 22:37–40; see 19:19).

Traditional spirituality always considers both the relationship with God — the vertical dimension — and the relationship with humans — the horizontal element. The former cannot be authentic without the latter. And love of neighbor can be selfish if not rooted in one's love of God. According to Gabriel Badalamenti, who cared for Solanus in his later years, "Father Solanus observed the first commandment to love God with your whole heart and soul. Everything else came from that." This "everything else" that flowed from the great commandment was the second: to love one's neighbor as one's self.

In a world where self-love was considered a vice, its appropriate expression constituted a strong basis for Solanus's spirituality; this was his response to his sense of having been loved first by God and significant others in his life. According to one witness:

I think one of the characteristic notes of his spirituality was the self-confidence he had. I might say it was a certain amount of self-assurance, or self-esteem. By all of this I mean that he was sure of

himself because he knew where he stood with God. He was optimistic. He expected good things to happen. First of all, God was the
source of his optimism. But I think it also came from the loving association he had with his family. He just believed that he was loved
by God, he was loved by his family, and from this relationship good
things just had to come.

In Solanus's spirituality the twofold dimension of love found in Matthew's Gospel constituted his life and what he defined as religion. Religion,
for Solanus, was the science of our happy relationship with God and neighbor; furthermore, it was the science of our providential dependence on
God and our neighbor. Combined it became "the science of our happy and
providential dependence on God and our neighbor."

In one of his reflections Solanus wrote that another word for religion
was "charity." In Solanus's mind the two key ingredients in any religion
constituted the twofold dimension of evangelical charity: its vertical dimension of a relationship and dependence on God and its horizontal
expression in a parallel relationship and dependence on our neighbors.
These two concepts are the focus of the following two sections.

The Practice of the Love of God

According to Solanus, living a life of love could be summarized quite
simply: "God loves us, let us love God." Or, as he once expressed it, God
"1. loves me, 2. is infinitely desirous of my love [and] proofs thereof;
[therefore] 3. I will love Him." In effect, his life was to revolve around God.

It has been said before that Solanus seemed to "breathe" the love of
God in his life. If this is so, it is because Solanus believed that God first
breathed that love in the form of grace in our souls. Brother Ignatius Milne
described his perception of Solanus's love of God this way:

> I feel that Father showed his heroic practice of the love of God in
> his openness to divine things. He always seemed to be able to speak
> about God or faith or the mysteries of God very spontaneously and
> without having to think about it. He evidently lived in God's pres-
> ence continually. He seemed to be completely absorbed with making
> God's goodness known to others, and he tried to show this, I be-
> lieve, in his own dealing with people. He was always able to accept
> whatever suffering or tribulations or difficulties he would have and

be able to thank God for them. This love of God was very manifest in his writings, which I read quite thoroughly.

An examination of Solanus's writings reveals that his love *toward* God was his "natural" response to his conviction of God's loving provident relationship toward him, others, and all creation: "As a reflection of the unity of God — a necessary feature of the Creator, all things created tend to become one. All things tend to unity," he wrote in a eucharistic sermon. "All creatures of good will are drawn by love and by the law of charity to unity among themselves and to union with God." He concluded, "Each individual in its way and all together as one, reflect the divine *unity* of the ever *adorable Trinity.*" In response to a letter of concern sent him by his sister, Solanus gently chided her by writing: "Dear Margaret, I see that you are just another piece of humanity like myself and like I meet with every hour of the day — inclined to worry and fret about the morrow as though Our Dear Lord had never spoken a word about His divine providence or proved His loving solicitude for each of us a thousand times a day."

In the letter Solanus recalls "the beautiful words of Our Dear Lord" in the Sermon on the Mount, which calls "attention to the birds of the air and the flowers of the field, etc: 'Be not solicitous for the morrow, for the morrow will be solicitous for itself.'" Reflecting on the passage, Solanus concluded: "I sometimes think we make a great blunder in the fact that, instead of thanking God for His goodness and kindness on every side and making acts of confidence in His loving providence, we just act as though everything depended on luck or on fortune, etc. Is it not true? And what a mistake!"

As children, both Margaret and Bernard Casey Jr. had God's provident love for them modeled in the "solicitude" of their "sturdy, honest, virtuous parents." When he joined the Capuchin Order, Solanus Casey immediately began by trying to grow in that love. On March 20, 1897, a few months into his novitiate, Solanus called himself to a "renewal frequently of resolve to strive for Love of God." A few pages later he outlined some "Means for Acquiring the Love of God," which included detachment from earthly affections and singleness of purpose, meditation on "the passion of Jesus Christ," uniformity of his will with God's will, mental prayer (meditation and contemplation), and intercessory prayer. He concluded this section with a quotation in Latin, translated here:

"Perfection," according to St. Bonaventure, "principally consists in charity, in that it is the most high perfection, when it excludes all covetousness, which is the enemy of charity. Covetousness however informs all things and will not voluntarily let go of them. Here then is the root of all evil: covetousness; thus the root and principle of perfection is most high poverty.

During Solanus's first assignment at Yonkers the people at Sacred Heart Parish developed their own rationale for why this priest could not hear confessions. As one woman recalled: "Father Solanus loved God so much that he could not hear confessions because he might not be able to take it if he discovered how many people were hurting God!"[74]

One of the most tender images Solanus used to describe God was "our Divine Sweetheart." God was also the "Heavenly Father," the "Good God," the "Dear Lord." His secretary Ambrose DeGroot recalls that Solanus's love of God was manifest "in the familiar way in which he used to speak about the 'Dear Lord.' His love for God was not an affectation, it was not phony, or put on. His life revolved around God. God was the pivot or the center of his life." Such references to God, as well as the fact that Solanus always found a way to steer conversations toward God, indicate that "even when he wasn't at prayer he would seem to be in the presence of God."

Rupert Dorn, who later became Capuchin provincial in the Midwest, points out that Solanus "seemed to take great joy in just talking about God. Even if we were out to dinner, it wouldn't be very long before the conversation in some way would get around to the business of God." Said another way, "You never talked to Father Solanus but that he talked about God." Solanus's way of talking about God revolved around love. His speech was centered on the Divine Presence. "Almost every other word expressed his love for God in one way or another," said Dorothy Fletcher. "I think when a person disperses God throughout his conversation it shows his love for God." One particular way Solanus manifested his love for God was in speaking of God's goodness. He would say, "Why be afraid of God? After all, He loves you, and He wants to help you."

Besides developing his own loving relationship with God, he promoted the same with his neighbor. "He instilled this love for God in others by the way he spoke to people about God." One of these people was Joyce Pranger. In her book *Rise Early to Meet Your Lord,* she recalls a visit she had as a thirteen-year-old girl with Solanus at Huntington:

His warmth and joy were contagious. He talked to me of the love of God and what a joy it had been for him to spend his entire life dedicated to him. Father's eyes were crystal blue like a mirror in which I could see the depths of eternity.

It was growing dark in the room, and he spoke, on and on, of the love of God. It didn't seem to phase him that a long line of people was still waiting outside to see him. He remained unruffled. He counseled me lovingly.[75]

Besides individual conversations with people like Joyce Pranger, Solanus's reflections on God's love constituted the heart of his reflections each week when people came for the blessing of the relic of the True Cross: "In his Wednesday devotions he often spoke of the sufferings of Christ as an indication of God's love for us," a layman testified, "and that we should have that same love for God." Besides manifesting a deep love for God at Mass and toward the Blessed Sacrament, the love of God also served as the core of his "fervorinos" at Mass.

Benedict Joseph Groeschel recalls that at such times he "would always preach on the love of God and invite the people to carry their cross and to suffer for the love of Christ who had suffered for them. He would be somewhat transformed when he gave these little sermons...[and] with great urgency would call the people to the love of God." Indeed, his very devotion at Mass itself was an invitation to others to share in God's love.

The motive of God's love manifest in Jesus' passion and death on the cross was often used by Solanus to invite people to make a similar response in love. Booker Ashe remembered one time complaining to him, as it were, about the corporal discipline that he, Solanus, and the other Capuchins practiced on Good Friday:[76] "I remember he lectured to me about the sufferings of Christ and what Christ went through for us. I would know of nothing that he ever said or did that would be contradictory to the heroic practice of his love for God."

For Solanus, if Jesus is the way to know God's love for us and our response to God's love for us, then Mary is the way to Jesus' love. "Indeed we cannot love Jesus as we ought to do, cannot be devoted to His Sacred Heart without devotion to Mary," he wrote as early as 1917. "Only through her and with her can we arrive at true devotion to the Sacred Heart of her divine Son, where the love of God is everything to the soul and the soul is everything to God."

Solanus nourished his intimate, loving relationship with God especially by constant prayer. His first biographer, James P. Derum, testified that he showed love of God by the long hours that he spent in chapel, even when he was tired, praying and particularly praying for others. This was related to me by members of the Capuchin Order as I talked to them in preparation for writing my book. It was related to me that oftentimes the janitor who would come in to clean up the Chapel in the morning at 5 a.m. would find Father Solanus in the Chapel, sometimes asleep, indicating that apparently he had been there most of the night. When the person who found him expressed his amazement at finding him in the Chapel asleep, Father Solanus in his wry humor stated: "Oh, it wasn't so bad, I was sleeping on the soft side of the boards." I believe that his deep love for God is illustrated by this incident.

The term "Divine Sweetheart," which Solanus used of God, must be understood in relation to its context of God's merciful providence — "notwithstanding our sins" — as well as Solanus's desire to live in loving union with God's will. The notion of God's merciful providence sprinkles the writings of Solanus. The response that was to be made to this divine providence was "grateful appreciation." However, the specific response to God's merciful providence was not to be limited to mere words; like any other familial situation, it demanded some kind of anticipatory reciprocation by making a promise to do something; this is what he called a "proposition":

> I find it always practical, especially in cases where all human scientific help is despaired of, to just turn to the Divine Author of all good — always solicitous to be asked for favors — and with all the confidence we can muster, to promise something that we are assured is pleasing to Him if we might only be spared (or be granted the certain favor).

Solanus recommended that others who wanted favors from God show their good will "by first promising some…little sacrifice of some kind." For Solanus the only real sacrifice "for a loving heart"[77] would be separation from one's friend. While this shows the familiarity Solanus had with God, it is clear that he also made "little sacrifices." As with St. Therese, this mainly meant loving acceptance of the people who came to him for help, "in accepting the stress of his work, of being in the office for hours upon end listening to the problems of the people. He certainly would not have done this from human motives. He would often speak of God, even just in the sense that we ought to thank God for the things that he has done for us and given to us."

As to the people's "little sacrifice," Solanus's confrere Cosmas Niedhammer noted that he invited people to "do more" to show their love:

> I think his love of God would be the reason why at times he would be stern with people who were not living the way they should and yet he never condemned them. He would encourage them to better practices in their life and in their religion. He would encourage them to go to the Sacraments. And if they had not been to the sacraments, he would encourage them to go to confession immediately. Usually a priest was available at all times to hear confessions of those people whom Father Solanus had encouraged to do so. He assured these people that if they would receive the Sacraments that those conditions which brought them to see him in the first place would be changed. Their lives would be improved, or their difficulties would be solved. When they did do what Father Solanus counseled them to do, their conditions did improve. Their lives were changed, and sometimes their illnesses were cured.

All these represent people's way of reciprocating to God's love, which is what Solanus continually told people to do. However, in some situations where people were not frequenting the sacraments or had stopped practicing their Catholicism, Solanus could be very stern. This was evident in the letters he drafted over a period of time to a Catholic doctor who was a benefactor of St. Felix Friary in Huntington, but who had stopped practicing Catholicism. Solanus wrote (assuming his deliberate missing of Mass was a mortal sin):

> According to the greatest theologians, the first punishment of sin is the withdrawal of sanctifying grace — of God Himself.... But, in God's blessed Name, who can claim exemption from such guilt? I, for one, could never dare think of such a thing. Can you, Doctor? Then, if "gratitude for favors is one of the first and surest indications of intelligence," then, in the name of everything that is logical, and intelligent and holy, let us be men enough to acknowledge our weakness, our stupidity, our real insanity and guilt in the sight of Heaven. By such humble acknowledgment — how mercifully simple and easy — we may recover our friendship and our peace with our God in Heaven [who is] at once the divinely gentle and loving Gov-

ernor of the universe and the no less divine Avenger of the proud and
the stubborn who refuse to appreciate His merciful goodness and to
cooperate with His gracious condescensions.

Despite the strength of this letter, Solanus's use of the term for God —
"Divine Avenger" — is balanced with notions of God's mercy and goodness
and human friendship and peace with God. Unlike the pattern of the day,
Solanus rarely appealed to people's fear of God but rather to God's love
for them. One of his earliest entries in his novitiate notebook notes that
"the magnanimous man" does nothing for love of humans or for fear of
them; rather "it is for love of God and virtue that he is moved to perform
great actions; all other motives have no influence on them." One layman
testified that Solanus's love of God was manifest in the way he approached
God: "I believe that he certainly had this great devotion and love for God
because he frequently spoke of God."

While Solanus could be stern with people whom he sensed to be living in sin, he could be equally compassionate with people who feared,
because of their scrupulosity, that they were controlled by sin. On these
occasions he would "assure scrupulous souls: 'No, Jesus is no crank. He
knows that we are not angels but poor sinners — every one of us.'" People
were "poor sinners" in a church "consisting of and under the supervision
of poor sinners."

While he sought to have love overcome fear in people's relationship
to and dependence on God, the fear of God was not absent from Solanus's own relationship with God. Father Blase Gitzen, who served as his
secretary, recalls:

> He certainly had a fear of God in the reverential sense that he would
> fear to offend God. And while he had a horror of sin, he certainly
> was kind to the sinner. I think in one sense he was more afraid of the
> devil than he was of God. He was opposed to the devil and in giving
> the devil credit for anything, even such as naming a cake after him —
> "devil's food cake."

In Solanus's mind there was no doubt that the devil existed: Satan was
"Eve's garden advisor." Furthermore, the ploy used on Adam and Eve by
Satan reveals an interplay between discontentment and sin: "One of the
most immediate and necessary consequences of sin is discontentment....
The more we are inclined to sin...the more do we become discontented

and inclined to murmur. History proves this from the time of Adam till the present day and will prove it till time and men are no more."

According to Solanus, the interconnection between sin and discontentment was not limited to the level of individuals; it could be found at the social and cultural level as well. "Sin causes discontentment. Not only because society is made up of individuals and nations and generations in like manner, but there are sins of society and national sins which bring their special curse to society or to the nation." In 1914, when Solanus wrote these reflections, the examples he used of social sin dealt with secular education and divorce—the "curse of the age." However, whether the sin was individual or social, it invited conversion.

Solanus saw conversion as twofold: It involved turning from sin as well as turning more to God's grace. His own conversion and that of others— that they might be brought to God — was the "one goal that he had set for himself in this life." Reflecting that "some people have an even queerer idea of conversion" than they do about "religion," he explained to a woman who seemed to fear whether her past sins were obstacles to God's action in her life: "It seems to me, therefore, that to be converted means to receive the grace of God, one way or other, to come back more and more earnestly and more practically to know, to love and to serve God. And since we are all so inclined to go wrong and to sin — even [being] born in sin — we can always be converted." In this sense of converting, Solanus regularly asked people to pray for sinners' conversion — beginning with himself. In 1954, with only three years left in his life, he wrote below a picture of himself: "Still only half converted — at it since October, 1870."[78]

In 1918 Solanus wrote in his notebook a quotation from scripture about fear: "*He will* do the will of them that fear Him and He will hear their prayer and save them." Such is a "holy," "happy" fear, "the beginning of wisdom." However, again, the emphasis is on the positive rather than the negative; such was the approach he used to invite himself and others to conversion. Given such a happy, dependent relationship on God's providence, one need not even fear death, for only someone "worldly" fears death.

In 1898, two years after joining the Order, Solanus quoted St. John Chrysostom, who said, "I fear not death, which is my gain." "Why fear death?" Solanus wrote while making a retreat in 1943. Two years later, again on retreat, Solanus penned similar reflections on death:

Why be afraid of gentle sister Death? Why be anxious about dying? Why? Rather ask, why *not* fear and avoid the cause of death? Only the unbelieving worldling fears death rather than sin, its cause. In other words, only [in] the crazy world that refuses to believe in the wisdom and power and goodness of God to provide a Hereafter for His faithful (and therefore, who fail to foster hope in this exile) is death a subject of horror. Again, since to sin is the climax of insanity, therefore only inasmuch as we have been so crazy as to have sinned, only in so much [should we] have cause to fear death or to be afraid to die.

After all, if God has given such striking manifestations for us all during our temporal existence of His love for us, why not leave death to Him too? Why not, as often as we think of it, just say, "Thank you Jesus ahead of time for the death ahead of me. That is your business."

When death did approach Solanus, he met it unafraid because he had practiced what he professed; his life had been grounded in love of God. Gerald Walker, Solanus's provincial at the time of his death, declared:

Yes, indeed, he had a love for God. I think the thing that impressed me most about his practice of this virtue was that he seemed to be more concerned about pleasing God than receiving from God. One of the last things he said to me before he died was, "I look on my whole life as giving, and I want to give and give until there is nothing left of me to give. Therefore, I have been praying that when I come to die I will be perfectly conscious so that with a positive act I can give my last breath to God."

The Practice of Love toward Neighbor

While it may be true that Solanus wanted to consciously give his last breath to God, he also said not long before he died that he wanted to live to see all people united. The love he had for God, which translated into his love for others, led him to seek their unity in God. Father Walker remembers that when he came to visit him in the hospital during his last sojourn there, he found him in great pain. He leaned over and asked him where it hurt: "His face was literally radiant, and he said, 'Thanks be to God. I'm offering my suffering that we all might be one. If only I could live to see the conversion of the world.'"

His loving approach to all people might be considered a twentieth-century translation of St. Paul's canticle of love in Corinthians (1 Cor. 13:4–7). Those testifying variously characterized his personality as simple, humble, peaceful, gentle, patient, kind, compassionate, and, especially, cheerful. A confrere from his earliest days recalls: "He was a cheerful person. He had a good sense of humor. He could tell stories, and he could also take a joke on himself and laugh about it." A layman who attended the services conducted by Solanus recalls:

> He had a good sense of humor. I remember one time at one of the Wednesday afternoon devotions when he was exhorting people to enroll themselves or their loved ones in the Seraphic Mass Association, he told the story of a woman who had enrolled her husband in the Seraphic Mass Association. When his condition — whatever it was — didn't improve she came back and wanted to know if she could get her 50 cents back.

Rupert Dorn, who later became provincial of the Capuchins, was inspired by Solanus:

> He was very kind, simple, and straightforward. One of the things that impressed me was the fact that Father Solanus never tried to impress anybody else by his actions or words or any other thing. He merely said what had to be said, as though this is what God wanted to tell people. When he talked with people, they received the impression that, at that moment, they were the most important people in the world to Solanus.

George Lauhoff testified:

> I think among the characteristic notes of his personality would be his sincerity, his concern for the people. He was a cheerful sort of person, very soothing in the way he talked to you. I know that I have been at the monastery waiting to talk to Father Solanus and there would be other people waiting, but he gave you the impression that when you came to the desk to talk to him that you were the only person that existed in the world at that moment. He was completely intent upon what you had to say. He was always encouraging in what he had to say to you. He was very positive in trying to encourage trust in God, and to have hope, and the courage to accept the trials of life. . . . He had to be aware of the fact that these thousands of people came to see him, and yet he was never puffed up by this knowledge. He had an unshakable faith and love for God.

Solanus had a certain predilection toward children. He was always "delighted to see children. He always kept a little bag of candy in his desk drawer to give to the children when they came to see him." Something about the man at the desk appealed to them. Dorothy Fletcher recalled that she would take her six children to visit him, "and even the little ones would sit there for an hour and not cry, or be fussy, or disturb anybody."

Given Solanus's charitable disposition, he did not need to seek others out by personal contact or communication; they came to him. Indeed, within a short time of his arrival at St. Bonaventure's in Detroit, the front office had to be expanded to accommodate the growing numbers of people. He would never refuse to see anyone or to try to help them.

James P. Derum, who wrote the first biography of Solanus Casey, testified of Solanus's time at St. Bonaventure's:

> [That] Father Solanus exercised the virtue of charity toward his neighbor...is illustrated in the hours that he spent in the Office listening to the troubles of people who came to him. After he had left Detroit, Father Solanus wrote a note to Brother Leo of St. Bonaventure's Monastery relating that fatigue that he experienced in spending these hours in listening to people and their troubles. It is evident from the tenor of this note that he had to exercise a great deal of will power to continue to do this work. I think his dedication to the people in the manner I have spoken about indicated that it was beyond the ordinary. Practically most of his life was spent in the Office of Porter listening to people from 9:00 a.m. to 9:00 p.m. almost without interruption.

In the eyes of many witnesses, the countless hours Solanus spent with the people in the front office manifested his deep love for human beings. "I would think that the hours that he spent with the people, instructing them, counseling them, encouraging them, alone would be a great evidence of the love that he had for his fellow man," one testified. "I think that these were more than just insignificant things. I think it took a great deal of love, patience, kindness in order to put up with all of this." The people's needs overcame any intrusions on his time.

When Solanus was interrupted, it was to fulfill his responsibilities as a Capuchin to the regular times for praying the Prayer of the Church (the Divine Office, as it was called then), as well as eating and participating in the proscribed period after lunch for "recreation" in common. "There might have been times when he would be late for meals or choir, but it was approved by the superiors to the extent that they never complained because he was late," Capuchin Ambrose DeGroot recalls. "It was understood that if he were busy dealing with the people that he had a sufficient reason to be late. When he was late he would come in, excuse himself to the superior, kneel down before him and kiss the floor to show his submission to the superior."[79]

On the days the friars spoke, Solanus took part in the fraternal bantering that not only revealed his fraternal charity, but his nonjudgmental nature and sense of humor as well. One day at table he was seated next to a brother who was a little obese, and when the cake came by this brother took a rather large piece. Father Solanus then helped himself to a very small piece. The brother said to Father Solanus: "Why don't you take a bigger piece like the one I have?" Father Solanus looked at him and merely commented: "Big furnaces need a lot of fuel."

Brother Ignatius also reported that if somebody wanted to see him, he would leave immediately, whether he had just started his meal or even only partially finished it. As Solanus said, "The food is not as important as trying to help others." The same thing would happen if Solanus was at the friars' "recreation" period after the noon dinner. His confrere Cosmas Niedhammer noted:

> He would come into the recreation room after the noon meal like the others. He liked to play pool or billiards. Often as not, though, he would pick a cue and start to shoot and his call bell would sound. Then he would have to put it right back into the rack, but never with any expression of impatience.
>
> It was remarkable. And it meant that when he was called he would be in the office until supper time. And sometimes he was so tired that we knew he would have to go into the last room of the office and lie down on the floor for a few minutes to take a catnap. He would just take off especially if he had an interruption.[80]

Cosmas also recalled what a good "community man" Solanus was during those recreation periods with the brethren when stories were shared, jokes told, and memories recalled.[81]

Solanus's whole life was ordered toward achieving oneness, or charity, with his family, his fellow Capuchins, and the people to whom he ministered. Since that unity was to image the love of God, love without discrimination, Solanus showed neither preferences nor prejudice. Capuchin Pius Cotter, who lived with Solanus both in Detroit and Huntington, verifies this: "Father Solanus was impartial to all people. There was no class distinction, no color distinction, no religious distinction in his mind among people. He saw them all as the children of God."

Despite the testimonies from those who actually knew him, one of those asked to give a theological opinion on the writings of Solanus questioned if the Servant of God might not have shown prejudice toward African American, Jewish, and Japanese peoples.[82] Far from evidencing prejudice, Solanus's use of words about various groups of people reflected the terms in usage among sensitive people at the time.[83]

His use of the word "darkie" for African American people echoed the usage of the period. The fact that he bore no "antipathy" or harbored no "inflexible generalization" regarding black people is evident in the letter that he wrote noting the presence of an African American at Huntington: "Thank God we have a very promising bouquet of brother-candidates, including a very carefree, happy darky." This particular candidate is now Brother Booker Ashe, who, as we have already seen, testified:

> He was a man who had great love and compassion for his fellow man. I believe that he treated all men equally. I am the first black member of the Capuchin Order in the United States and I think he was ahead of his time in the way he treated me. At least I felt nothing of the racial character in the way he treated me or the way he accepted me. He saw all persons as human beings, the image of God; their physical characteristics were mere accidents that he would pay no attention to — whether it would be race, color, or creed.

With regard to the possibility of anti-Semitism in Solanus's writings, there is only one possible questionable reference, to "*financial* Jews," and in that reference Solanus is quoting Father Coughlin. It seems, from the context, that he may have used this term to distinguish Jews connected with the large banks, which he felt were discriminating against the poor. As his *Collected Writings* show, he had nothing but respect for the many Jews who visited him, such as a doctor he knew who was "a Jew, a good, God-fearing fellow."

Finally, regarding Solanus's periodic use of the word "Japs," the censor accurately conflates what today is a cultural slur against Japanese people with a word absolutely void of such connotations at the time Solanus used it. "Perhaps this reflects the period of time when the United States was at war with Japan. It may simply reflect the rhetoric of the day." On the contrary, despite the fact that Solanus Casey's priest-brother Edward was imprisoned by the Japanese during the Second World War, he never used a derogatory remark for the "enemies" of the United States and persecutors of his brother.

Solanus's unbiased approach was evident in the way he ministered to people in the front office. According to his namesake, Sister M. Solania Manturuk of the Felician Sisters:

> I believe that Father Solanus was always impartial, just and prudent in the exercise of his charity toward others. I don't think he ever showed preference among people. I know that at times when I waited in the office to see him, there would be all types of people and he would never rush one person in order to take care of somebody else. Each one had as much time as they needed.

If any people did receive special solicitude from Solanus Casey, they were those suffering infirmity and poverty. He said that his "favorite people were the poor and the sick"; in fact, his whole life was dedicated to them. While "he accepted and welcomed everybody the same, that is, very warmly," Capuchin Elmer Stoffel recalled, "the poor were his specialty. He loved the poor." Or, as another person testified, "The poor were always on his mind." In this approach to the poor Solanus reflected the manner of ministry promoted by Pope John Paul II of a "nonexclusive preferential option for the poor." While he manifested "complete dedication to the needs of his fellow man," the poor received his special concern.

While he was still in formation one of Solanus's earliest notations reveals that the reality of the poor demanded a response from him. He quoted a statement of Pope Clement XIV, made while he was still a cardinal: "Be not contented with giving, but also lend to him that is in need, according to the precept of the Scriptures. I do not know a more contemptible object than money if it be not employed to assist our neighbor." Shortly before his ordination (1904) Solanus reminded his sister Ellen to "admonish" their brother Owen "not to neglect the most salutary [deed] — almsgiving for the poor and orphans."

From the beginning of his ministry Solanus evidenced a concern for the poor and marginalized. In Yonkers the parishioners noted that when he was portering,

> Solanus would feed the "tramps," as the wandering homeless were often called in those days. People recalled seeing him sweeping the sidewalk in front of the friary. When strangers arrived needing help,

he'd get them a big bowl of coffee, as well as whatever else might be available. The parishioners told each other that Solanus even would give the poor his own food.

Stories like these among the parishioners at Sacred Heart seem to have taken on a life of their own.[84] Loretta Brogan (now Sister Dolora Brogan) was in grade school while Solanus was in Yonkers. She relates the parish stories about Solanus:

> He could never be entrusted with answering the doorbell around mealtime because there were these soldiers of fortune or whatever you want to call them, [who] would come begging for something to eat. He would take his dinner and give it to the people. Then he would go fasting. He was very slender; he couldn't afford to fast. And stories like that were told about him, admiring his tremendous charity and feeling for others. He was not allowed to answer the doorbell at that time. I don't know how much truth there is in this, but these are things [that] circulated around the parish.

While he may have voiced concern about poor people, in his early years of ministry his regard did not always get translated into action. In a 1918 entry he chides himself for his failure: "Refused 5 cents (one time and) 2 cents to unfortunate." Two entries away from this notation about refusing aid to the poor, he quoted what Deuteronomy said about the way poor people should be treated: "Therefore I command thee to open thy hand to the needy and poor that live with thee in the land (Deut. 15:2)." This entry is the last self-admonishment found in his notes regarding his neglect of the poor.

Some sort of deeper conversion took place regarding his concern for the poor, as evidenced in the testimonies of people who knew him. Brother Dan Brady, who lived with Solanus in Detroit, relates:

> His love for God overflowed into his love for his fellow man. I know when I was the cook at the monastery during my novitiate days, Father Solanus would come into the kitchen and I might have a pie sitting there which he would take to give to somebody who had been at the door and was hungry. I would remonstrate with him, saying this was for dinner. He would say to me, "As long as there is one hungry person, this food does not belong to us."

As to the motivation for Solanus's response to the poor, Dan Brady surmised: "I think he saw in every human being the image of God, and therefore he had a great love for them as he had for his God." Dan's insights are confirmed by Solanus's own words: "What a marvelously different society we would have here, and what an ideal world to live in if we all would keep in mind the assurance of Jesus, 'What you have done to the least of my brethren, you have done to me.'" In Solanus Casey love of God and love of neighbor became conflated.

According to Sister Mary Cecilia Eagen, when Solanus ministered to the poor, the love of God "came through in everything he did. You knew everything he did, he did for God; it wasn't for himself. When he went out and collected food it wasn't for himself. He was doing it to feed the poor because this is what he thought would be the will of God. His love for God came through in everything he said."

Solanus not only involved himself in ministering to the needs of the poor, he involved others as well, even if it might be with the "widow's mite." Clare Ryan offers this example:

> One time when I went to see him, I had 78 cents in my purse and that's all the money we had until Friday which was a couple of days away when my husband would be paid. He said to me, "Whatever change you have in your purse, I want you to put in the Poor Box." He walked over and pointed out the Poor Box to me. So I put the 78 cents in the Poor Box and I can say that since that time I have never wanted for money in the sense that whenever I had bills to pay, I would somehow have the money to pay them.

Sister Dolora recalls that during his days at Yonkers Solanus had a way of discovering people in need — and a way to help. He also knew "some affluent people and didn't mind calling them up and saying, 'Tom, so and so needs this,' and Tom would provide it because Father Solanus asked him to. That's how he took care of people who were really in need at this time." At other times, especially while he was in Detroit, he involved people in helping the poor by their support of the Soup Kitchen. His "concern for the poor" led him, his provincial explained, to be "instrumental in the starting of the Soup Kitchen in Detroit, and [he] did a great deal to persuade farmers and companies to donate food for this particular work."

In Solanus's eyes, solidarity with the poor was an essential element of the Gospel life of Capuchin Franciscans. As he explained: "Our lot has been cast among the simple lives of the poor and our object is to give them spiritual aid and, if possible, material help as well." While the spiritual and corporal works of mercy implied here will be discussed in the next section, it can be said that the reality of the poor demanded Solanus's efforts to alleviate whatever it might be that caused their situation.

To conclude this section on Solanus's love of God and love of neighbor, the recollection of Ignatius Milne strikes true about Solanus Casey. In speaking of the "readiness in which he was willing to make himself available to others," Ignatius concluded that two words expressed his approach: "equanimity and magnanimity. He seemed to be totally concerned with two things: the glory of God and the service to his fellow man."

Chapter 10

The Works of Mercy

Although references to the spiritual and corporal works of mercy as such cannot be found among his writings, the whole life of Solanus Casey testifies that he admonished sinners, instructed the ignorant, counseled the doubtful, comforted the sorrowing, bore wrongs patiently, forgave all injuries, prayed for the living and the dead, fed the hungry, clothed the naked, gave drink to the thirsty, visited the imprisoned, sheltered the homeless, visited the sick, and buried the dead.

All these concrete manifestations of the spiritual and corporal works of mercy represented, for Solanus, humanity's response to God's merciful plan for each person: "Hence the little verse: 'God condescends to use our powers if we don't spoil His plans by ours.'" From the testimony of those who knew him, God used Solanus's powers through his practice of the works of mercy in a way that did not spoil God's plans but revealed them to others. Indeed, of those asked about Solanus's work, the vast majority referred to ministries of counseling and concern for the sick and the poor as the chief characteristics of his life.

Possibly because he knew himself so well and recognized God's mercy in his life, people sensed that Solanus *understood* them. Solanus, however, explained that much of this "sense of others" really flowed from his understanding of the human condition itself. To a young man who commended Solanus on how he was able to help so many people, Solanus merely replied: "Oh, that is not difficult. All you have to have is a knowledge of human nature." The ministry of mercy exercised by Solanus, however, reveals much more than simple knowledge.

The Spiritual Works of Mercy

The first spiritual work of mercy is to admonish sinners. Any admonishing of sinners Solanus may have done flowed from a sense of his own sinfulness. Thus Solanus continually asked people to pray for the conversion of poor sinners, beginning with himself. In noting that "he referred to himself as a sinner," one witness testified that he "said to my husband and myself, 'We're all sinners.'" "Notwithstanding our sins," Solanus noted, "God's merciful providence" was manifest continually.

Solanus's zeal for souls made him zealous for the conversion of sinners. In commenting on his practice of the spiritual works of mercy, a woman who knew him well said of Solanus: "He certainly was eager for souls and for the conversion of sinners to God. I believe that he offered up his day for these people [and] that he prayed for them."

Not only did he pray for their conversion, but "in dealing with them he tried to inspire in them the fact that there was a merciful God who would deal gently with them." Solanus urged those who had turned from God and the sacraments to turn back to them. Solanus asked a man who came asking for help for his ulcers whether he went to the sacraments. The man said, "No, Father." Solanus asked him how long it had been since he had gone to church. The man responded, "Twenty-one years. The day I was married."

> Father Solanus said: "Twenty-one years since you've been to Mass! Why don't you go in and kneel and thank God you're still walking after all these years. No wonder you have ulcers. Now, if you promise me right now that you will go to confession and go to Communion, your health will be returned. Will you do that?" The man said: "Yes, Father, I will."

Solanus arranged for another priest to hear the man's confession and then said:

> "Okay, go in the chapel and go to confession and God bless you. Kneel down and I will give you my blessing." Father Solanus blessed him and said: "You are going to be all right." This man lived for ten or fifteen years after that. He was hale and hardy and had no more trouble with ulcers. He told me: "I never had any pain after I saw Father Solanus."

Although he could not hear people's confessions and thus reveal to them God's mercy, Solanus often recommended mercy to those priests who celebrated the sacrament with those Solanus recommended. One of them, Father Cyril Langheim, commented: "I know that on many occasions, we priests who had the faculties would be called down to hear someone's confession. And he [Solanus] would say to us, 'Now be good to them; don't scold them; be kind to them.'"

Various people noted that Solanus was gifted with discernment and able to use that gift to invite people to conversion. Daniel Ryan testified about a man who roomed in a house owned by Mrs. Connie Casey. The man's father was quite old and was unable to go to church:

The father wanted his son to bring him to see Father Solanus, which he did, and Mrs. Casey went along with them. The son told Father Solanus that his father was worrying because he was old and couldn't get to church. The son said to Father Solanus that he thought he ought to tell his father that he didn't have to worry anymore because he felt that he had done his part. Father Solanus then said to the son, "Yes, he has done his part. When are you going to start doing your part?" At that, Mrs. Casey intervened and said, "The son does do his part. He goes to Mass every Sunday." And Father Solanus said, "Are you sure?" The young man admitted then that he didn't, that he hadn't been to church in almost six years. He would leave the house, and Mrs. Casey would think he was going to church. But he ended up going to a saloon. Father Solanus then said to him, "It's time you start doing your part."

Solanus challenged anyone he thought might be in need of conversion, whether friar, relative, or Capuchin benefactor, as in the case mentioned earlier of the doctor-benefactor who had ceased practicing his religion. Solanus wrote: "I feel that I would not be your friend or even a decently grateful patient were I to be silent as to dangers ahead of you." This letter, written in May of 1947, was apparently not sent, because six months later Solanus wrote another letter, in which he alluded to the struggle he was having in writing. Despite his difficulty in confronting the doctor for fear of embarrassing him, Solanus persevered:

Now Doctor, I want to assure you that it is not to embarrass you that I am writing you thus. On the contrary, I positively feel that I could not be your friend without making as strong an effort as possible to save you fearful embarrassment unquestionably ahead of you unless, by the grace of God, you open your eyes and cease trying to *do without Him,* without God!

This letter may not have been sent either, but it is clear from a letter that Solanus wrote his sister Margaret that he did succeed in confronting the doctor at some point.

Besides being stern with such sinners when it was necessary, Solanus also found gentle ways to get people not only to turn from sin but to turn more fully to God. To a woman who wrote Solanus about her husband's "affliction," Solanus responded: "Try and have your husband and friends go to Holy Communion more frequently with you. Nothing like frequent Communion to bring peace into a family or into a soul. At the same time it fosters faith in God and heavenly relationships, with all God's dear ones gone ahead of us."

The second spiritual work of mercy urges the instruction of the ignorant. In this, Solanus was the first to be taught, as his notes on moral theology (in Latin) indicate. The same can be said of his many retreat notes. Although he was not a teacher, Solanus Casey found many ways to instruct the ignorant. "I am sure that he was as kind and patient with the ignorant as he was with the learned," one person stated. "He treated all persons the same."

Besides his day-to-day reflections with people, his "fervorinos" at the Wednesday blessing, and his homilies at Mass, Solanus's desire to promote *The Mystical City of God* reflects his desire to help people come to know Jesus and Mary more deeply. When he could not help people sufficiently, as with Germans who needed instructions, he would find someone better versed.

The entries in a notebook he kept during his first assignment at Yonkers indicate Solanus's effort to instruct altar boys in the divine liturgy and respect for things holy is evident. His sermon notes at Yonkers show the same. As one of the sermons pointed out, "The more we learn to know of His divine majesty, the more we are drawn to reverence Him, to love Him, to adore Him. The more thoroughly we understand any of his works, the more we must admire the wisdom of the Creator."

The two volumes of letters written to his family and those who confided in him attest to the varied ways he instructed the ignorant. For example, he praised a wealthy couple who were considering paying for "the education of a candidate for the Holy Priesthood." Nevertheless, Solanus deferred to advice on the matter from the provincial of the province. Referring to the tradition of the province in instructing the ignorant, Solanus wrote:

I do know that the education of poor students and candidates has always been quite a problem in our educational institutions. Often some of the brightest and most promising students come from poor families and I am quite sure we have never as yet "turned down" [any] on account of financial shortage.

The third spiritual work of mercy — counseling — might be said to have characterized Solanus's very life. Although this has been treated at length throughout part 1, some examples are appropriate here.

Father Anthony Kerry, a diocesan priest who came to Solanus for counsel, says: "I think he tried to inculcate in the people a confidence and trust in God. I believe he also tried to instill in people the idea that our prayers could be answered even if it meant accepting suffering. He seemed to have an intuitive knowledge of those who would be helped and those who would have to bear suffering." Those who may have been "belligerent toward God because of their illnesses or ill-fated lives, he was able to turn about, and to accept God and accept the will of God."

Because of his wise counsel, all kinds of people (including other priests) came from near and far and at all hours to listen to his advice. "He was always available to the call of the people," one of his confreres noted. "I personally know that at times he would have been called at two o'clock in the morning. But whatever and whenever he was called, he was available without complaint." Uncomplaining about the demands made on him, Solanus brought peace and hope to those seeking his counsel. In a world that now has all sorts of "counseling techniques," one of his superiors commented:

He didn't have any special program for these people. He merely offered them spiritual advice and consolation urging them to prayer and the practice of faith and the reception of the sacraments. He carried out his activities with all types of people. There were no particular groups that came to him. Protestants came to him as well as Catholics. I certainly think that he made a great sacrifice of himself and of his time. I recall an instance in Huntington when there were several groups of people there and different parlors were filled. I happened to walk by and I didn't find Father Solanus in any of the parlors. Then I looked into another small room and there was Father Solanus with his head down on the desk taking a short rest. In other words, he literally was wearing himself out and he just took time to recoup his strength.

The chief way Solanus exercised his ministry of counseling was at the door at Yonkers, Harlem, the Lower East Side in New York, Detroit, Brooklyn, and Huntington. While some thought that Solanus's manifestation of the spiritual works of mercy was reflected primarily in his counsel, at least one other person believes his main ministry was in comforting those who came to him, especially those in trouble or experiencing sorrow. Often in his response to letters Solanus's compassion was evident in the way he referred to their situation as "pathetic," that is, evoking pity, sympathy, or compassion.

With some people, such as a nun experiencing various difficulties in her life and work, Solanus shared a poem called "Consolation," which was written by his brother Edward as a young man:

'Tis pain that purifies the human heart. Let this a gentle
     consolation be
When bright hopes fade and dearest friends depart and love itself
     seems but a memory.
The hours that fill the soul with silent grief, that flood it with
     unutterable woe
Become, when time hath given calm relief, the fountain whence a
     hundred virtues flow.
The mourner's tear hath furrowed kindly faces and left the light of
     love abiding there
Sweet sympathy and tender deeds are traces of pain and sorrow,
     soothed in silent prayer.
Christ wrought Redemption from despair and sin. By his dear Cross
     the clouds of grief
This Beth'lem and Calvary that win, from pain and sorrow, the seeds
     of heaven were riven.

In some ways counseling the doubtful and comforting the sorrowful paralleled each other, as is evident in the way Solanus counseled another nun who was encountering doubt and sorrow about a "failing" she had experienced. Two paragraphs of the letter evidence the way he tried to encourage her to hope:

My Dear Sister Mary Dorothy:

     God in His infinite wisdom and merciful power give you His peace! He will give it to you — sooner or later. He must have a purpose, however, in permitting you to fall, even like the rest of us. . . . He is the Master and the Judge, [who recognizes] the depth of our guilt and of our humiliation as well as how high above ourselves in His own good time He will raise us. Only we must have patience till he changes His attitude, because God is always figuring on our best. *"God condescends to use our powers if we don't spoil His plans by ours."* And all this even though we be stupid sinners. For that we all are, though the whole world proclaim us heroes and saints.

But why dear Sister be so anxious about tomorrow? The morrow like yesterday is in God's keeping. To worry about the past or the future is really to no purpose. Quite a different thing is to regret our blunders (God knows we have all made plenty of them) and humbly deplore them. But worry and fret? No. Because that's what hell wants us to do. Rather draw good out of them by praising God for His mercy to us and His infinite patience in not kicking to blazes us good-for-nothings.

The anxiety of the sister who received the letter from Solanus was eased by his comforting and insightful words. These reflected human as well as divine wisdom. This combination is evident in his understanding of the life stages of people who came to him for help. Thus, decades before people wrote of "the midlife crisis" in men and women, Solanus wrote to a woman experiencing depression: "As to that depressed feeling, etc., you complain of or lament, it may be from your age. It seems most women have an experience similar to what you describe, for a time after they are about forty-five." He noted that such women need to cultivate patience "with themselves and others. At all events," he concluded, "try and keep up courage and shake off anxiety as much as possible."

While many people experienced from him comfort in their psychological depression, others who experienced the loss of loved ones found that his consoling words strengthened them for a future without those they loved. This was true even when the loved one was a wife and mother of small children, or parents who lost a child, such as Mr. and Mrs. Frank Dineen.

The Dineens had a son, Jackie, whom they brought to see Solanus when the child was only a year old. He told them that their son would get better, and he did. However, two years later the boy died of whooping cough and pneumonia. As the mother explained it, the loss they experienced was assuaged by Solanus's comforting help:

I felt it was through the prayers of Father Solanus that he was left with us that long. I think it was all made much easier because of Father Solanus. He talked to us like, "Now you are not going to have him long. You will have him a little while, but you could not keep

him." Father Solanus made it more bearable. It was as if the Lord
prepared us that he loaned Jackie to us for a short time.

Solanus did not profess to have an answer to why children should suffer, much less be separated from their loving parents by death; however,
he deeply believed that somehow this too was part of God's merciful providence. Thus he wrote to his brother Owen and sister-in-law Martha at
the death of their young son that they might "confidently trust in God to
manifest someday a merciful design, not only in your case of such sorrow,
but in every case where he has permitted suffering in order that little children may come to him." Then, noting the connection with the Christmas
season, he concluded: "How happy you ought to be in reality this holy season! To have your little Owen, not only an altar boy, but one of the great
heavenly army of holy Innocents. In this thought... I console with you."

The fifth and sixth spiritual works of mercy invite Christians to bear
wrongs patiently and to forgive all injuries. Evelyn Cefai recalled: "I know
that he would tell the people [in the parish] and tell us, even if a person
has done something against you, pray for him, do not despise him, love
him. This was his constant teaching." While Solanus urged such mercy in
others, he also evidenced it in his own life the relatively few times such
incidents occurred. One of his superiors, in fact the one who told Solanus that he was to be transferred from his beloved Detroit on a day's
notice, recalled: "He never complained... about people who might have
harmed him in any way." Another witness has offered a possible reason
why Solanus was so merciful to those who may have harmed him: "As
far as forgiving people who might have injured him I don't think that he
would have ever considered himself having been injured by others. I think
he was so humble that he never took affront at anything that might have
been said or done to him."

In his middle years, especially in his early days at Detroit, his co-worker
(and boss) Brother Francis tested Solanus's forbearance to quite a degree.
One of Solanus's later superiors gives this account:

> Among the trials of Father Solanus were many humiliations arising
> from his work at the office. Much of it came from Brother Francis,
> who was really the chief porter of the monastery. Brother Francis was
> a very efficient person and couldn't stand Father Solanus's slow easy
> manner, letting people talk on, and letting people wait for hours to
> see him. He [Brother Francis] felt you had to keep people moving.
> He would scold Father Solanus before an office full of people, calling

him, "Casey," when he was piqued. Brother Francis would tell people that they could bring their enrollments to his desk and he could take care of them. Father Solanus would acquiesce and say that Brother Francis could enroll them also. Of course people would want to wait for Father Solanus and did so no matter how long it took. But it was a humiliation, and before all these people.[85]

In his later life the only friar who seems to have treated Solanus harmfully was Elmer Stoffel. Although he testified without any negative remarks about Solanus, Elmer often inveighed against him in varying ways while he lived. Elmer's accusatory remarks, however, "couldn't get him angry." On the contrary, as another confrere recalled: "I never knew Father Solanus to hold a grudge against a person. All of the people who have come in contact with him seem to consider him as a personal friend."

The final spiritual work of mercy involves praying for the living and the dead. For Solanus this came almost as naturally as breathing. "His life was almost a constant prayer," the doctor who attended Solanus in his last illness remarked. "He was uttering prayers with almost every sentence. It was 'Thanks be to God,' or 'If it pleases God,' or similar statements." For one whose life revolved around prayer, both as a Capuchin and as an individual, praying — including prayers for the living and dead — constituted his daily routine.

The first entry in his copy of the *Rule and Testament of St. Francis* carries this notation: "I labor for eternity, not $100 per day or $1,000 a month." This prayerful God-centeredness was clear in his novitiate notebook and continued until his dying breath, when he declared, "I give my soul to Jesus Christ."

He was raised in a family of faith, and prayer was the context for Solanus's life with his relatives. In a letter to his sister Margaret after the death of her son Frank, this underlying dynamic of prayer is assumed in varying ways for both the living (reconciliation) and the dead (for eternal life):

Remembrances of late have been whispering again and again of you and of poor dear Frank with your big family and prosaic handicaps and withal. Nevertheless [you have] your God-given faith to carry on in face of so many difficulties! Oh, the Faith!...

I wanted to tell you [about] our planning for months before poor, dear brother Guss died, in some way to smooth off the "friction" between him and someone else and about how beautifully the dear Lord took care of that for us. I felt all along that it was nothing more than a misunderstanding between them. Such it turned out to be, Deo Gratias. They both wrote me beautiful letters about it. In fact months before Guss got sick he wrote me asking prayers for the other party. Later on, shortly after his first operation and after the really beautiful understanding between them he wrote me again, quite resigned to the probability of what actually came [his death] and appealing to the Sacred [Heart] as his only source of hope of rescue. How beautiful. He died on the Feast itself.

Having experienced many deaths in his own family, Solanus made prayer for his relatives living and dead part of his daily routine. For those "straying the way of worldlings," he felt it would not be his "presence that will work anything worthwhile. Rather it will be someone's prayers." To his sister Margaret he wrote: "God bless you and yours. I hope this finds you all in good health and resigned to the cross [of] the recent bereavement God has seen fit to visit you with. Poor dear Frank Junior. In so many ways fortunate these days. 'R.I.P.'" Four years later Margaret and Frank lost another son, Edwin, after a long illness. Solanus's response testifies to his theological convictions about the afterlife (purgatory and heaven) and whether we pray "for" or "to" those who have died:

> I received your telegram of poor, long-suffering little Edwin. Confident that this was a happy transition rather than a death in the usual sense, I rather congratulate you on having such a chosen one to give to God, and consequently, on having one of your family in God's mercy, we hope. [This is] the second one to make intercession for the rest of us, still "viatores." Of course I nevertheless sympathize with you on the temporal loss and separation you must for some time expect to experience in his regard....
>
> Miss him? Indeed. And for a time and in a way perhaps more than you'd miss any of the others had someone else gone instead. Poor, dear Edwin! How often I have remembered our privileged little visit with him five years ago and wished I could visit him again and again! Well though, I think we can pray to him with good results; yet because it is easily possible too that he is still detained from the great, final Goal of the saints, it is no doubt our first duty to keep up our prayers for him and rather multiply them at least for a time. This I at least propose to do, with the help of our Guardian Angels and the grace of Almighty God.

In the midst of his own suffering Solanus prayed, and he urged others to pray in their own pain. He regularly remembered people in his prayer, especially at Mass. "God bless you and yours" was the regular way he began and/or closed his correspondence. In many of his letters, as well as in private conversations, he urged people to join him in praying for his and their conversions. Father Benedict Joseph Groeschel recalls: "He had a particular care that he often expressed for people who lived in countries where there was religious persecution, and he showed a great zeal in asking us to pray for these people, especially those who lived behind the Iron Curtain."

Solanus used people's gifts to him as reminders to pray for them. He encouraged people to "storm heaven" with prayers. He prayed for and in response to good weather, for relatives, for sinners, for the needy, for benefactors, for justice and peace, for the "triumph of God's church," and, above all, in thanks. He prayed with perseverance for everything, including perseverance. He considered Solomon's prayer for wisdom one of the outstanding prayers of history.

Having discerned his own vocation to the Capuchins during a novena, he urged prayer in discerning a vocation. To Brother Leo and the novices and candidates who wrote him name day greetings he replied:

> We hope and pray they all pray for vocations to multiply all over the world, in every Order and every society and phase of Catholic action. Thus they will at once be doing real missionary work and insuring their own holy vocation and perseverance therein. For no one who appreciates his vocation, as such a grace deserves, and is duly grateful, will fail to pray for a multiplication of further vocations.

He also prayed to and for the canonization of Father Stephen Eckert, who shared the same Capuchin vocation in the same province and, in fact, the same first ministry in Yonkers.

The Poor Souls were the objects of many of his prayers and devotions. His second notebook contains a page with reflections for a sermon entitled "For Poor Souls" on November 3, 1916, which reveals the theology of purgatory that guided him. Brother Ignatius remarks: "His concern for the souls in purgatory was very evident in the many letters that he wrote to people which I have read and studied quite thoroughly. This was something he would recommend in the event that someone was asking for a favor, that they should pray for the Poor Souls in purgatory." In his mind, the Poor Souls "hardly ever fail."

Solanus often encouraged people to pray for the Poor Souls, "to have

Masses said for them, and to enroll them in the Seraphic Mass Association." In addition, he prayed for the Poor Souls, and he prayed to them. Sister Mary Solanus Ufford, who was named after Solanus, recalls:

> He had a devotion to the souls in purgatory and urged it in others. He would tell us that if we, by our prayers and sacrifices, freed a soul from purgatory, we would then have another intercessor for us in heaven. I feel that this was like missionary work for him, to work for the souls in purgatory.

Because enrolling the Poor Souls was "missionary work" for Solanus, who had once thought of being a missionary, as he wrote to his brother Maurice Joachim:

> You've long since wanted to be a real missionary. So has your brother [Solanus]...who also wished indeed to be a missionary. When are we to start? Whither shall we turn to find a field wherein our zeal will be profitable to souls and appreciated? Shall we go to the ends of the earth, or shall we, convinced that charity, rightly ordered, begins at home? Shall we begin right in our own heart?

By enrolling the Poor Souls, he believed, they would become "missionaries with us." In this sense, a thin line existed between Solanus's devotion to the Poor Souls and his passion for the missions themselves. He noted: "Prayers for the missions and for the missionaries is mostly what they need."

The Corporal Works of Mercy

The missions and Solanus's involvement with them, especially through the Seraphic Mass Association (since 1988 the Capuchin Mission Association, CMA) linked the spiritual and corporal works of mercy for him. The very fact that Solanus himself toyed with different names for the SMA testifies to his effort to lay greater stress on people's loving financial support of the missions than their "buying" of SMA enrollments entitling them to remembrance in the Masses and prayers of Capuchins daily around the world.

For Solanus, membership in the SMA made one "indirectly a foreign missionary." Besides supporting the missions financially, he explained that "members of this association are asked to pray for our foreign missionaries and their work and for one another; those members of course who can pray. Also those who can afford to do so are asked to help with an offering of some kind besides by prayers and Masses."

Those coming to Solanus for help invariably heard him invite them first to do something more for God and God's people; usually the concrete expression of this would be their enrollment in the SMA. The Capuchin who served as provincial the last year of Solanus's life testified:

> He was known throughout the Order for his support of the Seraphic Mass Association. But I think it was not just the enrollment of the people in the Association that was important. I think he inspired them with a realization for the need of supporting the missions. I have been told by lay people that if they went to him and they didn't have the fifty cents or whatever the donation might have been at the time, that he would enroll them in the Association anyway. He would also promote in their minds the missions themselves. He also had a great belief in the efficacy of the value of the Mass and the prayers of the Association. This would be another reason why he would enroll them in the Association without an offering.

From the beginning of his portering ministry at Sacred Heart in Yonkers until the very end, Solanus promoted membership in the SMA. So great was his ministry promoting the SMA that in 1953 the minister general of the Capuchin Franciscans sent him a document of commendation for his service to the missions. His zeal for souls was legendary. It is safe to say that much of the present missionary effectiveness, and indeed, the overall provincial financial effectiveness of the Provinces of St. Joseph and St. Mary, still are due in large part to Solanus and his commitment to the missions through the CMA.

While Solanus exemplified all the corporal works of mercy and was involved directly in prison ministry (1922–23), without question he is most renowned for his concern for the sick and the poor. According to a diocesan priest who knew him well, Solanus's "chief apostolate was to the sick."

Fellow Capuchin Ignatius Milne was aware that Solanus's compassion and concern for those who were suffering "either physical, spiritual, emotional or mental difficulties" led him to "go out of his way to visit them at every opportunity he would have, very often taking what little free time he had outside of his work in the front office."

As early as Yonkers Solanus was called to people's homes when they were sick; they would ask for "the holy priest."[86] Later, in Detroit, Solanus usually led the weekly "Blessing for the Sick" on Wednesday. At other times he would be driven to hospitals and nursing homes to visit people there. Georgia Gietzen, whose husband he visited, remembered this incident:

> When my husband was in the hospital, I called Father and he told me not to worry, that my husband would be fine, and he would be down to see him in a couple of days. I didn't think my husband would live a couple of days for Father Solanus to get to see him, but my husband did live and Father Solanus did visit him.

Solanus also demonstrated his oft-stated adage that "charity, properly stated, begins at home" by the way he ministered to his own brethren who were ill. While he believed Capuchins were called to suffer and did not ask for their healing, he made a point of visiting the friars when they were ill. One of these was a brother who was not always charitable to Solanus, Brother Gerard. Cosmas Niedhammer recalls:

> Brother Gerard was an assistant to Father Solanus as Porter. He was a rather irascible person. He was very impatient at times too. He could be difficult to those who were under him. He was also very impatient with Father Solanus. The Office was supposed to close at 9:00 p.m. and sometimes Father Solanus would be talking to persons and would not be finished at 9:00 p.m. Brother Gerard would up-braid Father Solanus for being late. Later, Brother Gerard was in the hospital, suffering from cancer, and Father Solanus went to visit him. Brother Gerard was sitting in a chair. Father Solanus approached him, got down on his knees and kissed his hands.

Another Capuchin who received frequent visits from Solanus was his classmate Father Damasus Wickland. The two had spent years together in the clericate; now Damasus was blind. Many times Solanus could be seen taking his violin to play Irish songs in his friend's infirmary room. Capuchin Father Colman Boylan recalls that the two sat next to each other in the refectory:

> With patience and calmness, Father Solanus took the food that was being served by the novices. After he took his own meager portion, he then took all that Father Damasus could eat and put his food into his own dish. Then he would cut up all the large chunks of meat and potatoes into small pieces which would be easily edible so that Father

Damasus could enjoy his repast. This Father Solanus did at all meals during the two years I was with him stationed at St. Felix Friary.

When people died, Solanus made a point not only to pray for them, but to visit the home, bless the corpse, and console the families of the deceased. Whether bringing solace to families who lost loved ones during the First World War or enrolling the deceased in the Seraphic Mass Association, Solanus was known to be deeply solicitous of those who died.

The final, and perhaps the best-known manifestation of his expression of the corporal works of mercy involved his efforts to feed the hungry. While people recalled him giving food to the needy as early as his first ministry in Yonkers, it is his part in the creation and running of Detroit's Capuchin Soup Kitchen that is most remembered.

Previous to the establishment of the Soup Kitchen, "if somebody came to the friary door and was hungry, he would go into the kitchen and find some food for them." Father Cyril Langheim remembered "many occasions when he would go back into the kitchen and bring a bag of food from the refrigerator to give to some poor individual who needed it." Sometimes his sharing with the poor would be the actual food being prepared for the friars. If any friars objected, Solanus would simply remind them, "The poor have as much right to the food as we."

During the late 1920s, as the first signs of the Great Depression began in the car industry in Detroit, more and more people began appearing at the door, not just for counseling, but for food. At times there were as many as 150. As Capuchin Ignatius Milne explains:

When the Depression of 1929 came upon us, Father was very concerned about feeding the hungry. Because of the great numbers, he was not able to take care of this within the friary office and had asked the superiors to use the Third Order Hall located next to the monastery. He also got many businessmen to donate monies or donate supplies in order to feed the poor. Working with Father Herman Buss and the members of the Third Order of St. Francis, the Soup Kitchen was created. Soon thousands of people were being fed each day. While Solanus was not always there physically, Father Herman sensed his spiritual presence: "Even though he wasn't there all the time or directing the thing, through his holiness I believe he is the one who helped us to get help from Divine Providence. God was blessing the operation because we had a holy man right there."

Once established, Solanus "would go out and beg for the food in order to supply the Soup Kitchen." He "did a great deal to persuade farmers and companies to donate food for this particular work." Such people might be those whom he invited to "do something" in response to their request for help; others even included mayors of the area.[87]

Another who helped a great deal was Earl Eagen, whose farm was about forty miles northeast of Detroit. Often Solanus would join those going to the farm, praying at least one rosary and glorying in the beauty of creation on the way. Brother Ignatius remembers:

> Very often he accompanied the truck out into the country to bring home supplies from the farmers. Between the years 1940 and 1942 when I was stationed with Father Solanus at St. Bonaventure, he very frequently went out into the country to bring home these supplies. I would very often run into him as he got home late in the evening after spending the day in the country. I feel Father Solanus was generous in giving himself to others because I really feel that he knew he was serving Christ in other people, and had a genuine compassion to alleviate whatever sufferings they were enduring.

When he had the chance, Solanus would leave the front office and visit the people in the Soup Kitchen's lines. There he often heard stories about joblessness; consequently he would contact the many people he knew to try to find the unemployed good work.

In all he did Solanus reflected a life of mercy and compassion. He was bonded with others and they with him; together they were bonded with God. Truly society was improved and the world was made a bit better because he became a living witness to what he once wrote to a woman seeking his help:

> In the promotion of mutual and common charity, next to our happy dependence on Almighty God Himself, he has made us mutually dependent also on one another. And, incidentally, what a marvelously different society we would have here, and what an ideal world to live in if we all would keep in mind the assurance of Jesus, "What you have done to the least of my brethren, you have done to me."

Chapter 11

The Cardinal Virtues

In reflecting on how the cardinal virtues of prudence, justice (toward God and human beings), fortitude, and temperance were exemplified in Solanus Casey's life from the perspective of what others said of him and from his own writings, one must go beyond the words to the values they represent. The reason is that no references for "fortitude" and "temperance" exist among his writings. Except for just two references to "prudence," the only cardinal virtue to receive extended comments from Solanus himself was "justice." However, while Solanus Casey may not have elaborated in writing on their theological nuances, his life manifested each virtue quite clearly.

Prudence

In a 1937 letter to his sister Margaret, Solanus asked her to pray that he might learn "something more of prudence." While it is quite clear that Solanus Casey was gifted in the area of supernatural prudence, he recognized his need for growth in natural prudence. He admired St. Frances Xavier Cabrini, for example, for her prudence. In the testimonies the vast majority of witnesses indicated Solanus's virtue of prudence without making any distinctions between supernatural prudence and its human form. Some believed he excelled in both kinds of prudence, an equal number distinguished between the way the "natural" and "spiritual" prudence were expressed in his life, and two testified directly that Solanus may have been lacking in *human* prudence. The reason for the distinctions made here is that this is the one area where some questions, even though they be minuscule, may exist regarding Solanus's practice of virtue.

Specifically, these questions relate to concerns about his promotion of *The Mystical City of God* to some people rumored to be unable to understand and/or afford the volumes, his support of those who might have

217

capitalized on his friendship (as some suspected of Ray Garland), or his objectivity when he was too close to a situation (as with his psychologically impaired brother, Maurice). In these cases it is important to distinguish between divine (supernatural or spiritual) prudence and human prudence. While no one raised the possibility that he was not gifted with the former, a few did raise the question whether he might lack some of the latter, given his tendency to believe in people's good will, to give them "the benefit of the doubt." In the examination of these questions in the paragraphs below it is good to recall, as did one of the Capuchin witnesses who testified about these concerns, that Solanus's human "simplicity counteracted any human imprudence" he may have shown.

Some have questioned whether Solanus exercised enough prudence regarding *The Mystical City of God,* not so much in his promotion of it but in the way Ray Garland, the distributor of the volumes, may have capitalized on it. Although we will not reiterate what has been explained already, their testimony cannot be overlooked. Rupert Dorn, who later became a provincial in the province, testified to his conviction that Solanus had spiritual or supernatural prudence as well as human prudence. Yet he recalled other unnamed "superiors" who "questioned his recommendation to the people to read *The Mystical City of God.* Sometimes I think that the people thought he imposed an obligation upon them, perhaps to buy the book, and this might have created some problem." While no obligation was ever imposed, and no record of *any* kind of complaint has been recorded for anything he asked, one can understand how people might misinterpret a recommendation as a demand. Father Rupert Dorn's reflections were echoed by Monsignor Edward J. Hickey, who was chancellor of the Archdiocese of Detroit. He testified that the chancery did receive "a few" complaints about Ray Garland's sale of the volumes. These were twofold:

> First about the cost of the book. I believe that the people were being charged in the neighborhood of $24.00. The archbishop felt that perhaps those who were publishing the book [i.e., Ray Garland] were charging too much money. The complaint was not directly against Father Solanus in the sale of the book, but only indirectly insofar as he was advising the people to read the book. The second part of the archbishop's objection was that he did not personally approve of *The Mystical City of God,* and he felt that the people who read it might become upset in their own spiritual life, and rather imagine that they were having their own visions or revelations.

As agent of the archbishop, Monsignor Hickey visited Solanus's superior about the matter. The actions taken by the provincial and guardian were decisive. Solanus wholeheartedly adhered to his superiors' decisions, which included his transfer to Brooklyn, even though he probably believed in his heart that Ray Garland had not abused their relationship.

Father Rupert also noted that some people *might* have questioned whether "the human advice" Solanus gave to married couples was always prudent.[88] However, as chancellor, Monsignor Hickey never heard any complaints and, on the contrary, recalled "the good advice" that was given to people by Solanus. His counsel to all people seemed "to fit" the situation and problem at hand.

Solanus — like millions of others — was an early supporter of Father Charles Coughlin, the "Radio Priest." Both were initial supporters of Roosevelt's "New Deal" and staunchly anti-Communist. In the early days Solanus once (in 1937) referred to the Detroit-based priest as "our prophet." For his part, Coughlin considered Solanus a "heroic priest." The Coughlin-Casey connection has been discussed elsewhere; no evidence has been shown indicating any support for Coughlin once the latter became anti-Semitic in his writings and speeches. However, a further rationale for Solanus's indebtedness to his "friend" can be found in Coughlin's involvement in a Capuchin and Casey family difficulty in 1939. Solanus's psychologically unstable brother, Maurice, had gone to the seminary, dropped out because of depression, lived in depression, then reentered the seminary. He was ordained a diocesan priest, decided to join the Capuchins, and was received (as Maurice Joachim) but not allowed into the First Order. He remained as a Third Order member for about ten years, and then left disenchanted. He wandered around until he found his way to an asylum in Baltimore, and ended his days in a small hospital in Minnesota.

Maurice Joachim became frustrated with his life in the Capuchins in 1939. He left St. Anthony's Monastery in Wisconsin and went to Detroit, the provincialate of the Capuchins. But instead of going directly to St. Bonaventure's, he went to Royal Oak, the Detroit suburb where Father Charles Coughlin served as pastor. Solanus recalled that his "friend" served as a kind of mediator between Maurice and the Capuchin provincial. A meeting was arranged at the provincialate with the provincial, a kind of apology was made, and Maurice received a "letter of 'exit.'"

Because of Coughlin's personal help in easing this truly difficult situation, which sapped much of Solanus's energy at the time, it is understandable that Solanus did not cut off all connections to him (and this was never asked). However, it seems that after 1939 little contact occurred between the two. Furthermore, despite their friendship Solanus never publicly or privately indicated support for Coughlin's political positions. He was able to walk the thin line between support for the person and non-support of his actions.

Gerald Walker, who served as Solanus's provincial in the last years of his life, recalled the criticism he received because Solanus wasn't "hard and harsh enough with sinners." Gerald explained: "I think perhaps he won more by his kindness and his compassion than he did by being difficult. I do not believe that he ever would have encouraged anyone to remain in sin, or to have compromised any principles. I just feel that his dealing with these people was a prudent way of doing it."

The source of Solanus's gift of prudence was his faith and confidence in God. This prudence was expressed in the kind of advice he gave to the many people who came to him. Mrs. Regina Devlin shares her experience of Solanus's prudence

> in the advice that he gave and the way that he gave it. For example, my brother-in-law was ill. We went to Father Solanus to ask for his help. He did not give us the encouragement that my brother-in-law, George Devlin, would get better. He did tell us that he did not think that George would need the surgery, which was the point at issue when we went to see him. But he also left us with the impression that perhaps George would not survive. But at the same time he put it in such a way that we gained great strength from the words that he said to us. George did die in about six weeks, and yet we were somewhat prepared for it.

Because of this and other experiences, Mrs. Devlin concluded: "I feel that in all his dealings with us in counseling us that he was always prudent." Her thoughts about Solanus's counseling and prudence were shared by many. Mrs. Dorothy Fletcher, in a situation similar to Mrs. Devlin's, recalls:

> I think that Father Solanus was a man of prudence. I think he showed it in the way he counseled people. I know he did not give people false hopes, that is, to encourage them to expect a cure, or a miracle, when he knew that they should rather be preparing themselves to die. I known in the instance of my own father, I had asked Father Solanus to pray for him, and my father spoke to Father Solanus on the phone.

In speaking to him, Father Solanus urged him to pray for a happy death. Eventually my father did die a happy death, and realized that this was what he should have been praying for. I feel that as a result of Father Solanus's talking to my father that he had properly prepared him for that.

Because so many women came to see him, Solanus needed to exercise great prudence lest his dealings with them be questioned. One time a woman came to the office who had some sort of affliction on her thigh. In asking Solanus for a blessing, she gave "an indication that she was going to pull her skirt up so that he could touch it, but Father Solanus stopped her and said he didn't need that, that his blessing could go through the garment." Except for rare occasions when the situation demanded utter privacy, his dealings with women (as well as men) were conducted in the open. At all times he was careful and circumspect with the opposite sex. While a kind of shyness with women was noted, in reality, he probably treated them no differently than anyone else.

Another way Solanus maintained his integrity was the way he honored confidentiality; he never spoke of what transpired between him and his counselees. Sister Dolora Brogan recalls that, despite the many people he met each day, Solanus maintained his prudence by being "very circumspect in what he said. He never repeated or never in any way insinuated what had been told to him or what he picked up through the conversation of other people."

Solanus prudently sought the advice of others when he did not know how to respond to situations. Sometimes this meant consulting priests regarding theological or moral cases of complexity. Other times he contacted doctors. Regarding doctors, the Archdiocese of Detroit did receive one unsigned complaint from a doctor through the Catholic Physicians Guild. The "complaint was that when one of the physicians made a recommendation for a patient to go to the hospital, Father Solanus would, on occasion, advise against that." Whether or not this is true was not substantiated. Furthermore, while he was known to have said things like "do what the doctor says," he never was known to give rash advice. This does not mean, however, as we know from other stories pertaining to Solanus's gift of discernment, that he always necessarily agreed with the human opinion of all doctors.

For instance, Sister Mary Solanus Ufford recalled that Solanus once counseled a sister in her community to change doctors. Because Solanus did not know the doctor, Sister Solanus thought this was strange advice. Yet "it turned out that the sister did change doctors, and her condition improved." Because people hung on his every word, had confidence in everything he said, and told of feeling better and more committed because of his counsel, prudence was a *sine qua non* for Solanus. Father Benedict Joseph Groeschel points out:

> Considering the reputation and fame of Father Solanus and the num-ber of visitors and letters that he received, it was very important for him to practice the virtue of prudence. He could easily have become carried away by the immense number of calls that he received. In-stead, he seemed always to fit everything into the schedule and tried to practice moderation. Although he was pained when he was not able to see people...he expressed no rebellion or even judgment on the decision of the superior. When he was ridiculed in some small way, there was apparently no response at all to this kind of behavior. It was perhaps the most prudent thing simply to ignore it, although he did not do this in any way that was judgmental to the others. I never observed anything in his behavior contrary to the virtue of prudence.

While Benedict Joseph noted that Solanus never responded to ridicule, it is equally true that he never was an occasion of injury or ridicule regard-ing anyone else. This was probably because of the great sense of charity that characterized his relations with all people. Thus it can be said that Solanus, despite possible slights in prudence from a human perspective, certainly manifested the gift of prudence, its supernatural expression, in his ap-proach to others. Whether or not he exercised human prudence in the unstinting way he served others or the way he treated his own body may be another question. Despite his "jogging"[89] and "health foods," it may be questioned if he, like Francis, always took proper care of his own needs.

Justice

From his writings, it seems that Solanus was fond of the quotation from Jeremiah about God's justice:

> Thus says the Lord: Let not the wise man glory in his wisdom and let not the strong man glory in his strength, and let not the rich

man glory in his riches. But let him that glories, glory in this, that he understands and loves me, for I am the Lord that exercises mercy and judgement, and justice in the earth. For these things please me, says the Lord. (Jer 9:22–23)[90]

As early as 1922 Solanus wrote of God's "eternal justice" and humans as living in a world wherein those people who were "bitterly hostile to justice and truth are hostile to God Himself who is eternally both." If justice can be considered "giving all their due," Solanus practiced this virtue in a significant way. Whether these "all" were other human beings who became his concern or his concern for the way they would come to God, the words of Capuchin Cosmas Niedhammer ring true:

I believe that Father Solanus practiced the virtue of justice. I know he tried to give to everybody his due. For instance, the office could be crowded but he never hurried one person in order that he might let the other persons get in sooner. He dedicated himself to the needs of the person who was talking to him at the time. He never hurried their visits. I would like to state that he also gave God all that was due to Him. His love of God was exceedingly great. He would be the first to rise in the morning and to be in Choir usually before the rest of us. And...he would be found in the chapel at night. I even observed him once playing his violin before the Blessed Sacrament. This was his way of showing his particular love of God.

Justice was not just his way of showing his love for God; love was his way of ensuring people their rights as well. Conversely, his very practice of justice was evident in everyone's love for Solanus.

Solanus's Justice toward God

Not because of any obligation, but out of love, Solanus was intent on giving God what was due God, namely, his life, thoughts, and actions. Because "God was the center of his life," he therefore "always tried to fulfill what was pleasing to God and to obey all of his commands." A layman recalled, "I believe in regard to justice he gave to God what was his due. I know in speaking with Father Solanus, almost the first thing he would talk about would be God. God in his life was number one. He, therefore, I believe, gave to God what was his due."

Solanus found that fidelity to the common life and spiritual exercises of the Capuchins was a key way to return to God the good shown him. One witness summed up what many said: "Father Solanus's whole purpose in life was to fulfill the will of God." Solanus was convinced that the Rule and Constitutions and the province's *horarium* specified that divine will for him. James Maher believed that Solanus "became a religious in order that he might do God's will and do it to the fullest." For Solanus, obedience to his religious superiors was due them as representatives of God, to whom all obedience was due. This did not mean that he did not indicate his own desires, however, as one witness testified regarding Solanus's request of his superior to serve in a local parish on weekends:

> Father Cefai...was the pastor of the Maltese parish that existed in Detroit at that time, and he went to the monastery seeking weekend help. The superior at that time was Father Marion, and he responded that he had no one that he could send to Father Cefai. He said that he had priests but they were too old to go out on such work. Just at that moment Father Solanus happened to come in from outdoors. He immediately knelt down and kissed the hem of the superior's habit and asked for a blessing, according to the usual custom of the Capuchin order. Father Cefai asked Father Solanus, "Would you help me by coming on weekends and saying two Masses on Sunday?" Father Solanus said that he did not go out. He asked him in front of Father Marion if Solanus was willing in case he received permission. Father Solanus indicated he would be willing. Thus cornered, the superior acceded to his request. So Father Solanus obeyed his superior and helped Father Cefai for a period of almost seven years.

While people would give Solanus credit for the good that came to them through his prayers and compassion, Solanus knew that any good he did for others had to be credited to God. Solanus "always tried to do what was pleasing to God," "encouraged others to give to God that which was His due," and "always himself gave credit to God for all the things that happened," says Dorothy Fletcher. She recalls that "one time I called him when he was in Huntington to pray for me, for an intention of mine. He said, 'Dorothy, you can pray to the Lord,' indicating that it wasn't through Father Solanus but from God that the favors would come."

Solanus maintained fidelity to the assignments given him by his superiors by being conscientious in the duties of his office. Since his main ministry was to counsel people, he communicated the need to be faithful to God to the people coming to see him. "I believe in regard to God, Father Solanus certainly practiced the virtue of justice," one regular visitor recalled. "I am sure that he always sought to do what was pleasing to God and fulfill His will. It was that spirit that he instilled in us, the people to whom he spoke. He made us feel that we had an obligation to serve God in the same way."

While Solanus did not always show great concern about the monies themselves that people sent for SMA enrollments or for Masses, "he was particularly scrupulous about the offering of Masses for the intentions that he was given. He kept very careful records of donations that were sent to the Seraphic Mass Association, and took a great deal of time in responding to the benefactors." So much of his time was devoted to responding to benefactors, we have seen, that he needed full-time secretaries. When people criticized God for unanswered prayers, Solanus would "defend" God by "showing to them that God was, indeed, a Just Person."

The unique way that Solanus gave God proper due was by his continual thanksgiving. While the dimension of gratitude connected to hope has been discussed in the section entitled "Hope" above, it might be said that Solanus considered gratitude something *owed* God; thanksgiving flowed from him naturally. Gerald Walker, his former provincial, declared that thanksgiving to God was Solanus's way of showing justice:

> Any good thing that ever happened to him was always answered with, "Thanks be to God...." I believe, that whatever happened to him, he saw it as coming from the will of God, and he would be willing to accept it. I think even if he fell and broke his leg he would say "Thanks be to God" because it was the will of God that he should have broken his leg at that time.

Solanus's Concern about Justice among Peoples

It is a truism about Solanus that "because of his great love for God he would in turn have to be just in regard to his fellow man." If he showed his justice toward God through his thanksgiving, this same gratitude was expressed toward the Order that nourished him and was shown to those benefactors who helped him and his concerns. Sister Cecilia Eagen, daughter of the farmer who gave to the Soup Kitchen, remembers his gratitude: "He certainly was grateful to his benefactors. I know he made us feel that whenever we gave him food for the poor that we were really doing something worthwhile, and he certainly demonstrated his gratitude for all that we did." "He was grateful for anything that you ever did for him, no matter how small it might have been," another benefactor recalled. "We used to bring him hard candy because we knew he liked to give this candy to the children who would come to see him. He would be most grateful for this small favor that we had done for him."

Solanus's gratitude toward his benefactors could not be demonstrated in a material or financial way, so he oftentimes "showed it by his prayers and spiritual favors that he did for these people." His justice toward others was also shown in the very way he dealt with all people and, especially, his readiness to serve them. "He literally poured himself out for the people. He was available to them at all times."

Solanus viewed the cofounder of his province, Francis Haas, as "zealous for justice." Faithful to that justice that had come to characterize the province, Solanus once noted: "If we are to be considered children of God, we must pursue justice and peace." "Have you ever fathomed the fact," he asked, "that every crime against justice is at once an outrage on truth and an act of idolatry?"[91]

Solanus's concern for justice was not limited to the world beyond the friary walls; for him, it had to be found within as well. In one of the longest letters extant, Solanus wrote an extended argument to a provincial in favor of one of the brothers whom he felt had not received "a fair deal" from a local guardian.

As early as his first assignment in Yonkers, Solanus manifested deep concerns about social justice. He seems to have studied seriously the social teachings of Leo XIII. In 1917 he quoted the pope as saying: "Our lot has been cast in an age that is bitterly opposed to justice and truth," and again, "The social problem is not a question of charity or of donations but a question of right and of fundamental Christian justice."

Solanus's first known concrete effort at promoting issues of justice came in the same year. The incident involved the "unreasonable and unjust eviction" of the Graymoor Sisters from their property after they converted to Catholicism. Despite this being done by Anglicans, he wrote the sisters before the eviction was finalized: "I am fully confident that there are too many upright lovers of justice even among our separated brothers and sisters...ever to hold their peace while an act of such injustice was perpetrated as would be perpetrated should your community be ejected from Graymoor." Eight months later, another letter to Reverend Mother Lurana, the head of the Order, indicated the deed had been done. To Solanus, this action was a "farce against common justice and charity," which invited the sisters to be consoled and encouraged "at all events [by] the words of our

Divine Master, 'Blessed are ye when they shall revile you and persecute you...unjustly for my sake.'"

Commitment to the cause of justice, for Solanus, also involved solidarity with the "Irish Cause." The grandson of a man killed by the British while defending the Blessed Sacrament, Solanus followed the Irish Rebellion of 1916 with great interest.

For him, the Irish cause and the justice of God were intertwined. The editors of a newspaper noted of Solanus in 1922: "An Irish American by birth, he is zealously devoted heart and soul to the Irish Republican cause. He frequently expressed to us the view that that cause cannot fail because it has arrayed on its side God's justice which must prevail in the end." However, his commitment to the Irish cause made Solanus wary of any individuals who might seek aggrandizement. In this he found the quotation from "the dear Carmelite Father McGinnis, now General of his whole Order" apropos: "The moment a man or a machine or an organization or a clique gets bigger than the cause, get away from any or all of them because they have ceased to be of any good and have begun to do harm no matter what the past record of any or all of them be."

As Solanus's concern about the "Irish Question" and the justice issues connected with it grew, he prayed about it and wrote very clear and strong letters to the editor of various papers about the issues involved. In these letters, as elsewhere, he was not afraid to speak "his mind on justice issues." Believing that the mainstream press was "bitterly hostile to justice," his letters appeared in the Irish press in New York. While chastising the occupying forces in Ireland, he prayed that "the honest members" of the groups supporting the Irish cause would be blessed with a sense of "unselfish justice and consistency and unaffected charity."

Solanus's letters on the Irish issue attest to the debating skills he learned as a young man. His arguments indicate clearly reasoned positions and a keen ability to challenge people he considered unsupportive of the Irish cause or not supportive enough. Among the latter, at least in one letter, were the bishops of Buffalo and Baltimore. On the other hand, he was very willing to praise a bishop like Michael J. Gallagher of Detroit for being supportive; as Solanus remarked, he "undoubtedly loves Ireland and justice."

While justice issues related to Ireland were concerns for Solanus in the teens and 1920s, justice for workers and others deprived of their livelihood became his preoccupation during the Depression of the 1930s. With so many people without work, Solanus, like many others, was initially attracted to Detroit's Father Charles Coughlin. As "one who first tried to promote the idea of social justice, [who] favored the laboring class, the development of unions to protect their rights and that type of thing," Solanus became "a supporter of Father Coughlin."

Parting with Coughlin after he became anti-Semitic, Solanus became a staunch anti-Communist in the post–World War II period and the 1950s when there were so many "perverters of truth and justice" whose materialism and atheism made them "little better than fools." He found that the increasing atheism connected with that period was characterized by a disregard for the claims of "justice and truth." He believed it would incur the "avenging sword of justice." More specifically, he cared deeply about the imprisonment of Catholics in China and churchmen like Cardinal Jozsef Mindszenty. He wrote:

> It is hard to reckon the extent of modern martyrdom the church has suffered these several decades and probably less possible to surmise what seems still shortly to follow, the judgement awaiting enemies of Truth as the glory reserved for those who will have persevered, suffering for justice, for Truth.

Solanus did not find atheism in China or Eastern Europe only. It seems a doctor friend of his, William Koch of Deaconess Hospital, was involved in some actions pertaining to justice that were getting him in trouble with people Solanus considered atheists. Solanus also wrote about another doctor's cause and the sacrifices he endured. These "flagrant injustices" against Dr. Kraus arose from his fight against the activities which he saw opposed to "the very principles of *justice and truth — of religion against atheism*."

With the Cold War raging during the mid-1950s, Solanus became more concerned about the need to pray for world peace and for guidance in how to attain it. In this he was inspired by Pope Pius XII, whom he considered "so imbued with a love of peace... of truth and of justice." He copied the "Prayer for Peace" being promoted by the Archdiocese of Detroit and shared it:

PRAYER FOR PEACE

> Almighty and Eternal Father, God of wisdom and mercy, whose power exceeds all force of arms and whose protection is the strong defense of all who trust in Thee; enlighten and direct, we beseech Thee, those who bear the heavy responsibility of government throughout the world these days of stress and trial. Grant them the strength to stand firm for what is right and the skill to dispel the fears

of discord. Inspire them to be mindful of the horrors of atomic war for victor and vanquished alike, to seek conciliation in truth and in patience. To see in every man a brother so that the people of all nations may, in this our day, enjoy the blessings of a just and lasting peace. Conscious of our own unworthiness, we implore thy mercy on a sinful world in the name of thy Divine Son, the Prince of Peace, and through the intercession of his Blessed Mother and all the Saints. Queen of All Saints, pray for us. Queen of the Holy Rosary, pray for us. Queen of Peace, pray for us.

Solanus noted that those pursuing justice would be persecuted. Yet he noted, "As we see in the lives of the saints it is only after many a battle and a long struggle with ourselves and against the injustices of the world" that we come to learn the "sweetness that patient suffering unfailingly brings in the end, often long before the end." In the meantime, though, the other virtue that sustains people in their martyrdom is the virtue of fortitude.

Fortitude

When Solanus Casey was still in simple vows his notebook contains an entry indicating that he had made an "indignant remark," which was followed by consolation when he "acknowledged my fault." He then notes the contrast between Saints Athanasius and Basil and concludes with a strange comment: "Fortitude in different colors...."

Fortitude was expressed in "different colors" in Solanus's life, both in his early formation and in his later years.

> He must have had the virtue of fortitude to survive the difficulties he had as a young man at home on the farm, the problems that he had with his studies, and at least persevering to the point of being ordained a priest. I would think he showed fortitude in fulfilling his office as porter in the difficulties that he had to put up with in merely doing that work, and the long hours that he spent in the office listening to the problems of the people.

This section examines areas in which Solanus Casey exemplified the virtue of fortitude. These examples, plus the exemplary way he practiced long-suffering with his various illnesses and his manner of death, testify to the heroic way he lived out this virtue.

Barney Casey's first teachers in fortitude were his pioneering parents. Although in his early years he changed from job to job, once "called," Barney put "his hand to the plow" and did not look back (Luke 9:62). While some might falter when their initial dreams seem shattered — as happened when Barney Casey was told that he would not be able to be a diocesan priest — Barney sought counsel, prayed, and remained committed to proceed with what he sensed his vocation might be. Once in the Capuchins, excepting for the one period of doubt experienced in the postulancy, it seems Solanus Casey courageously proceeded to live his life, despite any obstacles.

Within the first year of his life with the Capuchins, Solanus Casey's fortitude was put to the test when he was required to sign a statement attesting to the fact that he joined "the Order of the Capuchins in the Province of St. Joseph with the pure intention to follow thus my religious vocation." In addition, he would "leave it to my superiors to judge" whether or not he was suitable for priestly studies. This was further tested three years later before he took final vows when he had to reiterate his submission to the will of his superiors vis-à-vis his possible future as a priest. Finally it was put to the test before his ordination when he discovered that he would never be able to hear confessions or preach formal sermons. His response? There was never once the slightest complaint about this, nor later about anything else.

Referring to St. Thomas, one witness testified that, for Solanus, fidelity to the Rule was his long form of martyrdom. Even when he was in his seventies and eighties Solanus "did not ask to be excused from the practices of the house, or the discipline of the house, or the observance of choir.... If there was any relaxation on his part of the Rule, it was always at the command of the superior that he should take more rest or eat more food." He accepted all assignments and duties without complaint. This uncomplaining attitude carried over to the way he lived in community, exercised his ministry, and accepted transfers. Father Benedict Joseph Groeschel, who was a Capuchin novice at St. Felix in 1951, recalled one way Solanus exercised fortitude in community living:

> Father Solanus never complained. When we were novices, we were aware that the superior was rather severe on all of the professed friars, and that Father Solanus was treated with the same severity. In fact, we would have thought it unthinkable that he would have complained. Some friars engaged in harmless humor about the su-

perior, but Father Solanus never participated in any of this humor. He seemed simply to accept things as they came. To my knowledge there was no violation of this virtue of fortitude. Solanus never complained about his superiors. Further, when he experienced rejection of himself or his ideals, he remained silent. The same could be said of how he accepted ridicule. While most of this was not hostile, such as comments about his violin playing, Solanus took it all in stride.

In his active ministry Solanus sought to fulfill his tasks joyfully and readily. Despite his long hours in the office, he did not complain. While this has been discussed at length in other contexts, those hours "he spent in the office just doing his job is evidence of his practice of this virtue [fortitude]. Sometimes he put in eighteen hours a day. All of these hours were not spent in seeing the people. Long after he saw the people, he would spend his time in writing letters to those who had written him."

One laywoman who testified believed that God had to be the source of Solanus's virtue of fortitude: "He must have had the fortitude from God to fulfill the job that he did. He would be in that office as late as 10 o'clock at night listening to the people and consoling them in their troubles. He always seemed to be so joyful in the work that he did. He was always present there in the office." In the office, with the people, he maintained confidence and courage and encouraged these manifestations of fortitude in others.

Solanus practiced what he preached about fortitude in the way he accepted his transfer from Detroit to Brooklyn, at the height of his fame. "When he was transferred to another Friary, he never complained and prepared to go immediately," one witness testified. "This was true particularly after he was transferred away from Detroit where he had been for so many years and where he had made so many acquaintances or friends, or at least spiritual friends, but he did not complain about this transfer."

Throughout his life, Solanus Casey accepted all difficulties in stride, including illness and physical problems. Solanus experienced physical suffering, including respiratory problems and a high-pitched voice, which resulted from his childhood bout with black diphtheria. While he was in New York, Solanus had some kind of gangrenous infection but quietly bore the pain. As he recalled the episode: "I had been in agony for at least forty hours, though no one else seemed to know it, and while I tried to thank God for it all, my principal prayer — at least a thousand times repeated — was 'God help us.'"

While he seems to have experienced normal aches and pains during his middle years, his seventies and eighties found him facing increased suffering. Accepting all of these sufferings from God, he offered them back to God. "I remember Father Solanus saying, 'If courage is half of the battle, confidence in God is victory assured.' I would say that he accepted whatever problems came his way because he didn't consider difficulties a problem but rather a privilege. He felt whatever came his way he could offer up to God."

When he was seventy-five years old, having been at Detroit from 1924 until 1945, Solanus's health problems, especially with his legs, as well as difficulties discussed before with the promotion of *The Mystical City of God,* resulted in his transfer to Brooklyn. Father Michael Cefai was one of those concerned that something be done to preserve his health:

> I knew of the terrible condition of his varicose veins. His legs were encrusted with scales and he had a blood infection. He never complained. I knew he would never excuse himself from seeing anyone as long as he was assigned at the monastery. I, therefore, asked the chancellor that Father Solanus be transferred from Detroit. As much as I wanted to keep Father Solanus, I thought he was being crunched down by the demands of the people and I was concerned for his survival. He was then transferred to Brooklyn, New York.

The year he spent at St. Michael's in Brooklyn seems to have been relatively free of sickness. However, when he moved to St. Felix in Huntington in late spring, 1946, the combination of age and skin problems increased rapidly.[92] "Solanus never bothered others about his sicknesses," Capuchin Ignatius Milne (who lived with him) commented. "He often tried to take care of them himself. He did not want to be a burden to others in this regard. He never asked to go to a doctor. He usually went to the doctor only after some of his confreres would see his problems and bring them to the attention of the superior."

According to Father Blase Gitzen, who once served as Solanus's secretary at Huntington, the friars who lived with him, and who knew him well, could tell Solanus was not feeling well only when he changed some of his habits, such as walking up and down the stairs instead of running. Father Blase also noted an incident in 1949, when Solanus returned to Huntington from Milwaukee, where he had gone for a celebration of the unveiling of the statue of the Servant of God Stephen Eckert. After dinner "a couple dozen affected by ptomaine poison[ing]," including Solanus, had to be hospitalized. Upon his return, Father Blase noticed Solanus walking very deliberately up the stairs to his room. "I noticed something was wrong with his feet and legs."

> After a bit of persuasion he finally let me look at them and they were as raw as a piece of meat. We bathed the sox off and sent him at once to...the hospital in Fort Wayne. There the doctors recognized the seriousness of his condition. Fearing the loss of blood circulation, they prepared an operation room for probable amputation. Every three minutes a nurse checked his circulation....
>
> His attitude toward his illness was one of such lack of concern, that I was curious whether he knew how seriously ill he had been and brought up the subject on the way home from the hospital. Yes, he knew that his legs might have to be amputated, but he had the attitude: "If they come off, it was alright; if not, that was alright, too." He showed absolutely no shock, surprise, worry or upset.[93]

As he recalled his experience at the hospitals in Milwaukee for the food poisoning and in Fort Wayne for the feet problem, he wrote that while it was "to nature a very unpleasant experience; but thanks be to God! I feel that my soul profited greatly by the experience." He continued: It was a "bitter pill that turned to sweetness of soul and body," as St. Francis tells us in the holy Rule, with regard to his personal experiences with the poor, dear lepers of his day, and as many chaplains and soldiers tell of what they went through in the Second World War.

While Solanus had these extreme problems in the decade he spent at Huntington, for any other problems he may have had he often relied on self-medication, probably "to conceal these things so that he wouldn't be taken away from the work that he had to do with the people." One of these home remedies was something "he teasingly called 'the good Irish medicine.'" Made by his benefactors, it consisted of flax seed, simmered all day, honey, lemon juice, and whiskey.

Increasingly the seriousness of his sicknesses demanded hospitalization. In 1955 he was admitted to a hospital for bronchial pneumonia and congestive heart failure. In the next years the varicose veins and arteriosclerotic vascular disease of his legs advanced. This caused poor blood circulation and resulted in an edema.

According to Father Rupert Dorn, when Father Solanus returned to Detroit, primarily for doctoring: "His skin was literally raw; he must have suffered a great deal and yet he bore it very patiently and without complaint." This attitude toward his suffering characterized his whole life. Brother Pius Cotter, who made a habit of closely scrutinizing Solanus, recalled that he manifested fortitude "particularly in regard to some of his illnesses. You could tell that he was in pain. He almost had the look on his face of asking the Lord, 'How much more can I accept?' and yet he would never outwardly complain about these problems." Sometimes, as on the Sunday before Lent in 1957, he asked for "the good Irish medicine" to relieve the pain.

Solanus was hospitalized on May 15, 1957, for erysipelas, a severe and toxic skin disease. He was treated, improved, and returned to St. Bonaventure's. However he was readmitted on July 2, 1957, with a recurrence of erysipelas. The admitting doctor states:

> At that time he had a severe penicillin reaction with exfoliative dermatitis, and he had a questionable myocardial infarction. He also had chronic arteriosclerotic kidney disease with uremia, that is, nephrosclerosis. The difficulty on his second admission, that is in July, was that he did not respond to treatment with various antibiotics. I think his immune system was expended. I don't think even the newer antibiotics that we have today would have had any effect.

The doctor realized that Solanus knew death was impending and prayed frequently. Yet he "was not disturbed or upset by the thought of death. I might say that his whole life was a life of prayer." This prayerful attitude fortified him in his last days as well, despite his great pain. His attitude of thanksgiving, which accompanied him during life, also attended the suffering he experienced as he was dying. Father Gerald recalls:

> He was thanking God for it. He was totally disposed whenever God wanted him. One of the priests who visited him in the hospital had told him that we were praying for him, and said "Wouldn't it be nice" if he died just before the feast of the Portiuncula, which is August 2. Father Solanus said: "I don't want to die on the Portiuncula or any other feast. I want to die when God is ready for me to die."

Solanus Casey would die two days earlier than the Feast of Portiuncula, on July 31, 1957. The attending nurse relates: "He was extremely patient and never complained. If you were in the room with him you couldn't help but feel that he was Christ-like. It was a great exertion to raise him. The orderly was raising him just before he died and heard him say: 'I give my soul to Jesus Christ.'"

Temperance

In the early 1950s a young man by the name of James Maher entered Solanus Casey's life. To say that he was deeply devoted to the well-known Capuchin would be an understatement. Maher remembered many of their conversations and gave very helpful testimony, including the story of one drive from Detroit to Huntington. On the way Solanus insisted that he pick up a hitchhiker. In his recollections of that and other encounters with Solanus, particularly in his reflections on Solanus's practice of temperance, Mr. Maher's comments on the virtue serve as a microcosm of how others perceived temperance expressed in Solanus Casey's life:

> I believe that he was a temperate man. I know that I asked him one time how to quit smoking. He told me: "I wouldn't know. I have never smoked." On the trip to Huntington, we were looking for a place to eat. We came upon one place and he said: "Here's a place." Then he said, "No, we can't go in there. It's a restaurant-bar." In other words, he would not go into a restaurant where there was a bar connected.[94]
>
> I think he was a very patient man. As I indicated, while we were delayed in getting started on the trip to Huntington because of my car, I seemed to be upset about it, but he wasn't. In fact, he took the time to go to the church to say his rosary. After we had dropped off the hitchhiker, he said: "Now see the strange ways in which God works. If we hadn't been delayed, we would never have been able to pick up this man. He hasn't eaten in two days, he has lost his job, and he was on his way to Chicago. Because we were late, we were able to do something for him."

Besides patience as described by Maher and others, the main quality of temperance that describes Solanus's personality is his gentleness. People described him as meek, even-tempered, and in "possession of himself."

Solanus's patience was almost legendary. One person — among many — who came to the front office commented: "To my knowledge he was never impatient. I know that when you went in to speak to him, if there were a lot of people waiting he never rushed you, never hurried up, never showed impatience in this regard." This same patience extended to those who called him during his front office hours. One of these "regulars" was a woman who called on a particularly busy day. After listening to her for quite some time, Solanus gently put the receiver down and continued talking with the person at the desk. Every now and then he picked up the telephone and made a few sounds of recognition. Once, as he picked up the telephone, he realized that many of those in the front office were watching this routine. He placed his hand over the mouthpiece and whispered to them with a wink of his eye, "She's still there!"[95] When Solanus would be called to the office, "even though he might have felt a certain amount of frustration at being called away from whatever he was doing, his sensitivity to the needs of the people countered whatever feelings he might have had at the moment in order that he might serve the people."

Given the endless repetition of needs from the never-ending lines of people coming to see him, Solanus once confided to his confrere Brother Leo Wollenweber that the monotony of it led him near to collapse. However, he immediately added that the model for his patience was the Lord: "In such cases it helps to remember that even when Jesus was about to fall the third time, he patiently consoled the women folk and children of his persecutors, making no exception.... Thanks be to God that he has such divine patience with us."

At various times Solanus showed his thanks for God's patience, which he identified with God's mercy. In his mind, patience was a gift of God. He found in Jesus a model of the patience he sought. He admired his classmate, Father Damasus Wickland, for the patience he had found, especially in his last days. He urged "patient progress" in virtue. The reward would be great, for "God is always planning wonders for the patient and the humble." "Patience, therefore," he urged and then recalled his brother Edward's poem, which he quoted often: "God condescends to use our powers if we don't spoil His plans with ours."

While he was still in temporary vows, Solanus cautioned himself to have "patience, therefore, *with* your own faults!" Forty-seven years later, in a letter to a nun experiencing frustration, he linked patience with humility:

> I hardly know what to advise you, other than that you simply practice patience with yourself as well as with your neighbor — whether in the classroom or in the convent or elsewhere. For we may be sure that we come nowhere in the practice of virtue or in spiritual progress with[out] patiently humbling ourselves in the face of the difficulties wherewith the divine jealous Lover of our poor souls is pleased to check our self-conceit and pride.

One of Solanus's favorite pastimes during his "quiet" days at Huntington was being with nature, working in the orchards or among the bees collecting their honey. However, whenever he was called to the office or the phone from the fields he responded immediately without any sign of impatience. Capuchin Colman Boylan relates:

> While performing his labor of love, he was often called to the front office of the friary to see a visitor or to take a phone call. The signal that he was wanted was a bell attached to the monastery tower bell. Upon hearing this call, he immediately left his work, went quickly to the office, took care of the business in the office, and returned to his beehives. This procedure went on day in and day out. Never once did Father Solanus show any signs of annoyance as he trudged back and forth from the fields to the office, and back to the fields in that hot and humid weather. He was always the personification of patience, and always ready to make himself available to the needs of others.

While there is one reference where Solanus recommended that someone model her living on the "Blessed Mother" and her "temperance," the aspect of temperance that he most recommended to others was patience. "The last sermon any of us will be able to give," he once wrote, "[is] on *patience* and *holy resignation.*"

To say that in his later years Solanus Casey never became impatient or angry would not be truthful, but his expressions of impatience and anger clearly arose equally from his sense of impropriety and injustice. Invariably his impatience and anger were goaded in response to deliberate or careless actions by others, as with altar boys who misbehaved during Mass or devotions,[96] people who did not participate regularly in the sacraments, friars who made a sloppy genuflection toward the Blessed Sacrament, or a person who might question the existence of God or authority.

While he was at Huntington, Solanus's anger became very evident when someone indicated that he was undermining the authority of the bishop of Fort Wayne. According to Father Francis Heidenreich:

> One time when I was superior at Huntington, I was called to the office of Bishop Pursley. He told me that there was a group of people there who were opposed to some of his programs in relationship to the schools and other matters and that Father Solanus was supposedly backing these people in opposition to the bishop. I assured Bishop Pursley that I did not think that this was true. I returned to the monastery and asked Father Solanus about this. This is the only time I saw Father Solanus close to being angry or at least he was very

indignant that anyone would think that he would lend his name to any opposition to a bishop.

Toward the end of his life the only thing that seemed to frustrate Solanus, if not make him angry, was people's restricted access to him. Father Rupert Dorn recalls that, while he submitted to his superiors' decision to limit people's access to him, it was not easy to take, humanly speaking:

> I think the only time I ever saw him show any feeling of impatience was during the latter part of his life when his superiors restricted his seeing people because of his health. I think he felt at times that he should have been allowed to see these people whom he felt needed him. Brother Gabriel was kind of put in charge to see that people didn't get to see him. The one remark that I remember Father Solanus saying was, "Oh, Brother Gabriel is so officious." That would be about the extent of the impatience that he ever showed.

Not one to share such feelings about people behind their back, Solanus quite clearly made his frustration known to Gabriel himself. "He was really a little bit upset with me because I was restricting his practices, but I took care of him and I got him better." It also could well be that what impatience Solanus did have with Gabriel happened because Gabriel made the superiors' restrictions stricter than even they intended.

Any strictness in his observance of the Rule and Constitutions in the Capuchin Province of St. Joseph at that time would have to be considered from the perspective that, among Orders, the Capuchins were considered very strict and, among Capuchin provinces, the Detroit province was known for its austerity. As a result, Solanus participated in the fasts observed (from Epiphany for forty days, Lent, from the Feast of St. Michael to All Saints, and Advent) and the days of abstinence (every Wednesday and Friday of the year). While such fasts were meant for self-discipline, Solanus remained mindful of others. He sought no dispensation from them, even when he got older; in fact, "he refused to do so." In his mind an expression of mortification of the body "brings one nearer to God and endears [one] to the Sacred Heart." Indeed, as he wrote while still in temporary vows, there can be "no progress in virtue without mortification." In the novitiate he quoted Romans 14:21 in his notebook: "It is good not to eat flesh and not to drink wine, or anything whereby thy brother is offended, or scandalized, or made weak." As the years went on, Solanus lived out what he had written. He never seemed overly concerned about food. He ate what was placed before him. He never asked for any special foods, nor was he accustomed to having delicacies. According to Evelyn Cefai, the housekeeper at the rectory where Solanus supplied help on weekends:

> He was a person who kept his natural desires in subjection. He never desired special foods or asked for delicacies. I know he would eat whatever I put before him, but he did enjoy my spaghetti. He was not given to alcoholic drinks other than enjoying a small glass of wine. I might point out that he never asked for a second glass. He drank what was put before him the first time and that was all, even in eating the spaghetti!

Miss Cefai also made Maltese cheesecakes, which Solanus liked, and Mrs. Bernard Smith and Mrs. Clare Ryan made him Irish soda bread. Mr. Ryan recalled: "My wife used to bring him Irish bread, which he thoroughly enjoyed. But he never asked her for these things."

He was moderate in what he ate. And because he ate in such small amounts, he remained thin. Periodically he would come to the refectory to share in the friars' afternoon snack. He would have a cup of coffee and "at the most he would take with that...just a plain slice of bread, no butter, no jelly, nothing on it, so he would simply satisfy his appetite, but not the sensual appetite." Sundays were special, and a sign of his "indulgence" for the festive day was to take butter on his bread.

Once in a while Solanus took a little brandy or his "good Irish medicine"; other than that he did not smoke or drink alcohol. On special occasions he would take some wine. For community recreation periods, Solanus "might take a small glass of wine and some cheese and crackers. But I never recall seeing him drink alone." One time, for his health, he was under obedience from his superior to have a glass of wine after his evening meal.

While all the Capuchins arose at 4:55 a.m. to begin their day, Solanus usually preceded them to chapel far in advance; when they retired around 9:30 or 10:00 in the evening, he was often just closing the office. Consequently, he did not get much sleep. Because of "the long hours that he spent with people...and because of his lack of sleep the night before he might excuse himself from the office for a period of five minutes and go into the refectory and lay down on a bench just to regain his strength."

Given their strict ascetical life, Capuchins of Solanus Casey's era did not frequent baths or other places for "cures" or take unnecessary trips. However, they were allowed vacations. In the Detroit province a two-week vacation could be taken seven years after a friar's first profession. Two weeks could then be taken every five years after that. For special occasions, like ordinations, exceptions were made. Due in part to the fact that his family moved out of the province's territory (Montana to New England) to live in Washington and California, Solanus took vacations only in 1911 (to celebrate his brother Maurice's ordination), in 1913 to Seattle (for his parents' fiftieth wedding anniversary), and in 1945 to Seattle again (for his nephew John's ordination as a Jesuit). On this latter trip Solanus also visited Los Angeles. Even in these faraway places, Solanus's renown seems to have preceded him. His sister-in-law Martha recalls: "I had the honor to drive Father to the different churches and convents out there, where all were begging him to say Mass or give talks and his blessings."

Chapter 12

The Evangelical Counsels: Poverty, Chastity, Obedience, and Humility

In 1918 Solanus wrote in his notebook various scripture references dealing with vocation. The first is a passage from Philippians: "I have learned in whatsoever state I am, to be content therewith" (Phil. 4:11). Given the patience that characterized his life, Solanus's contentment with his vocation, whether as a baptized Catholic or a Capuchin Franciscan and priest, flowed from his commitment to follow wherever God's will led him. "Notwithstanding my prejudice" about the Capuchins — whom he felt called to join "half against my will" ever since he heard the call "Go to Detroit" — Solanus Casey came to believe deeply that it was *God's* specific will (not his) that he be a religious and, more specifically, a Capuchin Franciscan. James Maher testified, "It was my impression that Father Solanus became a religious in order that he might do God's will and do it to the fullest." Despite one brief period of doubt in his postulancy, he never wavered. Maher remembered:

> I asked Father Solanus if, after he had entered the Capuchins, he had any doubts about his vocation, or had any thoughts about leaving the Capuchins. He told me that he never had any such doubts. His words to me were: "Once I was invested, I had no further doubts." He was grateful for such a vocation to such an Order and, I might say, especially for the grace of learning so quickly to love the Order.

Solanus also "had a great respect for his vocation as a priest." This is all the more understandable when one considers the difficulties he had in the diocesan seminary and in his early days as a Capuchin seminarian.

In 1947 Solanus made a retreat at St. Felix Friary, preached by Father Marcellus of the Pittsburgh Province of Capuchins. In his retreat notes he described reasons related to "Why a Religious?" In the main, his remarks

241

dealt with "reparation": for personal sins, for the conversion of sinners, for the suffering holy souls in purgatory, and for supplying what is wanting in the bitter passion of Jesus Christ. Possibly Solanus shared the same reflections about his call as his retreat director; however, his writings and those who knew him never mentioned images of "reparation" related to his vocation to religious life. For him, it seems, his was merely one call among many that invited him to fidelity and thankfulness. Yet that call to be a Capuchin Franciscan was one he cherished deeply: "How can we ever be grateful as we ought to be for such a vocation," he wrote to his confrere Brother Leo Wollenweber, "in the Seraphic Order of the Poverello of Assisi? Thanks be to God that he has such divine patience with us."

Solanus prayed for vocations and urged others to pray for vocations as well. He encouraged others to enter religious life and be faithful in it. One of these was Booker (Agathangelus) Ashe, the first black brother in the history of the United States Capuchins. He testified:

> In regard to religious vocations, I know that on occasions he would encourage an individual to try the religious vocation. Also to us younger brothers, he would encourage us to be faithful to our vocation and would encourage us by reminding us that the religious life wasn't as difficult as we thought it was.

The following pages describe how Solanus Casey lived his specific religious life though the practice of poverty, chastity, obedience, and humility.

Poverty

Solanus Casey's fidelity to his vow of poverty can be found in his own personal simplicity of life and in his commitment to the poor themselves. While the latter has been discussed previously, his own personal expression of poverty and attitude toward material things will be discussed here.

Material things never seemed to be a preoccupation for Solanus Casey. As a young man, Barney Casey shared the income from his work with his family when they were in need. As a Capuchin he lived the austere expression of its poverty in an exemplary way. He dealt with very large sums, yet never seemed to be interested in the money. In fact, when people gave him money, he almost seemed careless about it. His unconcern about money was so total that, when people gave him money, he would merely put it in his habit; he did not keep good track of it, unless it was for something specific, like the SMA or Masses. Brother Ignatius noted:

> He seemed almost to have a contempt for money. I recall that one time when I was assisting as a porter, he came in and gave me some money for Masses, that is, Mass stipends. I made the remark: "It's too bad that we have to be involved with money." His reply was, "Yes, it is," as though he would rather not have to bother with this. And yet, during the years that he was porter, he dealt with thousands of dollars that he received in Mass stipends and enrollment in the Seraphic Mass Association. And yet, he never showed any sense or desire to possess it.

Solanus once confessed to a relative: "As for the financial or business affairs...I just do not like to dabble into them." Because of the large amounts of money given him and his seeming lack of interest in it, it was decided that he should have someone to help him account for it. "This was one of the reasons I acted as his secretary, because of his little concern for money," Father Blase Gitzen testified. He recalled: "One time the superior had me go through his room and collect whatever monies were there, and I found over a hundred dollars. It wasn't that he was keeping it; he just disregarded it."[97]

People noted Solanus's simple way of life. He had a minimum of things and these things contented him well. He made no special demands. His room was very plain, even for a Capuchin. "I know on one occasion when his regular confessor was absent, he asked me to hear his confession, and I went into his room; there was nothing to speak of in his room," Father Cyril Langheim recalled. "There was nothing on his desk except a book of spiritual reading. I would say that most of us had other books or we had little personal mementos in our room. Father Solanus had none of that." The only thing he did have on his desk was a small hand-lettered sign reading: "Blessed be God in all His designs."

Even when he was old and sickly Solanus did not expect treatment that might have compromised his austere interpretation of the vow. Father Rupert Dorn noted:

> I know on one occasion when he was at Huntington, Indiana, because of his illness he had to keep his legs elevated. His superior came into his room and found his feet propped up on an orange crate. When the superior offered to get something more comfortable,

Father Solanus wasn't concerned about it. He said the orange crate served the purpose and there was no need for anything fancy.

His own clothing was minimal. He had but one habit. He seemed unconcerned when it became threadbare. When this would happen, he held the habit together with safety pins. Inevitably, when he would visit the Immaculate Heart of Mary Sisters in Monroe, a side benefit would be that his habit would be repaired by a seamstress sister. On occasion his lack of care for it did make him embarrassed to be seen in it. Capuchin Pius Cotter recalled: "His habit was, to say the least, old and maybe not as clean and neat as it could have been, but it didn't seem to bother him a great deal. I know on one occasion he asked to borrow my habit because his was pretty dirty. I think he was ashamed to wear it to the office to see somebody."

In his community living Solanus was not reluctant to remind his brothers of the interconnectedness between the vow of Capuchins and the needs of others. Brother Daniel Brady recalls: "He used to chide us in the kitchen about bakery goods, which were donated every Friday after the bakery was closed. We would sneak out one of the better cakes for ourselves, and I think he knew this. He would remind us that this was not really according to the spirit of poverty."

Solanus wore his habit all the time, except when he went on more extensive trips. Then he wore clerical clothes. However his suit and hat seemed to have been the ones with which he entered the Order. His shoes were old and his "luggage" was a cardboard box. His sister-in-law Martha Casey recalled that his ancient attire seemed to amuse the priests he visited when he came to visit his family in Seattle:

> Father arrived in Seattle in the same old black suit he had when he entered the Order. Some of the Fathers laughed at his dress and funny little hat, but were very much ashamed when this holy man went on his knees and asked for their blessing. They remarked that they should have been the ones to get on their knees and ask his blessing.

After he died, Martha gathered his personal belongings together and took them to the monastery. But what he had left was minimal. Father Rupert Dorn commented: "When he died there was very little among his possessions that had to be disposed of; as a matter of fact, I don't think he even had his violin at that time."[98]

In his ministry Solanus's poverty was manifest in the way he lived for others, trying to meet their needs. He once noted that he surely "sympathized with so many poor people in the world" who had to "struggle, struggle, struggle." For material things he was allowed to dispense, he seemed only concerned with having enough to give to others. The almsgiving he was able to practice he encouraged in others. For instance, to his brother Owen he recommended almsgiving as the "most salutary" act of all. In one of his last notes he reminded a man who seemed to be very busy that the Lord would be very sensitive to him as long as he would "have a heart for His poor."

When people wrote him notes, he often returned his comments on the same piece of paper. And while he received much money from benefactors, he never kept it for himself. He turned everything over to the superior. Brother Booker Ashe marveled: "When I think of all of the things that he received as gifts from the people who came to him, you would expect his room to be filled with the little trinkets or mementos, and yet his room was very bare and plain and he had none of these things in his room."

On weekends during the 1940s Solanus ministered in a parish pastored by Father Cefai. "When I arrived at St. Paul's Maltese Church there was a debt of $62,000. If I mentioned contributions in my sermons, Father Solanus would say to me, 'Don't talk money so much.' He was not venal and the things of this world were unimportant to him."

One of Solanus's many benefactors was Clare Ryan. She learned quickly how unimportant material things were to him. "He had no concern for material or temporal things. If you brought him a gift, as on occasion we might bring him a bottle of liquor, he would smile and thank us and say, 'The Fathers will enjoy it.' He considered nothing for himself." When people brought him things to the front office, often they were disposed of almost immediately. As Doris Panyard testified:

> I believe he followed the dictum of St. Francis that if you have something that you have no use for, give it away. I know one time when I was visiting him he had a small plaque on his desk and he asked me if I would like to have it. It occurred to me that it would be a keepsake of Father Solanus so I said I would like to have it. He gave it to me. This I think would be typical of his attitude.

Solanus's detachment was also very evident when he celebrated his various jubilees and received much money, many mementos, and expensive gifts. "Everything he had he gave away," Dorothy Fletcher said. She went on to illustrate:

He received a chalice on the occasion of his fiftieth ordination anniversary, and he gave that to a priest who was going to the missions.
He had nothing of his own. He wanted nothing of his own. I think he
excelled others in the exercise of this virtue because he had absolutely
no concern for temporal things. His habit was a tattered remnant of
what it should have been, but that didn't seem to bother him. He just
had no concern for worldly things.

Solanus's unconcern for "worldly things" flowed from his spirit of
poverty. In his mind, everything available to humans came from God.
Consequently "material things were to be used merely to help get us to
heaven."

While he was asked to seek alms for the Order, he never treated people
with more money differently from those with less, or none. In fact, when
people wanted to enroll in the SMA and had no money, he would enroll
them, making up for their poverty with monies given him for this purpose
by others.

Chastity

Solanus's approach of relating to all people was very evident in the way
he exercised his vow of chastity. Respect for himself and his vocation as a
Capuchin Franciscan and as a priest grounded his life of chastity and was
translated in the way he related to others. As one diocesan priest who knew
him well reflected on Solanus's practice of chastity:

> I believe that the life of the priesthood is a total consecration to God.
> I believe that a priest who has this total consecration is happy. You
> can see it in his demeanor, his actions. Father Solanus was such a
> priest. He was always happy and content with what he had and what
> he was doing. For this reason, I believe he was totally consecrated to
> God and to His service and the service of his fellow man. I know of
> nothing that would be contradictory to the practice of this virtue of
> chastity and purity on the part of Father Solanus.

Women, whether children, young women, middle aged, or older, were
treated the same. But it might be equally said that he treated women in
the same way he treated men. In an Order whose Constitutions urged all
friars to avoid frequent contacts with women, Solanus lived his life in full

contact with them, yet he exemplified chastity in all his dealings. "I never saw anything in Father Solanus that would have suggested that he did not observe this virtue of chastity," his last provincial recalled.

> First of all, his language was always proper and modest. I don't think he would ever permit anyone in his presence to speak in a way that was not wholesome and chaste. Certainly in his conduct with persons of the opposite sex he showed nothing irregular. He would treat them the same as he would treat men. He was very natural with them as he was with men. As far as I know he did nothing that would be contradictory to the exercise of this virtue.

As a young man Barney Casey definitely manifested normal sexual inclinations toward young women; his request for the hand of Rebecca Tobin in marriage attests to that. However, when he was twenty-five years old and felt the call of God, he made his own private vow of chastity.

Once in the Order, it seems that people who knew him interpreted Solanus's ways of dealing with women differently. While it is generally agreed that nothing he said, wrote, or did was against chastity, some people answered questions about his practice of celibacy from a perspective that might indicate their own understanding that men should be somewhat removed from women. For instance, one person noted, "In my opinion I think he was just maybe a little bit scrupulous in regard to this particular virtue"; another testified that he didn't look directly at women, while more than one or two noted that he kept himself a bit aloof from women. However, it seems more correct to say he was not aloof from women (or anyone else); he was merely circumspect. One woman, Marguerite Baker, seems to describe his approach best: "He was never aloof from women, but he was always circumspect in his dealings with them. He was not forward in any way. He never showed any particular desire to be in conversation with women alone."

Mrs. Baker's comments about Solanus not having any particular desire to associate with women rather than men found reinforcement from other testimony as well. However this does not mean he was afraid of women. In his eyes, women and men were all images of God, all were equal. No one, consequently, was considered special. His nonsexist approach to people has been well described by Capuchin Ambrose DeGroot, a moral theologian:

> I never saw anything on his part that indicated any preference to be with persons of the opposite sex.... He was kind of oblivious to this

type of thing. I'm sure that he might have had temptations, as we all do, but it would not have been indicated in his manner of action. He was neither naive nor a stoic, but he lived so much in the aura of the supernatural that I would have to feel he had the natural pretty much under control. God, as I said before, was the center of his life, and all of mankind were his children, and he just accepted them all without preference.

While Solanus was in control of himself in his dealings with all people, including women, that control was not something that made him rigid or hard; it was expressed in a kind of reserve or modesty evident immediately. He believed it was not without cause that, after the Fall, Adam and Eve fashioned "aprons" for their bodies. He was not one to give affectionate embraces; indeed the touches he did give seemed limited to those connected to blessings. This modesty and reserve were important because so many women consulted him. One of the women who visited him was Leona Garrity. She explained:

> In regard to the virtue of chastity, Father Solanus had a very modest demeanor. I know that in the conversation I had with him he was very circumspect. He was not overly interested in me as a woman. He was interested in me as a person who had a problem. I can only state from a general observation that seeing him at meetings at the monastery, he always conducted himself with persons of the opposite sex in a rather dignified and modest way.

With everyone he was reserved, proper, and beyond reproach. One definite expression of Solanus's modesty toward people of the opposite sex involved his conversations with and about women. He never made sexist remarks, uttered vulgarities, told off-color jokes, or made risqué comments. Indeed, "His conversation was always most edifying. It would have been unthinkable even in a jocose way to expect him to make any observations which pertained to chastity, sexuality, or any similar topic."

Not given to such ways of speaking, Solanus did not expect others to be so either. Others might have been reserved out of their deep respect for Solanus (as in the case of the friars), but if someone did make an offensive comment, the person would be challenged.

As a normal man, Solanus was well aware of the temptations coming from self and society that hindered a life of chastity, but he knew that "temptations against it [are] not necessarily sinful." Capuchin Rupert

Dorn recalls: "He recognized the problems, and said to me, 'If it weren't for the grace of God, none of us would ever succeed.'" Besides temptations against chastity coming from one's own natural drives, Solanus was concerned about addressing their sources in society. His sermon notes from 1917 show him urging the people to "fight against our own evil inclinations. We must beware of dangerous company, of dangerous amusement. We must cultivate the Christian virtues."

In challenging people to their own form of chastity, Solanus exemplified an uncompromising, but loving stance. "I remember one time in one of his Wednesday afternoon talks he spoke of modern dress, which was becoming rather immodest," a diocesan priest who attended this talk recollects:

> He certainly indicated his opposition to it, but he didn't rant and rave about it. Rather, he spoke about the need of modesty and that modesty was the guardian of chastity. It was in this manner in which he spoke that he would be very prudent in what he said so that he did not offend anyone and yet, nevertheless, he would speak what had to be spoken.

Besides finding the sources for temptations against chastity in one's own members and society, Solanus also attributed such temptations to their ultimate source: sin and the source of sin. For Solanus, this ultimate source of temptation was "the devil. He said that when we were so tempted we should get down on our knees and pray."

Besides prayer in the face of temptation, Solanus realized that his vow would be "guarded by mortification." Thus he practiced the means provided by the Order to preserve chastity, especially prayer, fasting, and the discipline. As Father Cyril Langheim stated, Solanus "observed the virtue of chastity" in the way he practiced corporal discipline in accordance with the Rule. "This discipline consisted of using a chain and striking yourself about the legs and the backside. This was done three days a week. He also observed the Fast very carefully, which I feel is a means of keeping one's desires in subjection."

Another way Solanus avoided unnecessary temptations against chastity was by not making efforts to initiate conversations or correspondence with women. A related way, which enabled him to be faithful to his vow of chastity and treat women respectfully, is found in his devotion to the Blessed Virgin. As one woman who visited him often recalls: "He was modest in his conversation and speech. He seemed to have no undue desire

to converse with women. He treated us the same as he treated everybody
else. The only one he ever spoke of with a great deal of affection was the
Blessed Mother."

Solanus was able to be helpful to others in their struggles with chastity.
One of these was the young Capuchin Pius Cotter. His reflections offer a
good conclusion for our discussion of Solanus and the vow of chastity:

> While I was stationed in Huntington with him, I had a period where
> I was being severely tempted in regard to this particular virtue to the
> extent that I was even considering leaving the Order. The tempta-
> tions were that severe. I went to Father Solanus and talked to him
> about it. I asked him if he had himself ever been so tempted. Father
> Solanus said yes, he had been, but through the grace of God he had
> been able to preserve this virtue.
>
> He admitted that women were attractive, but he felt that with the
> help of God we could control these attractions. He was also sharp
> enough to realize that in working in the office women seemed to
> enjoy talking to me, but he also pointed out that perhaps I was some-
> what responsible in that I made myself somewhat available to these
> persons. So he chastised me in a sense for putting myself in these
> occasions.
>
> For some reason, after talking to Father Solanus and reflecting on
> what he had to say, and perhaps the realization that a man like him-
> self would be so tempted, my own particular strong desires seemed
> to subside. I won't say that I didn't have problems after that, but they
> were never so severe.

Pius Cotter's conclusion aptly summarizes the testimonies of all those
who knew Solanus Casey and observed his practice of chastity: "I know
of nothing that Father Solanus said or did that would be contrary to the
practice of this virtue."

Obedience

Recently a Capuchin who was a novice in Solanus Casey's last year of life
recalled an incident involving Solanus, his respect for authority, and how
he sensed the Feast of Christ the King might be celebrated. The incident
took place in October, 1956 at St. Bonaventure's Friary, where Solanus
lived and where the novices resided at that time:

After the regular "Conventual Mass," the novices were gathered for breakfast in the refectory. The guardian (Father Bernard Burke), novice master (Father Elmer Stoffel), and assistant novice master (Father Giles Soyka) were all gone. According to procedures the senior Father was in charge. Today it happened to be Father Solanus.

Breakfast was always a very simple meal. Except for great feasts like Christmas and Easter, it was always taken in complete silence. On this day, however, we novices could sense a tension within Solanus. He wanted so badly to give us permission to talk, because for him this was truly a great feast day. But he knew if he did he would face the anger of the novice master who had told him never to interfere with the regular routine of the novitiate.

The tension lasted throughout breakfast until Solanus found a creative way out: if he could not give us permission to talk to each other, he would talk to us. And talk he did! He began to extol the glory of this feast by describing all the marvelous deeds the Holy Fathers had accomplished for Christ the King during the past hundred years, from Pius IX to Pius XII!

Inspiring as this might seem, it did not inspire us novices. Breakfast usually lasted no more than ten or fifteen minutes and, here at the end of breakfast, we were going to be subjected to a discourse covering a hundred years of papal history. We'd never get out! And besides, we had to do the dishes and prepare for the 9:00 Mass in the big chapel.

I do not know how far Solanus got in his hundred-year history before he realized this delay could be another reason for incurring the novice master's wrath. So he dismissed us with the prayer after meals.

Looking back, I don't remember anything Solanus said that day, but I will never forget the depth of feeling he conveyed. There was absolutely no doubt about his passionate commitment to Christ the King and his great admiration for the ministry of Christ's vicars on earth.[99]

For Solanus, obedience represented "the master stroke in the sacrifice of self to God's service." Solanus's obedience and submission to all forms of authority began with his desire to do the will of God and obey God in all things. Under the Lordship of Christ the King, Solanus envisioned all authority and obedience. While this included society, in a special way his obedience was directed to the authority residing among the leaders of the Catholic Church; thus he quoted Pope Leo XIII: "Only the Church of Jesus Christ has been able to preserve and surely will preserve to the consummation of time her form of government."

In church government, he envisioned that authority ultimately resting in Rome and the sovereign pontiffs. In the diocese, authority rested in the bishops. In the parishes, authority rested in the pastors. In the Capuchin Order this authority resided in the minister general and provincial and his local superiors. According to people's recollections and his own writings regarding all these sources of authority, Solanus Casey was never known, at any time, to have violated the spirit or the intent of his vow of obedience.

As a child Bernie Casey learned to obey his parents. When he discerned his call to become a Capuchin, he sought permission from his local ordinary. Once he joined the Capuchin Franciscan Order he deemed it a "privilege" to obey the Rule. For him, obedience to the Rule was the "best penance" he could imagine. More specifically, he willingly submitted to the authority of those the Rule declared would be representatives of God's will for him. Even in the smallest things, this seemed to apply, as Mrs. Lillian Lewins recalled: "One time I asked him if there was something I could do for him since I was able to type. He did state that he had something that he would like typed that he wanted to have published. However, he stated that he would have to have his superior's permission first."

Solanus deeply respected religious obedience, even when it might be manifested in apparently arbitrary ways. One of these occasions occurred when Solanus was "outside in the cloister when he was called to the Office and he started to run. Father Bernard, the guardian, saw him running and called to Father Solanus to stop. He immediately stopped. Father Bernard told him to walk and this is what he did."

Whether it was in such matters or even asking permission to leave the friary, Solanus submitted to his superiors' authority. This was not always easy, as Solanus discovered when he had to submit to his superiors' decision that taking the vows as a Capuchin in 1898 did not mean he would be a priest nor when it became clear in 1904 that priesthood for him would not include being able to hear confessions.

"I think his acceptance of his superiors' will that he should be ordained a priest simplex is a prime example of his obedience to the will of his superior," his niece, Sister Bernadine Casey, testified: "I feel that this must have been a great burden and humbling and embarrassing act." Perhaps his attitude toward this decision is best summarized in the reflections of Brother Ignatius Milne:

I think Father Solanus was imbued with the spirit of obedience. I never found him to criticize or complain or object to the will of his superior, whether it was fair or unjust. His attitude was that this is the will of God and if it is meant to be different in time, it will work out. In my own opinion, I feel that he must have really learned this, and certainly gave evidence of the spirit of obedience when it was determined that he would be ordained, but only as a priest simplex. This must have been a great disappointment to him and, yet, he accepted it. It was in this spirit that he accepted every rule, order, command, commission that was given to him.

Having accepted his superiors' decisions regarding his priesthood itself, he found no problems when they asked him to change assignments as a priest, even when he had become endeared to the people, as in Detroit. It was in this transfer — given and acted upon within twenty-four hours — that has testified to many as the clearest case of Solanus's unswerving obedience. As Bernard Burke, the superior who relayed the transfer, recalled: "Even when he was transferred from Detroit to Brooklyn, New York, it might be said that he was at the height of his popularity here in Detroit, and yet he accepted this change very calmly and without any complaint whatever."

After a year in Brooklyn, Solanus was reassigned to Huntington, Indiana. Once there he heard that he might be returned to Detroit. Shortly after, he wrote his brother, Edward: "There is a possibility I'll be sent back to Detroit, though I hardly think it is at all probable. I have not the least worry about whether I remain here or be transferred. It is after all, essentially quite the same." The reason for this equanimity in Solanus resided in his conclusion: "It is such a surprising privilege to know definitely that one is doing God's will by keeping the Rule and obeying."

When his superiors determined Solanus should return to Detroit in the last years of his life their decision to restrict people's contacts with him created him much pain; yet he submitted as his provincial at that time recalled:

I was the provincial when I brought him back to Detroit from Huntington [in 1956]. The first thing the guardian said to him was, "Father Solanus, we are not going to let you see the people or have the people see you because it will kill you." Now I know that bothered Father Solanus, but he never said a word in disagreement, and he certainly observed the command of his superior.

Father Lawrence Merten, who sat next to table in the refectory with Solanus, testified:

> Father Solanus was very obedient. About a year before he died, some people came to the monastery and were very insistent on seeing Father Solanus. Because of his physical weakness, the superior wanted to protect Father Solanus from fatigue and had forbidden visits to him. Sometimes, however, the superior had granted permission for limited visits. In the absence of the superior, I was the vicar.
>
> Once, when an insistent visitor continued to ask to see Father Solanus, I followed the precedent set by the superior and granted permission for Father Solanus to visit for thirty minutes. Now the people were always inclined to overstay the allotted time, and Father Solanus paid no attention to time as he just wanted to help people. So I went in at the end of thirty minutes and concluded the visit. Although it was hard for Father Solanus to say goodbye, as his natural inclination would be to spend a longer time, he nevertheless very readily acceded. There were never any arguments. His attitude toward authority was always marvelous.

To argue with or be critical of his superiors, for Solanus, would have been unthinkable. For him, it was simple: "Whatever the superiors wanted, he did." Mrs. Dorothy Fletcher, who knew Solanus well, testified:

> Father Solanus practiced the virtue of obedience. I know many of the priests who had been his superiors. They have stated to me that they have never had anyone who obeyed them as well as Father Solanus. I know he was always submissive to the will of his superiors. On the occasion of his eighty-fourth birthday, he asked me and my family to stay and attend that Mass with him because he was so delighted that they were going to let him sing a High Mass for the occasion. It seems to me that this showed that if this had offered him such great delight, that he accepted their will in not celebrating High Masses on other occasions.

Fortunately, among those who were Solanus's provincial and local superiors, many lived to testify about his exemplary manifestation of obedience. Father Gerald Walker, the provincial during Solanus's last years, declared: "I know of nothing he did that would have been contradictory to the heroic practice of this virtue." His guardian at Huntington, Father Francis Heidenreich (whose strictness with Solanus and visitors has been discussed elsewhere), recalled:

> In my own experience with Father Solanus as his superior, he was always submissive and obedient. When I was superior at Huntington one time the provincial on the occasion of a visit noticed Father Solanus in making his reverence before the Blessed Sacrament. He commented to me that he thought Father Solanus was getting rather old and frail and maybe should not be kissing the floor. He wanted me to inform Father Solanus that he was now dispensed from this act. Later, I noticed Father Solanus still kissing the floor. I reminded him that he had been dispensed by the superior and that this was practically [uttered] in the spirit of obedience. Father Solanus merely laughed and said: "Oh, I am getting old and sometimes I forget and by the time I have kissed the floor, I remember that I shouldn't be doing it." But, eventually he did conform to the will of his superior. I am sure that when he did kiss the floor it was not done out of the spirit of disobedience but rather out of habit. I think he was an outstanding example in showing the spirit of obedience.

Perhaps one of the more controversial dimensions of Solanus's life involved his promotion of Mary of Agreda's *Mystical City of God*. Aware of the controversy around the book, Solanus argued from obedience to its authenticity: "This work itself, *The Mystical City of God,* was written in holy obedience to rightly constituted authority and was unreservedly approved by the highest superiors both of church and state." Toward the end of his time in Detroit, especially 1944–45, Solanus's own sense and spirit of obedience received a strong test when his superiors decided he should sever visits with Ray Garland, the man he had endorsed to promote *The Mystical City of God*. While the reason for this has been discussed elsewhere, its connections to the virtue of obedience have been well articulated by his superior at the time, Father Marion Roessler:

> His obedience was severely tried in his dealings with a certain convert layman [Ray Garland], who attached himself to Father Solanus. At the time of the following incidents it seems this man was unemployed. Father Solanus, being an ardent client of the Blessed Virgin, sought to promote devotion to her among the thousands of troubled souls who sought his help and advice at the monastery office.

How the following got started, I don't know, but Father Solanus was accustomed to ask many of his clients to promise that if a certain petition for divine assistance would be granted, that in thanksgiving they would read the four large volumes of Mother Mary of Agreda's private revelations of the Blessed Virgin. The people felt that, if Father Solanus wanted them to make such a promise, they would have to keep it, regardless of whether or not they were financially able to purchase the books.

After this went on for a very long time, some of these poor people sent in complaints to the chancery office, explaining that they felt obliged to purchase these expensive volumes, and read them as they had promised Father Solanus. The chancery office contacted our Father Provincial, Father Theodosius Foley, about the problem, requesting that the people not be required to purchase these expensive volumes. Father Provincial spoke to Father Solanus about it, and to the best of my recollection that was the end of the matter.

The exactness with which Solanus followed his superiors' decision about the book sales and Ray Garland has been described by one of Solanus's friends and benefactors, Doris Panyard. It seems that, while he was in Huntington years later, Ray Garland's son called Solanus on the phone. She recalled: "He told me that he hung up on the young man because he was afraid that Ray Garland, the father, was present there at the same time and he would have been tempted to talk with him and this would have been violating the direction given to him by his superiors."

Solanus was obedient not only to his superiors; he accepted the advice, the suggestions, and the counsel of his juniors as well. This did not prove difficult for him, for, as one who lived with him recalled, Solanus "treated everyone as if they were a superior." Such obedience — to superiors as well as his juniors — served as an example to all the friars.

Because he manifested so evidently the vow and virtue of obedience, Solanus was able to instill obedience in others. Daniel Ryan recalled: "He tried to instill this spirit of obedience in others by encouraging them to keep the commandments, to go to Mass and the sacraments regularly, and to treat our fellow man properly."

Solanus's notion of treating others "properly" can be linked to his reflections on service to God — which represented the heart of his understanding of obedience. As early as his novitiate, Solanus noted that "willingly to serve God must be happiness," and that he did not want to live if he could not be in God's service; for him there could be no peace for creatures except in service of their creator. "To serve God" would be "to reign." Service was the way people were called to live in "the good God's wonderful universe."

In his mind, for human beings, the "primary purpose" for living, taught in the catechism, the "one thing necessary" involved "knowing God better so as to love Him and serve Him better and save our immortal souls."

For Solanus, knowing God resulted in appreciation; to love and serve God follows. Solanus Casey came to "know God," by knowing Jesus Christ; this knowing of Jesus revealed his obedience: "To do the will of his heavenly Father; the Second Person of the Blessed Trinity assumed mortal flesh to be an example for all mortals in being obedient, even to the death of the Cross," Solanus once wrote. Since Christ's obedience involved service, all service constituted the essence of vocation. This service offered "a privilege," whether it be in marriage, the priesthood, in the service Solanus himself exercised as a sacristan, or in his ministry to "our dear Lord's least brethren."

Among those who learned much from Solanus's practice of obedience were his own brothers in the Order. A novice who lived with him testified: "In speaking to the novices, he would remind us of the need of obedience. He would say Christ was God, and Christ was obedient; therefore we should be obedient. He would say that the guardian is the boss; therefore he is to be obeyed. He sought to instill in all of us that spirit of obedience."

> In terms of obedience to civil authorities, there is no doubt that he was very patriotic in his attitudes toward the United States of America. I know of one occasion where he wrote to General Douglas MacArthur, encouraging him to run for the presidency of the United States because he felt that MacArthur was a great patriot.[100]

As Solanus reflected on being a citizen of the United States, while he stressed obedience to civil authority, he perceived a rising atheism which was growing precisely because of humanity's unwillingness to come to know God.

Humility

In 1946, while he was in Brooklyn, Solanus Casey wrote a letter to a nun who was experiencing many difficulties in her life and relationships. The letter not only shows Solanus's compassionate way of dealing with people in trouble, but it also clearly reveals his thoughts on humility:

> We may be sure that we come nowhere in the practice of virtue or in spiritual progress without patiently humbling ourselves in the face of the difficulties to check our self-conceit and pride.
>
> If the dear Lord has deigned to invite you to more than ordinary virtue and if on your part you have, perhaps again and again, seen something of the privilege of such an invitation, finally consenting even half-generously to follow the *Crucified Spouse,* then you may quite naturally, rather logically, expect difficulties of some kind or of any kind to exercise you in the virtues that put the enemies of the Cross to shame and make heaven rejoice. Such virtues are, of course, first of all, humility from which all other virtues worthwhile in God's sight take root and nourishment....
>
> At all events and whatever comes, turn frequently to our dear Lord in the tabernacle, and next to Him, to our Blessed Mother Mary, begging for the grace to correspond to the graces that He is always lavishing on our unworthy selves and for patience and *humility.*

Among the many virtues attributed to Solanus Casey, humility ranks among the most notable. In the opinion of some witnesses, in fact, humility did become the virtue from which "all other virtues worthwhile in God's sight took root and nourishment" in Solanus's life. As Doris Panyard testified:

> Father Solanus practiced the virtue of humility to the highest degree of any person that I have ever known. He also had a great respect for that virtue in other people. At one time my brother Fred, who had four children, called me. He said, "Ask Father Solanus to pray for me. I have done everything I can for my children." He seemed to think that his children were not turning out well, although I thought the children were fine. Anyway, I spoke to Father Solanus about it. He said, "I will do something for Fred because he is humble." This is the one and only time I ever heard Father Solanus use the word "I." All other times he would say that he would ask God, or that God would do it. He always gave credit to God for all of the things that occurred.

When he was a novice Solanus cautioned himself: "Beware of congratulating thyself on the blessing wrought through any medium." That he remained true to his caution, especially in not taking credit for the grace of God worked through him, has been attested by many. James Maher stated that "he attributed any cures or good works that were performed to God and not to his own self. He was not a person who was blown up with his own importance. It was one of the things that impressed me, that he realized his own smallness in the sight of God and anything that came through him, came from God." When people would "speak in a way in which we would be giving credit to him for things that had been done, he would insist that this honor be given to God." More specifically, his confrere Father Blase Gitzen recalls:

> He never took any credit to himself for any of the wonderful things that happened during his life. They were attributed either directly to God or to the influence of the Seraphic Mass Association. He talked about certain cures, and there were a few that were special to him and that he did like to talk about. But never in the sense that it was through his doings. He was always extremely humble in this regard, and in giving credit to God or to prayer.

Casimera Scott remarked that she once thanked Solanus for his help at the time that her mother died. He merely said, "It was God who helped you, not me." At other times he would tell people it was their own prayers that helped them receive the favors they requested: "It's not me," he would say, "it's your prayers." The degree that Solanus attributed all such happenings to God, to the prayers of others, and to the saints and sacramental invoked — and never to himself — is best described in the reflections of Father Gerald Walker:

> It never seemed to dawn on him that God was using him in a special way. If cures were worked through his intercession, he never even seemed to advert to it. I think I would have been surprised if he had been surprised. In other words, he gave credit to God for all of the things that happened, and took none of it to himself. I also heard someone state that when they asked Father Solanus for his blessing he gave it willingly, but he also said, "You know, other priests are here who can give a blessing."

Solanus once wrote, "In his divine economy God has honored his creatures — most especially rational ones — by giving them each, according to his ability, a part of His own work to do — by participation in His own divine activity." Fidelity to that role implied becoming an instrument of

God's grace in the world. In the mind of Sister Mary Solanus Ufford, Solanus showed his humility "first of all, by always attributing to God the credit
for things that were done. He would refer to himself as only the channel
through whom God worked. . . . He never took any credit to himself for the
fact that so many people sought him out."

Solanus greatly revered the power of blessings from priests, and also
from others, like Brother André. In the last days before his death, when
he still could be wheeled to the hospital chapel, he would dip his fingers
in the holy water font and flip the water to all about him, saying, "Glory
be to the Father and to the Son and to the Holy Spirit." Then he would
bless himself.

Even though at this time people flocked around him, Solanus did not let
the people's admiration affect him. He showed no ostentation, pretense,
or vanity. "He didn't ever give any indication that he was anyone special. I think he felt that his relationship to God was the same to be found
in others." "He was never vain. He took no pride in the fact that people
sought him out or the numbers of people that sought him out. He merely
felt that he was helping them and that he was helping them to come closer
to God."

Solanus rarely spoke about himself; this made it difficult for people who
wanted to study his life to understand him.[101] However, self-forgetfulness,
he noted while still in simple vows, was the "most important quality"
of humility. Consequently, he spoke neither about his sufferings and
problems nor his successes and accomplishments.

In his retreat notes from 1945, reflecting on a conference on humility
and simplicity, Solanus wrote: "Of myself I am nothing. Only inasmuch
as I shall succeed in humbling myself can I expect to be anything in
God's eye, anything therefore in reality worth seeing. Humility and simplicity belong together and to one another more than do twin sisters." That
these twins found a home in Solanus is evident from those who testified
about his virtue. "Father Solanus possessed the biblical simplicity of the
dove, without having the cunning of the serpent," Father Marion Roessler
commented: "In his deep Irish faith, his Catholic practice was that of an
innocent child. His religious obedience was naturally linked to holy simplicity, even as St. Francis linked these two virtues. His humility made it
easy for him to realize his limited abilities in theory and practice."

While recent data indicate that Solanus may not have had the "limited
abilities in theory and practice" noted by Father Marion,[102] Solanus had
come to believe that he was not very gifted. When the superiors decided

he could be ordained but had to remain a simplex priest, his resignation to their decision not only manifested his humility, but exemplified it as his sense of the "truth" about himself. In his mind, "patient resignation [is] at once a great promoter and a fruit of Christian humility." Diocesan priest Father Anthony Kerry reflected: "I think the fact that he was ordained a 'sacerdos-simplex' is evidence of his humility. He accepted this. I never heard him complain about this restriction that was placed upon him."

The fact that two of his own brothers were priests with full faculties and all his classmates were as well,[103] while Solanus remained a simplex priest and served in the capacities given to lay brothers,[104] never seemed a source of personal humiliation. Solanus's niece Sister Bernadine Casey testified that the thing that impressed her "perhaps the most" was "his acceptance of the fact that he was ordained a priest simplex." She explains: "The more that I have come to understand what that means the more I appreciate his great humility and obedience in accepting this. Particularly when he would compare himself to his two brothers who were priests and to his confreres around him. And, yet, at the same time, to be so cheerful, joyful, resigned to his life."

If being told he would remain a simplex priest was humiliating to him, Solanus's response exemplified what he once declared: "In order to practice humility we must experience humiliation." Because he experienced humiliation he was able to urge humility to others, like Mildred Maueal. He noted that "confidence in God — the very soul of prayer — hardly comes to any poor sinner like we all are, without trials and humiliations." He counseled her to be free of considering herself a failure, but "rather thank God for having given you such an opportunity to humble yourself and such a wonderful chance to foster humility — and by thanking Him ahead of time for whatever crosses He may deign to caress you with, *confident* in His wisdom."

Solanus confidently believed that in God's wisdom he was supposed to remain a simplex priest. He never seems to have distinguished between the roles of priest and lay brother, for in his mind all roles revolved around service. When people came to him asking for some priestly service he could not give, such as confession, he would say to them, "I cannot hear your confession; I will send you to someone else." Yet never once did he complain about this. All who came to him found the same genuine person all the time; there was no counterfeit. He did not act self-conscious or stand on his dignity as a priest. Father Blase Gitzen remembers that "during the years he was at Huntington this was a novitiate, and he never used his position, as a priest, to lord it over the novices or the brothers. He treated each one of them as an equal." He conducted himself the same with all people.

His humility impressed all his visitors, and it made him attractive and approachable to them. Mrs. Elvera Clair recalled:

> I think his humility was one reason why so many people from all walks of life could come to him. He never put himself above anyone. He was never given to ostentation or vanity. He always wanted to be the least among us. He never wanted to have a fuss made over him. In spite of the number of persons who came to him, I am sure it never occurred to him that he was a person who was to be considered special. I think the fact that he was so Christ-like, persons were just content to be in his presence.

While others might think that the constant demands and requests of people coming to Solanus might cause him problems, Solanus once told Brother Leo Wollenweber, "That poor sinner Solanus...more than anyone else gave me trouble as long as I was in St. Bonaventure's." This notion of himself as a sinner was something that Solanus had no problem with sharing with those who came to him or wrote to him. "We're all sinners," he once said to a couple who visited him. Such a saying was based on a sense of what "false humility" and true humility revealed — something that he learned as a novice from St. Teresa of Avila: "False humility and the sadness we feel at the sight of our sins are among the most subtle of the devil's snares," he quoted her as saying. However, he added, "humility and sorrow which come from God console and pacify the soul."

Because he considered himself to be a sinner, he regularly asked people to "pray for my conversion." "I didn't understand at the time what he meant [by such a statement]," Margaret Baker recalled. "I felt that this was such a holy man. Why should we be praying for his conversion? I have come to realize now that he considered himself to be a sinner, to be lowly in the sight of God." One time when he asked Mr. and Mrs. Daniel Ran to "pray for my conversion," he explained that "he meant he could become closer to God, and when he passed on he would be able to help the people even more."

After his ministry at a parish on weekends, its pastor, Father Cefai, remembered: "Whenever Father Solanus would leave the parish to return to the monastery, he would get down on his knees and ask my blessing. I then knelt and asked his blessing. He would always say, 'Now, during the week until we meet, you pray for my conversion and I will pray for yours.'"

That such requests came from his heart is evidenced by the testimonies about Solanus's humility from those who lived with him. Father Francis Heidenreich, who acted as Solanus's superior, noted:

> He constantly referred to himself as the sinner and asked others to pray for his conversion. There was nothing counterfeit about his humility. When you have lived with a man for years, you know that it is a true and genuine humility and not just a show for others. There was certainly nothing ostentatious or vain about the man. I know of nothing that he did that would be contradictory to the heroic exercise of this virtue.

Capuchin brother Booker Ashe noted that, precisely because of the very fact that Solanus was "never vain or ostentatious" and never "tried to impress anyone" that "perhaps at the time that's why I wasn't so impressed by him myself, because he didn't make much of himself."

That he did not react negatively when his confreres humiliated him has been noted by them as a sign of the authenticity of Solanus's humility. That he took no personal credit for any cures attributed to him impressed them as well. The same deference was exhibited by Solanus when discussions revolved around his role in founding the Soup Kitchen. "He never once took any credit for having anything to do with the Soup Kitchen," Capuchin Daniel Brady marveled. "He would always give credit to others for the great work that it was doing. I know this because I was very much involved as a cook."

Another way Solanus exhibited humility is illustrated in the way he sought the counsel of others, especially in difficult theological cases. The way he did this was the source of edification to Cyril Langheim when he came to St. Bonaventure's as a young priest: "He did not hesitate to ask counsel of others, even priests who were younger than himself. When I came to St. Bonaventure's I was a much younger man than Father Solanus. Yet he would not hesitate to ask me for advice or counsel particularly in a theological or moral matter such as marriage cases."

Solanus's continual gratitude to God also expressed his humility. To a nun who described to him her discouragement regarding her limitations, Solanus stressed "the necessity of humble *patience* and patient *humility*." He then added: "At the same time just the weaknesses we experience — and who is so stupid as to imagine he is an exception — are naturally providential guards against one of the very greatest dangers to genius: The 'big head.' So instead of lamenting such weaknesses we really ought to thank God continually for them."

No matter what happened he would say, "Blessed be God in all his designs." His gratitude for God's goodness in his life echoed in his gratitude toward people who showed him kindness. "He also had the greatest sense of gratitude for anyone who did the slightest thing for him," one person recalled. "In other words, he didn't feel this was something that was being done to him or given to him because he deserved it. Rather, he felt that the people were great in their charity."

This sense of gratitude toward others, even those who may have hurt him, is evident in the way Solanus responded to the humiliations inflicted upon him by Brother Gerard Geromette. Gerard was Solanus's assistant as porter at St. Bonaventure's and would get very irascible when Solanus did not finish in the front office by 9:00 p.m. Later, when Gerard was in the hospital, suffering from cancer, Solanus went to visit him, "got down on his knees and kissed his hands." Later, when Solanus himself was in the hospital and Gerard visited him, he entered the room and, as was the custom for lay brothers toward priests at that time, knelt and kissed his hand. Father Solanus then rose, knelt, and kissed Gerard's hand. Brother Ignatius, who witnessed this action, concluded (as we can conclude this section on Solanus's humility): "Knowing Solanus's deep compassion for the suffering...and his gratitude for the goodness of others, I felt he was reverencing the suffering of Christ in Brother Gerard or expressing his sincere gratitude and appreciation for brother's visit in spite of his suffering."

Chapter 13

Conclusion

At the conclusion of this section on Solanus Casey's practice of the virtues, the words of Capuchin Bernard Burke, one of his superiors, aptly express the extraordinary way he lived his ordinary life:

> It is rather difficult to pinpoint specific examples of Father Solanus's practice of virtue, whether it be humility, obedience, or anything else. And perhaps this is one of the significant points that shows his practice of virtue because he did not make himself stand out in spite of the fact that he was well-known and credited even then with miracles, or at least with healings and cures. But he never pointed to himself as being outstanding because of these things. He was one of the members of the community, and he subjected himself to the rules and regulations of the community. So in that sense, he was not outstanding. Perhaps this in itself is, as I say, a sign of his great practice of his virtues.

Solanus Casey's practice of the virtues, while "ordinary" as described by Bernard, were "heroic" insofar as he practiced them all vigilantly, consistently, and constantly. As Bernard said elsewhere, Solanus practiced the virtues in a way that "could be called heroic, because, to my mind, his practice of all the virtues was for him habitual. It was just part of his very life. Certainly he was consistent in the practice of his virtues. By this consistency I mean that day in and day out his demeanor was always the same."

The notion of Solanus's consistency can be found throughout the testimonies of those who knew him best. Whether with friars who knew him for scores of years or those who knew him briefly the theme of consistency characterized their overall impression of Solanus's practice of the virtues. The oldest friar who testified declared: "Father Solanus was always the same. I never saw him have bad days and good days. Each day for him was the same. And because of his consistency in doing these things, it came with a great readiness and ease. It was never any effort on his part to be humble or to be obedient or temperate." James Maher observed:

> He was always the same. I would think that in the practice of virtue, he was very consistent. I never saw him impatient, angry, out of sorts. It seemed to me that his concern for his fellow man was always the same. If consistency is one of the notes of heroism, then I would think that he practiced virtues to a heroic degree.

That Solanus practiced the virtues in a heroic way has been declared by many who knew him. Because of his consistency and "the readiness in which he was ready to do the things that were asked of him or expected to him," his first biographer noted, Solanus "practiced the virtues in a heroic manner." Evelyn Cefai too attested to the heroic way he manifested the virtues: "He was always humble. He was always obedient. He was always willing to do God's will. He always said he could do these things only with the help of God.... He always seemed happy no matter what was given him to do. For this reason, I think he was extraordinary."

Witness after witness testified to examples indicating the "heroicity" or "extraordinariness" of his virtue: because so much good came to others, because of the consistency, because of the readiness, ease, and pleasure of his various tasks, especially the many hours in the front office.

Solanus Casey did not evidence all these virtues throughout his whole life; he grew in them, especially in patience. That anger and impatience were problems for him as a child has been stated above; however, that he struggled to bring them under control might not be so clear. Only someone who knew him well and who admittedly "observed" him, such as Capuchin Pius Cotter, knew that there were "times when he was given to either impatience or anger. Even at these times I could feel that there was a struggle going on within him to conquer this particular fault. He did not give vent to these feelings, but you could see that he could be upset."

That he harnessed his anger and impatience with others is testified in the reflections of Father George Gaynor, a diocesan priest who knew Solanus well. Father Gaynor described Solanus's patience as that virtue which most impressed him: "I know myself I would have become upset many times, but Father Solanus never seemed to be disturbed either by the hours he put in or by the number of people that he had to see." A reason for this can be found in his total concern for God's will and God's people who came to him in need. As Mrs. Georgia Gietzen recalled: "I believe [that be-cause] he had a great love first for God and then for his fellow man that the practice of these virtues became easy. I am sure there must have been things that upset him, although I don't know of them personally, but I think in his later years he showed a heroic practice of all these virtues."

If there had been no evolution or growth in the practice of the virtues of Solanus's life, one would question whether grace was evident. "The difficulties that he overcame in the pursuit of his vocation to become a priest and to remain in the priesthood" may have been signs of the extraordinary way he pursued fidelity to his vocation as a youth, but the way the fruits of the Holy Spirit progressively became evident in his later years testify to the work of God in his life. "I know of no one individual who ever excelled this man in the practice of virtue," Capuchin Blase Gitzen testified. "There might have been others who were better speakers, or more intelligent in solving difficult problems, but not in the practice of virtue. Father Solanus, in everything he did, reflected Christ."

Whether Solanus Casey will be beatified and canonized will be decided by the Vatican. However, among a constantly increasing number of people he has received the highest expression of holiness: edification and emulation.[105] One of these is Benedict Joseph Groeschel. He lived as a novice with Solanus and serves as the vice postulator for the Cause of the Servant of God Cardinal Terrence Cooke. He declared:

> In the course of my life, I have had the opportunity to observe several people who were known for holiness, some of whom are living and some of whom are deceased. These people all had reputations for heroic virtue. Father Solanus was the most extraordinary. I could easily say without any hesitation that he was the greatest human being I have ever known.

When people visited Solanus Casey they felt that "there was something special about him. You felt that he was a saint." "In my opinion he had all the virtues required for the making of a saint," one of his former Capuchin superiors testified of Solanus. Indeed, in 1898 Solanus himself noted while in simple vows "Traits of Saintly Characters" (that is, eagerness for God's glory, "touchiness" about the interests of Jesus, and anxiety for the salvation of souls.)

The volumes constituting his biography, testimony from witnesses about him, and this summary about his virtues and spirituality are now complete. It is the hope of those involved in the process that the Holy Father and the Congregation of the Causes of Saints will agree with the

Servant of God Solanus Casey's own words to determine if, indeed, his life on earth testifies to his presence now among the saints in heaven:

> According to the lives of the saints, we may, if we try, ascend to great sanctity and to astonishing familiarity with God even here as pilgrims to the Beatific Vision.

Notes

Introduction: Hagiography and Heroicity

1. The material in this first part of the introduction, on hagiography, was originally the introduction to the entire volume on the "Virtues" submitted to the Congregation.

2. Alasdair MacIntyre, *After Virtue* (Notre Dame, Ind.: University of Notre Dame Press, 1981).

3. Edith Wyschogrod, *Saints and Postmodernism: Revisioning Moral Philosophy* (Chicago and London: University of Chicago Press, 1990), xv.

4. Ibid., 257.

5. Ibid., xv.

6. Ibid., 256.

7. At the time this material was presented to the Congregation for the Causes of Saints, Solanus had been given by the Congregation the title "Servant of God." This was the first step toward canonization. When this material was accepted by the Congregation and Pope John Paul II, he was given the title "Venerable." This made Solanus Casey the first male born in the U.S. to receive this title. The next steps will determine if he will be able to be called "Blessed" and "Saint."

8. The material in this second part of the introduction was originally featured in chapter 11 of the biography submitted to the Congregation.

9. A copy of this letter as well as all other documentation noted in this chapter (unless so cited) can be found in the Archives of the Vice-Postulator of the Cause for Canonization of Solanus Casey at St. Bonaventure's in Detroit.

10. Michael H. Crosby, OFMCap., *Thank God ahead of Time: The Life and Spirituality of Venerable Solanus Casey* (Quincy, Ill.: Franciscan Press, 1998).

11. Catherine M. Odell, *Father Solanus* (Huntington, Ind.: Our Sunday Visitor, 1988).

12. Father Peter Gumpel, along with the whole process for canonization, has been highlighted by Kenneth L. Woodward in his book *Making Saints: How the Catholic Church Determines Who Becomes a Saint, Who Doesn't, and Why* (New York: Simon and Schuster, 1990). Interestingly, Frank Brady and his wife, who were beneficiaries of Solanus's concern, were Woodward's uncle and aunt.

1. The Family Background of Bernard (Solanus) Casey

13. Ann Taves, *The Household of Faith: Roman Catholic Devotions in Mid-Nineteenth Century America* (Notre Dame, Ind.: University of Notre Dame, 1986), 7.

14. Lynn Hollen Lees, *Exiles of Erin: Irish Migrants in Victorian London* (Ithaca, N.Y.: Cornell University Press, 1979), 193–97

15. I have based my division on Robert Broderick, "Paraliturgical Actions," *The Catholic Encyclopedia* (Nashville and New York: Thomas Nelson, 1976), 449–50.

16. Taves, *The Household of Faith,* 69.

17. Catherine M. Odell, *Father Solanus* (Huntington, Ind.: Our Sunday Visitor, 1988), 16–17.

2. Barney Casey Jr.'s Response to His Call

18. Peter Leo Johnson, "John Martin Henni," *New Catholic Encyclopedia* (New York: McGraw-Hill, 1967), 6:1017–18.

19. Editorial, *Milwaukee Catholic Citizen,* June 26, 1896. In Sister M. Justille Mc-Donald, *History of the Irish in Wisconsin in the Nineteenth Century* (Washington, D.C.: Catholic University of America, 1954), 207.

20. Cuthbert Gumbinger, OFMCap., "Father Solanus Casey: Capuchin Agreda Devotee," *Age of Mary* 5 (1958): 108.

21. Full "preacher's patent's" give a priest authorization to hear confession and preach all kinds of sermons, as well as to say Mass. Solanus would not be allowed to hear confessions or to preach formal sermons, e.g., the kind given on a retreat of a more doctrinal type.

4. Yonkers, New York, 1904–18

22. Celestine N. Bittle, OFMCap., *A Romance of Lady Poverty* (Milwaukee: Bruce, 1933), 306.

23. Don Brophy and Edythe Westenhaver, eds., *The Story of Catholics in America* (New York: Paulist, 1978), 99.

24. Cuthbert Gumbinger, OFMCap., "Father Solanus Casey: Capuchin Agreda Devotee," *The Age of Mary* 5 (1958): 110.

25. Julio Campos, "Marie de Jesus (D'Agreda)," in *Dictionnaire de Spiritualité, Ascetique et Mystique, Doctrine et Histoire LXIV–LXV* (Paris: Beauchesne, 1977), 511.

5. Manhattan and the Expanding Concern of Solanus for Justice in the World (1918–24)

26. Woodrow Wilson, quoted in James Hennesey, SJ, *American Catholics: A History of the Roman Catholic Community in the United States* (New York: Oxford, 1983), 223.

27. I.W., ed., Comment preceding "Open Letter to *Brann's Iconoclast,*" *The Irish World and American Industrial Liberator,* August 19, 1922.

28. SC, "To the Editor," *The Irish World,* ca. September 27, 1922.

29. Ibid.

30. Ibid.

31. Solanus read the autobiography of "The Little Flower" at least fifteen times.

32. Book of Minutes of the Friary Discreets at Our Lady of Angels, January 14, 1922 (New York, Our Lady of the Angels Friary).

33. Until the Second Vatican Council in the United States it was a custom to offer five dollars to pay for a "pagan baby" who would be baptized and cared for at an orphanage in some mission land.

6. The First Time in Detroit: 1924–45

34. According to Sister Agrippina, CSA, her brother was a novice in Detroit while Solanus was there. Assigned to be sacristan, he would get up at 4:00 a.m. to get things ready. "When he would come down to chapel, Father Solanus was already there in the corner praying."

35. The blessing continues to this day. The chapel is always filled, with people ministering to each other as each is blessed. Many use the occasion to spend extra time at the tomb of Solanus, which has been placed at the far left of the chapel.

36. James Patrick Derum, *The Porter of St. Bonaventure's: The Life of Father Solanus Casey, Capuchin* (Detroit: Fidelity, 1968), 168–69.

37. Ibid., 99.

38. George Q. Flynn, *American Catholics and the Roosevelt Presidency, 1932–1936* (Lexington: University of Kentucky, 1968), 235.

39. Paradoxically, while Solanus had eczema most of his life, he was seen by others as helping them be free of their own eczema. Father Cefai's sister, Evelyn Cefai, recalled "one occasion when a young girl who attended St. Paul's Church came to my brother. She had a severe case of eczema on her hands and although she tried many things she could not get rid of it. My brother took her to the rectory to see Father Solanus. Father Solanus blessed her and he touched her hands. The eczema disappeared immediately. To my knowledge the eczema never returned."

7. Semiretirement for an Untiring Solanus: 1945–56

40. At the time Solanus was at Huntington, Francis Heidenreich used his religious name, Thomas Aquinas. After the Vatican Council, he returned to his baptismal name.

41. Account noted in Catherine M. Odell, *Father Solanus* (Huntington, Ind.: Our Sunday Visitor, 1988), 176.

42. E. A. Bachelor Jr., "Detroiters Pay Homage to Priest," *Detroit Sunday Times*, July 18, 1954.

43. St. Felix Friary *Chronicle*, July 28, 1954. See the Provincial Archives for this, St. Bonaventure, Detroit, Mich.

44. Ibid., 4–5.

8. The Return to Detroit (1956–57)

45. St. Bonaventure's, *Chronicle*, December 2, 1956.

46. Jerry Sullivan, "Life in the Monastery in the Heart of Detroit," *Detroit Sunday News*, December 2, 1956.

47. *Chronicle*, December 2, 1956.

48. Sr. Arthur Ann, in James P. Derum, *The Porter of St. Bonaventure's: The Life of Father Solanus Casey, Capuchin* (Detroit: Fidelity Press, 1968), 260, 264.

49. Sr. Margretta Hughes, CSJ, in ibid., 264–65.

50. Milne, reflection shared with Michael H. Crosby, OFMCap., September 1, 1983.

51. Detroit City Council, Testimonial Resolution, passed August 3, 1957.

52. Necrology of Solanus Casey, the *Michigan Catholic,* August 1, 1957.

53. Father Gerald Walker, OFMCap., "Father Solanus Casey, OFMCap., 1870–1957," *The Messenger* 21 (Detroit: Province of St. Joseph, 1958): 35–36.

54. Father Gerald Walker, OFMCap., "Funeral Homily," in Derum, *The Porter of St. Bonaventure's,* 274.

9. The Theological Virtues

55. Solanus called Satan "the prince of diabolical deceivers."

56. Although for Solanus atheists were wanting in intelligence, he noted in a few places that the Sorbonne was atheistic.

57. See also Michael H. Crosby, OFMCap., *Thank God ahead of Time: The Life and Spirituality of Solanus Casey,* 2d ed. (Quincy, Ill.: Franciscan Press, 1997), 241–42.

58. Solanus quoted this passage from scripture in his retreat notes while still in the seminary, around 1900. The "damn(ed)" fool, of course, was Lucifer.

59. See also Crosby, *Thank God ahead of Time,* 219.

60. See ibid., 263–99.

61. Solanus was very close friends with the founder and foundress of the Atonement friars and sisters, Anglican communities that joined the Catholic Church.

62. William Tremblay, March 15, 1979. See Crosby, *Thank God ahead of Time,* 110. Solanus also challenged people when they came for ashes on Ash Wednesday but did not receive Communion.

63. For more on the devotion to the Sacred Heart in the Province of St. Joseph, see Celestine Bittle, OFMCap., *The Romance of Lady Poverty* (Milwaukee: Bruce, 1933), 306.

64. This title may have been taken from the poet William Wordsworth.

65. For a humorous account of Solanus's penchant for praying the rosary while in a car, see Crosby, *Thank God ahead of Time,* 170–71.

66. Sometime between 1946 and 1949, on the Feast of St. Joseph, "Father Solanus was celebrant of the Community Mass. No homily was scheduled but after the Gospel, he turned to the Community and began to speak to St. Joseph, but shortly after he began, tears welled up and he was unable to continue the homily."

67. St. Anthony also was a recipient of Solanus's violin "concerts." Evelyn Cefai tells us of an interesting incident: "My brother, Father Michael Cefai, was called to go out on a sick call. He went to the church; my father went with him. My brother was looking for the keys to the Tabernacle and the cabinet where the Holy Oils were. He could not find the keys. In front of my father he turned his pockets inside out. He then sent my father to go back to the house to see if perhaps the keys were on his desk or on a table. When he came into the house, Father Solanus (who helped out in the parish on weekends) asked my father what he was looking for, and my father told him what had happened and that Father Michael could not find the keys. Father Solanus told us to kneel down and to say a prayer to St. Anthony. This we did. Then he told my father, 'Go and tell Father Mike that the keys are in his pocket.' My father went back and told my brother

to look in his pockets for the keys. My brother reminded him that he had looked in his pockets and turned his pockets inside out. My father told him that Father Solanus said to do this, and so he did it and he found the keys in his pocket. My brother said: 'Don't tell me Father Solanus is not a saint.'"

68. See also Crosby, *Thank God ahead of Time,* 56–57.

69. William Tremblay, March 15, 1979, in Crosby, *Thank God ahead of Time,* 279–80.

70. Confidence in Jesus could be fostered by appealing to the Blessed Virgin Mary. James Maher testified that he thought Solanus's message for today "would be to have confidence and trust in God. I know the last time I saw him, this was the impression that he gave me. As I left him he reached out and handed me what looks like a scapular. It is a picture of the Blessed Mother and the Infant Child, both with crowns on their head. On the back is a simple prayer that says: 'My mother, my confidence.' He just handed it to me, smiling; but didn't say anything."

71. Crosby, *Thank God ahead of Time,* 219.

72. Daniel Crosby, OFMCap., June 7, 1984, in Crosby, *Thank God ahead of Time,* 255–56.

73. See also Crosby, *Thank God ahead of Time,* 268–69.

74. This person was quoting an unnamed person in Crosby, *Thank God ahead of Time,* 51.

75. Sr. Joyce Pranger, *Rise Early to Meet Your Lord* (Denville, N.J.: Dimension Books, 1977), 41–42, adapted. At the same meeting Solanus told Joyce that she would become a nun and do much good in new ways for religious women.

76. The "discipline" on Good Friday as well as the vigil of other major feasts consisted of beating one's bare back with a small metal chain as the Miserere (Psalm 51) and other prayers were offered. At other times (Monday, Wednesday, and Friday for the professed) the friars took the "discipline" together in a darkened room as the prayer leader of the week (hebdomadary) intoned prayers. For the "over-the-back" discipline, it was not allowed to draw blood. The purpose of the "discipline," the Constitutions of that period explained, was to help remind the friars of the passion of Jesus.

77. The actual quotation reads: "Separation from friends for a loving heart means sacrifice indeed."

78. There has been some confusion of Solanus's birthday. His baptismal record gives his birth date as November 25, 1870, and when he entered the Order he recorded that date on his Attestation of Freedom, written in 1898. However, when his novice master placed Solanus's record in the Book of Investitures, he wrote the birthday as October 25, 1870. Thereafter, each Provincial Directory from 1897 to 1957 listed Solanus's birthday incorrectly, and *October 25* is the day that became known to everyone as his birthday. Solanus never complained or asked to have the date corrected, and eventually seems to have forgotten the correct date himself.

79. "Kissing the floor" was a practice of all Capuchins before their superiors until after the changes inaugurated by the Second Vatican Council. It was to be a sign of humility before one's superior, who was recognized as a representative of God.

80. Father Cosmas Niedhammer, OFMCap., March 16, 1980. See Crosby, *Thank God ahead of Time,* 113.

81. Ibid.

82. The censor, like the other one, found nothing in the writings of Solanus Casey that might be considered questionable in terms of faith and morals: this theologian merely was asking that these three areas be addressed. In a response to this request, Michael Crosby explained the reasons for their use to the satisfaction of the Congregation.

83. A classic book on prejudice in the United States of America is Gordon W. Allport's *The Nature of Prejudice* (Garden City, N.Y.: Doubleday Anchor Books, 1954). He defines ethnic prejudice as "an antipathy based upon a faulty and inflexible generalization. It may be felt or expressed. It may be directed toward a group as a whole, or toward an individual because he is a member of that group" (10). Solanus hardly fits the definition!

84. The basis for these stories was grounded in statements by those who knew him during that time. Sister Agrippina Petrosino, CSA, for example, spoke of Solanus's concern for Italian immigrants: "He was extremely kind to them and to the poor and to the downtrodden."

10. The Works of Mercy

85. For more on Brother Francis's ill-treatment of Solanus, see Michael H. Crosby, OFMCap., *Thank God ahead of Time: The Life and Spirituality of Solanus Casey*, 2d ed. (Quincy, Ill.: Franciscan Press, 1997), 117.

86. See also ibid., 52–53.

87. Ibid., 120.

11. The Cardinal Virtues

88. In the interest of integrity this possibility has been included. However, in the interest of objectivity, no complaint was ever received formally. Hearsay and innuendo should not be used as the basis for any critical interpretation of any so-called imprudence of Solanus in the case of his counseling married couples.

89. Michael H. Crosby, OFMCap., *Thank God ahead of Time: The Life and Spirituality of Venerable Solanus Casey* (Quincy, Ill.: Franciscan Press, 1998), 210.

90. Scripture translation from Solanus's writings.

91. Solanus's letter to *Brann's Iconoclast.*

92. Crosby, *Thank God ahead of Time,* 202.

93. Ibid., 200–201.

94. In *Thank God ahead of Time,* Michael Crosby notes that Solanus did stop at a bar in Detroit while on a ride. There he had a beer. The bar was owned by a benefactor of the monastery (125–26).

95. Crosby, *Thank God ahead of Time,* 136–37.

96. See also ibid., 50–51, 86, 162.

12. The Evangelical Counsels

97. Father Blase's contention that Solanus "never really kept track of the money that was given to him, or the purposes for which it was given to him" seems contradicted by

the majority of others who testified he was quite clear about money when it involved obligations for the Capuchins or contractual relationships.

98. After Solanus's death, his violin was returned to Detroit. It had been used in Huntington by another friar.

99. Recollection of Father Daniel Crosby to Michael Crosby (Detroit: Archives of Solanus Casey Guild, 1991).

100. Solanus Casey's admiration for General Douglas MacArthur stemmed, in good part, from MacArthur's efforts to halt the communist advances in Korea.

101. Michael H. Crosby, OFMCap., author of *Thank God ahead of Time: The Life and Spirituality of Venerable Solanus Casey* (Quincy, Ill.: Franciscan Press, 1998), the definitive biography of Solanus Casey until this volume, found it very difficult to get to know the "self" of Solanus because of the few times he talked about himself. He was helped in probing his psyche by graphology (see 306, 309).

102. On the basis of graphological evidence, the contention of this editor is that Solanus possessed a higher-than-average IQ (about 135), but that given his long years in grade school, his lack of proficiency in German as an Irishman in a German-speaking province, and his highly intuitive approach, he was intellectually lazy. Because his teachers did not have proficiency in helping him with ways to combat his deficiencies and capitalize on his capabilities, it merely was assumed that he was not smart.

103. His classmates who were ordained simplex priests seem to have fought to receive full faculties. Solanus chose not to do this.

104. Roles traditionally given to lay brothers were given Solanus throughout his priestly ministry.

13. Conclusion

105. That there are over sixty thousand people who belong to the Father Solanus Guild testifies to this statement.